Word.

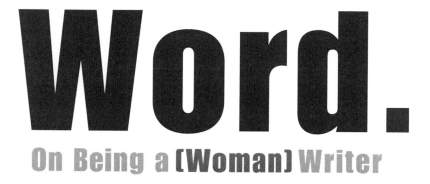

Word.
On Being a (Woman) Writer

Edited by Jocelyn Burrell

Foreword by Suheir Hammad

The Feminist Press
at The City University of New York

Published by the Feminist Press at the City University of New York
The Graduate Center, 365 Fifth Avenue, Suite 5406, New York, NY 10016
feministpress.org

12 11 10 09 08 07 06 05 04   5 4 3 2 1

First edition, 2004

Library of Congress Cataloging-in-Publication Data
Word : on being a [woman] writer / edited by Jocelyn Burrell ; foreword by Suheir
    Hammad.— 1st ed.
    p. cm.
ISBN 1-55861-467-2 (alk. paper)
1. Women and literature. 2. Authorship. 3. Literature—Women authors—History
and criticism—Theory, etc. I. Burrell, Jocelyn.
    PN471.W65 2004
    809'.89287—dc22   2003027988

Publication of this book was made possible, in part, by public funds from the National
Endowment of the Arts and the New York State Council of the Arts.

The Feminist Press is grateful to Helene D. Goldfarb, Barbara Grossman, Nancy Hoffman,
and Florence Howe for their generosity in supporting the publication of this book.

Text design and composition by Dayna Navaro
Printed in Canada on acid-free paper by Transcontinental Printing

If not for Karen, if not for Kimmie—
this is for many but because of you

And in loving memory of Martha Matthews Perry (1930–1999)—
I haven't forgotten, and neither will the world

The pen is ours to wield
—Ada

CONTENTS

Foreword

From the Margin to the Page

To illustrate the concept of marginalization to a class of Boston fifth graders last winter, I held up a sheet of loose-leaf paper and asked, "If you were to write a story, where on this page would you do so?"
"Right there," a chorus rang out, a baker's dozen of little fingers pointing to the body of the page.

"What about this space, in the margins, what do you write in here?" Blank faces, a few curious glances, the anticipation palpable in a classroom just before the teacher drops an answer on forming brains. Here I paused.

A story begins in the margins. It's where we do our math. Where we check our spelling. Where we dream.

The young people I stood before were under the caring tutelage of a college friend of my younger sister, who had invited me into their classroom to talk about being a poet. Michael had shared one of my poems with them, and had asked the young people to look up Palestine on their maps the day before my visit, to prepare us all for our time together. My own preparation was my morning cup of coffee and a quick prayer that I would be worth their time.

"So," I continued, "a marginalized voice is a voice that is part of the story, but that is left off of the 'main' page. Can you think of people whose stories we don't hear about on the news or read about in our schoolbooks? People you know have things to say and share, but who are silenced by their exclusion?"

I didn't have to state the obvious. One by one, these young people looked up at the paper I was holding in my hand, then down at their notebooks, and connected it all on their own.

The thing about getting older is that you don't really grow up. Standing in front of a coed group of ten and eleven year olds, I don't care how grown up you think you are, that part of you, that eleven-year-old girl, is awakened and alert. You want them to like you, to think you cool. You remember the smell of your first musk. The racing of your heart when homeboy/homegirl looked your way. Your first blush. And then all of a sudden, you are thirty years old and there are a bunch of little yous (hey, wait up, when did I get grown?) who are looking up at you, deciding whether or not you have something to offer them. All you have are your poems.

You, dear reader, are probably not eleven (but you could be), but there is an eleven-year-old right there, just beneath your hardened skin. By the time I'd gotten my first period I knew that my only escape from the boredom and many restrictions of my well-meaning parents' refugee immigrant apartment was books. My mother, who was entrusted with raising moral and obedient girls, nonetheless gifted me a library card before I was nine, and would take me to the library on 9th Street in Brooklyn once a week. There was a pathetic half shelf of Arabic language novels and weird reference books she would worry over, desperate for her own language in this lonesome foreign city, and I was set loose in the children's section to find my books for the week. I tried to take out one for each day. I know . . . I didn't have many friends . . . and my parents were happier seeing me in the company of hard copies than the "loose morals" of my classmates.

I read everything, a sentiment you will find sung out by the writers you are about to read. We will read the tissue box in front of us if there is nothing else around. We know the nutritional content and suggested serving size of the cans of ravioli we heat up for after school lunch (someone should really check to see if in fact my generation of poor school children were ever fed enough at school) because all of that is written on the back of the can, because we need something to read while we are stirring. I found a librarian in my junior high school library, Mr. Scheifitz, who allowed me to take out adult books as long as he could recommend books as well. So, while I was reading smutty off-limits romance novels, I was also checking out Tolstoy, Shakespeare, and Poe.

It wasn't until high school that I began to search out women writers, just as my body began to take its woman shape and "the rules" began closing in. But the escape world books offered me was built and tendered by men. I was (and remain) thankful for it, but my world needed windows into my self. And so it began, the slow plaiting of women's words into my fiber.

And the writers in this collection could only be readers. Only readers write, I have decided. Show me a poet who doesn't read poetry, and I can point to tendencies in her craft that will not stand the test of time. Only a woman who has had her breath taken away by a phrase will toil a line of words on a page over and again until it is just so. And again.

We will not entertain the nature versus nurture debate on women's literature here, or class biases, or the "cultural wars," or even the cold shoulder most women of color writers still experience from all limbs of the writing world. Look, we write out of our bodies. There is no mistaking a Hemingway novel for one by Alice Walker. And thank goodness for that. Thank goodness for the differences, and for those women who wrote up not only their own stories, but also the stories of their kin, their people. The women who braved societal and familial marginalization in order to write. Can you imagine? It is easy to take for granted now what it meant even one generation ago to be a woman writer. Or what it means to be one today, and, as that classroom of fifth graders reminded me, what it will take to be one tomorrow. Selfish, delusional, unrealistic . . . and other, meaner, words hurled at them to quiet them down, to still their pens and dampen their fire. Words meant to kill words.

This is what all exceptional writers do: they carry the margins over to the page. The mathematics of our lives, the practice runs that make up what we offer the public as real, are proven in the margins. We whisper there, perfecting what we want others to hear, often editing out truth. And yes, we dream there. It was where our societies' outsiders live. And where each of us, as lone individuals, dwell. Women writers have practiced our craft from the outskirts. Our lenses have been aimed at the public spaces which have marginalized our voices. And yet, we also write from the "in-skirts"—from our bodies and the intimate space around them. To find ourselves we hold up a mirror to the worlds we all inhabit.

These writers have left something for you. A glimpse into their private thoughts. A doorway into a different perspective. What an awesome thing to do, place words together, one after another, to create an atmosphere, a world. To literally compose a deeper reality, another dimension. Sounds like magic, doesn't it? But it is this same creative force that is busting out of our memories of traditional woman's work.

The recipes doctored to individual perfection. The order of a house edited down to the comma of a coffee table placed just there. The metric perfection of braids. We reclaim that same energy, that beautifying clarity that women possess that has had us burned at stakes, stoned to death, sexualized to sell automobiles. We manifest creation through the language arts. Because as Michael's ten and eleven year olds would tell you, the main page does not exist without the margin. Women, certainly, have always known that.

Read these words and be nourished. Read them and gain a sense of style. Read them and then go back over to your own page. What dreams have you scratched out in the margins there? What have you left out? What will you dare to carry over to the page?

Suheir Hammad
Turtle Island
2004

Editor's Note

Dort wird sie eingehn. (Here she will enter.)
—Gertrud Kolmar (1894–1943?)

It is my special honor to introduce this gathering of remarkable writers, especially as their work speaks for itself and really begs little if any introduction. Immediately this one reader's astonishing privilege is surpassed by the gift they offer us all through their work, play, and daily resistance with words. With words. From Bulawayo to Bedford-Stuyvesant, these writers and more are raising their voices against the night, they are dazzling us with the brilliance of their craft—and their daring to cast it on this difficult world. And as this small but powerful chorus will testify, to write in a world inscribed by violence, repression, poverty, and dread is more than a literary act. It is a last stand.

In *Word. On Being a [Woman] Writer,* twenty-four contemporary writers grapple with all that it is, is not, and could be to write as a woman in the world today. Here they argue and meditate on the nuanced pleasures and dangers of their work, revealing hidden censors; the complex terrain of familial and cultural influence; the thorny intersections of audience and identity, globalization and art; the often unexpected costs of critical/industry attention and the persisting marginalization of those who dare to write without it; and more. While their perspectives on writing vary as widely as their experiences as writers, it seems likely that at least one strategy is common to all: *Live by your word.* Judging from what follows in this collection, I imagine they would urge each of us to do the same.

That said, I encourage you to read the following selections, in every way that is important, as letters to you. Letters from exile. Letters from diaspora. Letters from zones of war and occupation. Letters from survivors of genocide, of enslavement, of ongoing and recent colonizations, of rape, of partition. Letters from jail cells and other prisons we call home. Letters folded lovingly and put away for the writers of tomorrow. And above all, letters of art, hope, resilience, anger, and love. These are letters to the world—the one we live in and the one we must imagine into being. We must. All with our words.

Awaiting yours,
Jocelyn Burrell
Boston, Massachusetts
2004

I.

Difficult Passages /
Dangerous Acts

■

It is dangerous for a woman to defy the gods;
To taunt them with the tongue's thin tip
—Anne Spencer

Ritu Menon

■

The Structured Silences of Women: Culture, Censorship, and Voice in a Globalised Market

Cofounder of Kali for Women, the oldest women's press in India, Ritu Menon is an internationally respected writer, critic, activist, and publisher. For three decades she has continued to break new ground in feminist publishing and in the global women's movement. An independent scholar, she is coeditor of several fiction anthologies and publishes widely on women and violence, media, partition, militarization, publishing, and fundamentalisms. She is also coauthor of the pivotal oral history *Borders and Boundaries: Women in India's Partition* and a driving force behind the first comprehensive study on the status of India's Muslim women.

In "The Structured Silences of Women: Culture, Censorship, and Voice in a Globalised Market" (2001), Menon expands upon disturbing findings from a recent ten-language project on "the gendered nature" of censorship in India. She launched this ambitious initiative as part of her work with Women's World Organization for Rights, Literature, and Development (Women's WORLD), which defines "censorship as any means by which ideas and works of art that express views not in accord with the dominant ideology are prevented from reaching their intended audience." Against the paradoxical backdrop of the information revolution (and a time when women comprise two-thirds of the world's illiterate), she argues, censorship is more broadly defined and emerges in complex ways, particularly for women writers. Along with the familiar mode of state-sponsored censure, Menon takes a hard look at the effects of more insidious but equally devastating censors that silence women: familial constraints and cultural pressures, the sheer force of market (in)tolerances, a literary establishment that determines largely who is read and what is deemed "publishable," and a damaging "aesthetics of silence" practiced by many women writing in India—and beyond.

■

3

"Although confined and deprived of a homeland, my father wanted me to write political poetry . . . I was expected to create political poetry while the corrupt laws and customs insisted that I remain secluded behind a wall, not able to attend assemblies of men, not hearing the current debates, not participating in public life. . . . Where was I to find an intellectual atmosphere in which I could write political poetry? From the newspaper my father brought home at lunch every day? The newspaper is important but it doesn't have the power to inspire poetry in the depths of one's soul. I was enslaved, isolated in my seclusion from the outside world, and my seclusion was imposed as a duty—I had no choice in the matter. The outside world was taboo for women of good families, and society didn't protest against this seclusion; it was not part of the political agenda. . . . My commitment to life weakened as I remained secluded from the outside world. My soul was tormented because of this seclusion. My father's demands may have initiated my turmoil, but the pain always stayed with me, taking different forms through-out the journey of my life . . . the process of maturing was a most painful experience in body and soul. I was oppressed, crushed; I felt bent out of shape. I could not participate in any aspect of life unless I pretended to be another person. I became more and more distant.
—Fadwa Tuqan

Women writers like Fadwa Tuqan make a breach in the wall of silence. They say things that may not have been said before and say them in print, where anyone can read and repeat them. This is a vital step in the creation of modern civil societies, for civil societies are based on discussion, the public use of free expression.

The twentieth century will surely be remembered as one in which the free flow of information was virtually guaranteed by the advent of cyberspace and the Internet. The democratisation of media that has resulted, and the autonomy that individual users now enjoy, is revolu-tionary, and it has transformed the very nature and business of communication. Practically every familiar feature of writing and pub-lishing, communicating and disseminating is being re-examined—either with alarm or exhilaration, depending on how you look at the whole phenomenon. The iconoclasts will say there is nothing sacro-sanct about authorship anymore, and that copyright or the assertion of intellectual property rights can fly out of the window. Authors, on the other hand, can say there's no real need for publishers anymore, because desktop publishing makes that particular intermediary redundant. And publishers may well say that retailers are irrelevant because e-commerce enables them to sell directly to buyers. The change is so overwhelming that some publishers find they have to review contracts practically every time they draw them up, because of the difficulty of satisfactorily monitoring any transaction. Although access to the Internet and a vast storehouse of information is still a privilege available only to a small number of people, at least in our country, those who have it virtually have the accumulated knowledge of the centuries at their fingertips.

It is almost inconceivable, then, to speak of censorship and silence in the year 2001; the very idea of such a force operating in the era of Internet is laughable. Yet, consider this: a serious weighing up of the pros and cons of publishing a controversial text is part of most publishers' editorial and marketing decisions today, no matter which part of the world they happen to be in. Whether extremist, militant, fundamentalist, or chauvinist, "thought police" exist in every part of the world and go about the business of silencing, as effectively as ever. And the trend is growing.

Last year, Bangladeshi writer Taslima Nasrin published her autobiography *Amar Meyebela* [My Bengali Girlhood] in Calcutta. Her first major work, written over the years that she has been in exile in Europe, it was banned almost immediately by her government. The event passed without comment in the world press, including ours, almost as if this was only to be expected. This is ironic because, of course, anyone who wishes to read her book can do so easily enough—it's readily available. But the point of censorship is not to keep people from reading a particular work, censorship is to keep them from writing it—and that is why it persists, despite the free and untrammeled flow of information.

My comments are based on an analysis done by Women's WORLD, a free-speech international network of writers, and on our ten-language project on the gendered nature of censorship in India. Our definition of censorship is broader than that used by most human rights organizations, which see censorship as the silencing of writers by "jailers, assassins, or official censors." We define censorship as any means by which ideas and works of art that express views not in accord with the dominant ideology are prevented from reaching their intended audience. Such works may be seized or banned; they may be ignored, defamed, diminished, or purposely misinterpreted in order to silence their authors and maintain the existing order.

> Scissors to cut with, a needle and thread to sew my lips with. If I write my subconscious, the earth will be covered with paper.
>
> —Anamika

For most women writers in the country, writing remains an isolated, solitary activity, often surreptitious, generally unacknowledged and undervalued. Although the number of women writers may well run into some thousands, they are still invisible, encounter all manner of obstacles in expressing themselves freely, and experience many forms of direct censorship, simply because they are women. Examples of this range from an outright ban on reading and writing or denial of access to education, to a kind of censorship by the market which decides which women can be published and when; as well as to all kinds of self-censorship which often come into play before any external silencing takes place. In between lie the constraints placed on women by families, communities, and society in general.

The enormous pressure exerted by cultural censorship on women's subconscious makes the conflict between public and private unbearable. Anamika said that in her fifteen years of writing experience as a poet and essayist, she had imposed a kind of "spiritual dieting" on herself. She spoke eloquently of the "needle and thread" syndrome in women's lives, keeping their lips properly sealed, observing a stern "aesthetics of silence." For middle class women like her, this aesthetics has been particularly oppressive. What are we so ashamed of and why? Who are we hiding from? she asked. Family honour, the compulsion to be a good daughter, a good wife, and a good mother locked her into the "good girl syndrome."

What is it that connects women to writing? And what is it that defines and determines the contours of that writing? What are the limits of the freedom that women are allowed in self-expression? Is a poem or a short story like an exotic sweet, a neatly embroidered handwork, or a well-trained voice to be displayed on occasion as a sign of feminine accomplishment? Marked by measured cadences and neatly drawn lines—never flamboyant, never demanding attention, just gently drawing praise with modest, womanly grace.

after being
planned to perfection with
weep like this walk like that laugh like this
comb out your very life like this—
when the tangled noose tightens
the dying declaration
flows effortless
like a rhyme learnt by heart
　　　　　　　　　—Kondepudi Nirmala

Can women freely write whatever they wish, whenever they wish? Is there a "proper subject" for women writers? Subjects—like religion, politics and sexuality—that are taboo? Who decides? And when we do write, are we generally accorded the serious consideration that all writers expect, or do our personal histories and private lives and loves become part of the literary assessment of our work? Can we be confident that gossip will not replace fair evaluation, derision and dismissal not silence a tentative articulation of what is deeply, often painfully, personal?

Who censors and when? Are men and women censored differently? Is censorship cultural, religious, official, familial, or internal? Is it necessary to challenge it? If we are to change the definition of censorship, what factors should we consider: experience and environment, social and political context, or language, form, and choice of subject?

These were the questions and confusions that haunted us during and after a series of ten workshops on women and censorship in India. Conducted in Urdu, Telugu, Marathi, Malayalam, Hindi, Gujarati, Kannada, Bangla, English, and Tamil, and held in different and varied surroundings, the workshops brought up new issues and allowed fresh insights into the nature of censorship that women face. The thread that ran through most of them was disconnection: the disconnection between what women said and what they wrote; between their spoken words and their silences; between their husbands' and fathers' apparent encouragement and support, and their explicit, disapproving silence when a norm was violated. Between women as the subject matter of writing, and women as subjects and writers. Between language, literature, and social movements, and the emergence of women's voices. Between language and gender, and gender and genre.

On the face of it, the writers said, women are not subjected to any kind of censorship, any curb on their freedom of expression, as women. We are writers, and like other writers are free to choose what we write about and how to write it. We are preoccupied with form and content; with language; with meaning and metaphor; with being read and critically appraised. And yet, when one of them said, "A woman's life is censored from start to finish, and if not censored, then severely edited," no one thought it either incorrect or exaggerated. Rather, on closer examination, and lengthier discussion of the circumstances in which women read and write—and are read and written about—it appeared that the very concerns that seem to be common to all writers, male and female, are gendered in ways that can, and often do, silence women. Take the question of language, said one writer. There is no way a woman can use swear words in Hindi, because they are specifically and abusively anti-women; to use them would be to deliberately endorse their derogatory intent.

Well-known Hindi writer Mridula Garg identified four kinds of censorship that women commonly experience: political, sociocultural, familial, and internal or auto-censorship. Political censorship almost always follows cultural, and self-censorship certainly does so. In her view, cultural censorship is probably more insidious and powerful than all the others, because it pervades all social institutions; for women, in particular, it introduces a powerful duality between the individual and the writer. Speaking for herself, she said that she had never experienced any censorship by her family. What troubles her is something else: she finds that she is torn between the cerebral/masculine and emotional/feminine dichotomy; drawn more to the former, she says her identity as a "woman writer" is thrown back at her by critics and the literary establishment, who tend to devalue it for this reason. The tension between gender and writing is ever present and, despite herself, she finds she censors what she writes.

For most of the other 160 writers in our workshops, however, marriage, motherhood, and the family encompass women and affect their writing, for better or worse. "I never write in love, always in anger. I write a lot, but not what I want to write," said Sudha Arora, who gave up writing for twelve long years after her marriage in order to prove that she was a good housewife. The "good girl syndrome" again. When she resumed her writing, she found she was censoring herself so spontaneously that she abandoned the autobiographical novel she was working on. Now she writes on topics from which she can distance herself. Her newspaper articles, radio scripts, and stories are all to do with women, but safely remote from her own experience. Maitreyi Pushpa has not even been able to begin writing her autobiography, and Chitra Mudgal was advised by her son to reconsider the whole project—after all, she had the family to think of. Almost every writer present said she had not been able to write about those subjects that involved the family, or those that they might object to as reflecting negatively on them. Gagan Gill spoke movingly and poignantly about how she confronted her mother, years after it had happened, about a sexual assault on her by a close family member. Not only did it alienate her from her mother, it lay embedded in her own psyche and had a profound impact on her all the years that she was growing up.

When asked which subject they found the most difficult to write about, the majority said: the family. To write honestly about it was almost impossible. And so this "household dimension" of women's writing itself becomes a powerful form of censorship. Apart from having to accommodate their writing to the demands of domesticity, women have to deal with the most intimate and deep-seated patriarchal prejudices within the home. As Azra Parveen said, "Censorship is nurtured in the home," and women are often willing self-censors. If not willing, then unwitting, and if neither of these, then they submit for the sake of sheer survival.

But there is also another kind of censorship at work, less remarked upon, and that is the censorship of the market and literary establishments; a censorship that is much more difficult to deal with because it is disguised as "literary quality," "saleability," "patronage," and subtle manipulation, which sometimes barely conceals outright bias.

Women's access to the literary market and the media have been important subjects for analysis and discussion by feminists, media activists, and practitioners for a very long time. These analyses have been very significant, and have unmistakably—even conclusively— altered our understanding of how media represent or accommodate women, and of how capital and ownership influence the amount and nature of space available to women in every area of media operation. I'd like to speak about a much-less discussed phenomenon, which is the denial of access to women writers through market censorship.

Every society has some degree of censorship which it carries out by its normal means of social organization and control. In a military dictatorship, censorship is exercised by the military; in a communist country, by the "dictatorship of the proletariat"; in a market-driven society, by market forces. My canvas is smaller, limited to India, demographic billionaire and home to twenty-two officially recognised languages, including English. The women in our workshops, representing ten major literary languages, spoke about their marginalisation in the literary establishment, about male patronage, sexual harassment by editors of powerful periodicals and papers, and about the oldest form of informal censorship we know—simply ignoring a writer's work.

Angela Carter, well-known writer, says, "I spent a good many years being told what I ought to think and how I ought to behave and how I ought to write, even, because I was a woman and men thought they had the right to tell me how to feel. But then I stopped listening to them and tried to figure it out for myself, but they didn't stop talking, oh dear, no. So I started answering back. How simple, not to say simplistic, this all sounds; and yet it is true." At the other end of the world Parvathy Devi, in our Malayalam workshop, said that as far as women are concerned, "Writing that reinforces or is uncritical of prevailing societal norms and values is praised, while that which critiques patriarchal values or promotes the idea of women as individuals provokes censure. Men who write differently are honoured, but women who do so are isolated."

Nirmala, a Telugu writer, told us that as long as she wrote "just ordinary poetry" her literary friends were very happy with her, but as soon as she started writing more "feminist" stuff, their attitude changed sharply. It took her one year to get "Labour Room" published and one editor said in disgust, "What sort of visual can we use for a poem like this?"

Labour Room

> See! It strikes you like a 3D film
> The violence of reality
> The reality of violence.
> Step into the labour room
> Framed in seductive white of

Sensuous silk
Scented jasmine
Sweetened milk.
You see alienation bondage exile
Each table turbulent with suffering
The walls wet weary
Tremulous with tears
Sobs, screams, save me o god
Splitting at the seams.
Living actions like
Walking, talking, laughing
Assume a different meaning here.
—Kondepudi Nirmala

Other writers spoke about how they were advised by literary "well-wishers" to avoid writing about certain subjects, if they wanted to be published, and if they were arrogant enough to persist, the attacks could be vicious. Volga, a major writer in Hyderabad recounted how feminist poetry was dismissed by Telugu critics as being full of "body consciousness, but devoid of social consciousness."

"Don't write feminist poetry, don't write about sex," was a common refrain; Sujatha said that when she took "A Wave Beneath an Eyelash," her story about a young woman married to a very old man dreaming about a romantic attachment, to be published, the editor told her, "If a woman wants a man, how does that make a story? What is there to justify this title? It's nothing but sex!" Lalitha Lenin, a well-known Malayalam writer, had her name changed by the editor of a magazine, without her permission, because he thought it was "too common-place." And another suggested she change hers because she belongs to a minority community!

Several writers, especially from Bengali, Kannada, Hindi, and even English, said they gave in to editors' demands just to get published. The situation is especially adverse in languages that have few literary magazines or other avenues for speaking and publishing; in at least two languages, Telugu and Gujarati, there has been a sharp decline in the number of literary magazines published, and almost all writers are forced to finance the publication of their books. Obviously, very few women are able to afford this. Even a language like Bengali, which has

7,000 little magazines, is inhospitable; and women writing in Bangla spoke openly about being asked for sexual favours by male editors in return for being published.

Although, as Satyavathi said, "We avenge the censorship we face in reality through our writing," any number of women censor themselves for fear of how their families or communities would react, or of being rejected. Censorship often takes place within the family, where manuscripts may be destroyed, suppressed, or altered by husbands, parents, or siblings because of what they reveal about "family secrets." Fathers or husbands may also suppress or appropriate the work of their daughters or wives because they do not wish them to have an independent identity, and feel that the work of women in their family properly belongs to them. The objection is often very violent. Ilampirai, a Tamil writer, told us that her ex-husband broke her right wrist for daring to write a poem about their divorce, and many others spoke about the physical abuse they suffered in the marital home.

Belittling, ignoring, or trivialising their writing is one of the commonest forms of informally censoring women; and identifying them with their female characters is a foolproof way of denigrating them. This happens very rarely with men. Indeed, when women writers are interviewed they are asked about the personal details of their lives, but when men are interviewed, they are asked about Life and Literature. Nor are they reprimanded for straying from their designated spheres, or for being "anti-Indian" if they question their place in traditional culture. It doesn't help that the literary establishment is male-dominated, that there are few fora for women to meet and interact, and that publishing in any language is highly competitive and bristling with politics.

The greater part of book publishing in the world today is controlled by three major conglomerates, thus effectively controlling our total intellectual output! The number of independent presses is shrinking rapidly, and the few that exist are finding it extremely difficult to survive in a market dominated by chain stores, heavy discounts, and planned obsolescence. Small autonomous presses—feminist, green, left, radical and progressive—that publish not for profit primarily, but for social change, are finding it even more difficult; the consequences of this for women's writing, and for their access to a very important means of cultural expression and communication, cannot be underestimated.

North and South, but especially South, women have spontaneously, consciously, deliberately, through handbills, leaflets, pamphlets, source books, magazines and periodicals, theoretical debates, books and journals, created another world and commented on the world they are in. In cultures where education is denied to women, they have demanded it; where it is handed out mechanically, they have insisted that literacy is more than being able to read instructions on an anti-diarrhea packet. Where access to print is difficult, they have innovated with posters, songs, and low-cost materials. Where women have been diffident about writing, they have organised meetings to encourage them, first to talk, then write—or they have taken down what they said and then published it. All the testimonies by women over the last few years have come to us through transcripts, interviews and documents put out by small groups of women, networks like Women Living Under Muslim Law and Women Against Fundamentalism; or like Red Feminista Latinoamericana y del Caribe contra la Violencia Doméstica y Sexual, Fempress, and many others. All the Debates Feministas, the magazines of information and analysis, the bibliographies on specific issues, monographs, and special journal numbers have made an enormous contribution to spreading the word, to disseminating theory, and to theory building, and they have been largely responsible for what is sometimes called the "democratisation of information."

If much of this history is available to us today, it is because feminist publications, periodicals, and magazines have documented and preserved it for us. Not only were they the record keepers and archivists of the women's movement, they also contributed to challenging existing canons and changing the way in which knowledge is produced. A feminist or gender perspective on issues ranging from militarisation to religious fundamentalism; the environment and access to productive resources; the media, arts, and technology; politics and economics, and so on is now neither a bizarre notion nor a laughable proposition, even though it may not always be given the serious consideration that other "isms" receive. And feminism's contribution to neutralising masculinist terminology is now universally acknowledged.

The widespread acceptance—indeed, even the "mainstreaming"—of women's studies and the demands of the women's movement should have made for a concomitant growth in feminist publications, feminist bookstores, reviewing periodicals, presses, binderies, and all the ancillaries of the book trade. It should, in other words, have made for the burgeoning of what has been called the Women in Print Movement. That this has not happened is abundantly clear. By far the greater part of theoretical or "academic" feminist work today is published by university or academic presses; certainly, the greater part of more popular or general interest writing is published by trade or mass market publishers, while feminist presses are now truly occupying a "niche," specialising in one or other particular genre or category: lesbian, travel, mystery, classics, and so on. Several movement-inspired magazines have closed down, and those still in print are struggling to survive.

The opening up of mainstream publishing to the broad range of women's writing offers women writers the freedom to choose from a variety of options, but as more and more of them exercise their choice in favour of trade and academic presses (for very valid reasons, it must be said), those very many women in print who initially took the risk—relying, as Linda Gardiner says, on "sweat-equity and tremendous word-of-mouth publicity"—find their survival at stake. The impact of bookstore chains on feminist bookstores, for example, has been devastating in the U.S. In 1998 their number dropped from 110 to 85, a fall of 25 percent, and most bookshops in towns where the superchains have opened have seen their book sales drop by about 15 to 40 percent. Only eight years earlier, in 1990, their combined sales were more than $35 million. Their expenses, however, remain the same, as does their commitment to their communities and to selling feminist books.

The importance of being economically viable is not lost on feminist publishers, but because our objective is primarily to be true to our politics, we walk a tightrope. The skill, as Susan Hawthorne says, lies in combining the commercial with the political—but there's the rub. Feminist publishing, or publishing for social change, is by definition a "developmental" activity in every sense of the word. It's a long-term investment involving the surfacing or excavating of hitherto unremarked or unacknowledged work; often initiating research or writing on subjects that have been ignored or discounted; working closely—and uneconomically, it might be added—over long periods with authors; and, above all, developing material, awareness, skills, writers, markets and, not least, developing a readership. This is more or less true generally, but particularly so in countries of the South. Not only are we unable to provide advances or other inducements to our authors, we are simultaneously engaged in publishing the kind of movement-related material that no commercial publishers will take up: reports, primers, handbooks, training manuals, and so on. Slow gestation, low returns, and difficult marketing characterise this kind of material, which many may not even classify as "books" or "monographs," for much of it is fragmentary and documentary in nature. Because it is unsuited to the retail trade, it needs to be marketed differently—through nongovernmental organisations, alternative networks, in training programmes and workshops, and at women's caucuses, conferences, and seminars. All of this requires networking and dogged perseverance of a kind that commercial publishing is unable—and, what's more, unwilling—to invest in because its interest lies in "movement as market," not movement as resistance.

It is in this paradoxical context that we have to work for change today. Cybernetics ensures that practically anyone's message can be disseminated worldwide instantly, yet death threats—and even divorce as censorship, as happened recently with Nawal el Saadawi—are on the rise. The attempt on the part of those who censor is not to prevent others from reading what we write, but to prevent us from writing or speaking in the first place. And, as we know from the discussions with writers quoted earlier, the most powerful censors are usually at home. The question before us, therefore, is: how can we enable women's voices, censored by culture, society, family and the market—and women's publishing, embattled and with its back to the wall—to continue working for progressive social change?

bell hooks

■

Women Who Write Too Much

With the modern classics *Ain't I a Woman: Black Women and Feminism* and *Feminist Theory: From Margin to Center,* bell hooks radically transformed U.S. feminist thought and emerged as one of its most influential critical voices. Also well-known as a provocative cultural critic, educator, filmmaker, and lecturer, hooks has distinguished herself as a "leading public intellectual of her generation." With over twenty published works on feminism, race, media, writing, and more, she is a prolific writer who often brings out two full-length books in the same year. But as hooks suggests, literary and intellectual productivity, when practiced on the margins, often exacts a strange and ambivalent response from reading audiences, from critics, and even from other feminist writers.

In this selection from her 1999 collection *Remembered Rapture: The Writer at Work,* hooks reveals the public's uneasy reception of "women who write too much"—and her own uneasy realization that the publishing establishment does impact her "capacity to write." Like Ritu Menon, hooks pulls into view hidden censors that not only silence women writers but punish those who break through what literary studies pioneer Tillie Olsen famously described as the silence of "exhausted achievement." Noting the hard-won marketplace success enjoyed by women writers in the last thirty years—spearheaded by feminist publishers and later co-opted by mainstream presses—hooks expresses dismay that "these changes have led to conflict and competition between women who write a lot and those who don't." hooks urges us to consider this paradigm shift in public discourse as a "significant advance for all women writers." Nevertheless, she remains dubious and warns us to beware: "Until the prolific female writer, and specifically the black female writer, is no longer seen as an anomaly we cannot rest assured that the degree of gender equity that exists currently in the writing and publishing world is here to stay."

■

There are writers who write for fame. And there are writers who write because we need to make sense of the world we live in; writing is a way to clarify, to interpret, to reinvent. We may want our work to be recognized, but that is not the reason we write. We do not write because we must; we always have choice. We write because language is the way we keep a hold on life. With words we experience our deepest understandings of what it means to be intimate. We communicate to connect, to know community. Even though writing is a solitary act, when I sit with words that I trust will be read by someone, I know that I can never be truly alone. There is always someone who waits for words, eager to embrace them and hold them close.

For the vast majority of my life I have longed to write. In my girlhood writing was the place where I could express ideas, opinions, beliefs that could not be spoken. Writing has then always been where I have turned to work through difficulties. In some ways writing has always functioned in a therapeutic manner for me. In *The Dancing Mind,* Toni Morrison suggests that the therapeutic ways writing can function are at odds with, or at least inferior to, a commitment to writing that is purely about the desire to engage language imaginatively. She contends: "I have always doubted and disliked the therapeutic claims made on behalf of writing and writers. . . . I know now, more than I ever did (and I always on some level knew it), that I need that intimate, sustained surrender to the company of my own mind while it touches another. . . . " Morrison's description of the urge that leads to writing resonates with me. Still, I believe that one can have a complete imaginative engagement with writing as a craft and still experience it in a manner that is therapeutic; one urge does not diminish the other. However, writing is not therapy. Unlike therapy, where anything may be spoken in any manner, the very notion of craft suggests that the writer must necessarily edit, shape and play with words in a manner that is always subordinated to desired intent and effect. I call attention to the way writing has functioned therapeutically for me as a location where I may articulate that which may be difficult, if not impossible to speak in other locations because this need leads me to turn and turn again to the written words and partially explains the sheer volume of my written work.

As long as I had only written and published one or two books no one ever inquired or commented on my writing process, on how long it took me to complete the writing of a book. Once I began to write books regularly, sometimes publishing two at the same time, more and more comments were made to me about how much I was writing. Many of these comments conveyed the sense that I was either doing something wrong by writing so much, or at least engaged in writing acts that needed to be viewed with suspicion. When I first took creative-writing classes from women professors who taught from a feminist perspective, we were encouraged to examine the way that sexism had always interfered with women's creativity, staging disruptions that not only limited the breadth and range of women's writing but the quantity as well. In a feminist studies course taught by writer Tillie Olsen I learned reading her essays on writing that prior to the 1960s it was rare if a white female writer, or a black female or male writer, published more than one book. We talked in class both about the material conditions that "silence" writers as well as the psychological barriers (i.e., believing that work will not be received or that what one has to say is either not important or has already been said). Knowing that black writers had faced difficulties that inhibited their capacity to write or complete works that had been started did serve as a catalyst challenging me to write against barriers—to complete work, to not be afraid of the writing process.

To overcome fears about writing, I began to write every day. My process was not to write a lot but to work in small increments, writing and rewriting. Of course I found early on that if I did this diligently these small increments would ultimately become a book. In *The Writing Life,* Annie Dillard reminds readers: "It takes years to write a book—between two and ten years. Less is so rare as to be statistically insignificant. One American writer has written a dozen major books over six decades. . . . Out of a human population on earth of four and a half billion perhaps twenty people can write a book in a year." Dillard's numbers may no longer be accurate as writers today not only have more time to write but have more writing aids (like the computer). Certainly as a writer who has hand-written, then typed or keyed into computer, all my books, I know how the computer and printer speed up the process. Typing and retyping a book takes much more time than keying in rewrites on a computer. I never approach writing thinking about quantity. I think about what it is I want to say. These days when I see the small yet ample stack of books I have written (usually seen at book signings), I know that this body of work emerged because I am again and again overwhelmed by ideas I want to put in writing. Since my interests are broad and wide-ranging, I am not surprised that there is an endless flow of ideas in my mind.

I write as one committed simultaneously to intellectual life, which means that ideas are the tools I search out and work with to create different and alternative epistemologies (ways of knowing). That I am continuously moved to share these ideas, to share thought processes in writing is sometimes as much a mystery to me as it is to readers. For I have writing comrades who work with ideas in the mind as much as I do but who are not as driven as I am to articulate those ideas in writing. A driving force behind my writing passion is political activism. Contrary to popular assumption writing can function as a form of political resistance without in any way being propagandistic or lacking literary merit. Concurrently, writing may galvanize readers to be more politically aware without that being the writer's sole intent.

A covert form of censorship is always at work when writing that is overtly espousing political beliefs and assumptions is deemed less serious or artistically lacking compared to work that does not overtly address political concerns. In our culture practically every aspiring writer realizes that work that is not addressing the status quo, the mainstream, that addresses unpopular political standpoints will rarely be given attention. It certainly will not make the best-seller list. Since I began my writing career utterly uninterested in writing anything other than poetry and fiction, work that I did not see as political, I was more acutely aware than most writers might be that by writing critical essays on unpopular political issues, I might never be seen by the mainstream world of critics and readers as an artistically "serious" writer. It has been challenging to maintain a commitment to dissident writing while also writing work that is not overtly political, that aspires to be more purely imaginative.

Successful writing in one genre often means that any work done in another genre is already marked as less valuable. While I have been castigated for writing critical essays that are too radical or simplistic, just "wrong-minded," the poetry I write along with other work that does not overtly address political concerns is often either ignored or castigated for not being political enough. Until we no longer invest in the conventional assumption that a dichotomy exists between imaginative writing and nonfiction work, writers will always feel torn. Writers will always censor their work to push it in the direction that will ensure it will receive acclaim. Everyone knows that dissident writing is less likely to bring literary recognition and reward.

Dissident voices are rarely published by mainstream presses. Many writers from marginal groups and/or with unpopular perspectives have relied on small presses to publish their work. Indeed, my writing would not have achieved public acclaim were it not for the alternative small presses publishing my work at a time when large publishing houses simply held to the conviction that writing about race and gender would not sell. Mainstream publishers showed interest in my writing only after sales of work published with small presses documented that an established book-buying audience existed. Significantly, the publication of my work by a mainstream press was also possible because many young college-educated workers in the industry were familiar with the work because they had studied it in school or knew that other students were excited about it and they could affirm the existence of an established readership.

My zeal for writing has intensified over the years and the incredible affirming feedback from readers is one catalyst. In my early writing years I thought this zeal was purely a function of will. However I found that rejection by the publishing world really affected my capacity to write. It left me feeling blocked, as though no one wanted to hear my ideas. No writer writes often or well if they despair of ever having an audience for their work. Knowing that readers want to hear my ideas stimulates my writing. While it does not lead me to write if I am uninspired, it does enhance my capacity to work when inspired. Long solitary hours spent writing feel more worthwhile when a writer knows there are eager readers waiting for new work. Oftentimes I write about issues readers have repeatedly asked me questions about at public lectures. My professorial work, which includes both classroom settings and public lectures, keeps me in closer touch with reader response to my work than I might be were I creating work in a more isolated manner. It is equally true that engaged dialogue about ideas is also a stimulant for writing. Sometimes I feel an urgent need to write ideas down on paper to make room for new ideas to arrive, keep my mind from becoming too crowded.

Historically the writers in our culture who were the most prolific were white males. Now this is changing. However, as more writers from marginal groups break silences or barriers that led to the creation of only one work, producing a body of work is often viewed with disdain or disparagement. While it is true that market forces lead the publishing industry to encourage writers to produce books that may simply be repetitive, poorly written, and uninspired simply because anything specific successful writers write will sell, it does not follow from this that every writer who has an ample body of work is merely responding to market-driven demands. Since I have never tried to make a living as a writer, I have had the extreme good fortune to be able to write only what I want to write when I want to write it. Not being at the mercy of the publishing industry to pay the rent or put food on the table has meant that I have had enormous freedom to resist attempts by the industry to "package" my work in ways that would be at odds with my artistic vision. Reflecting on the interplay between writing and the marketplace in *Art {Objects}*, Jeanette Winterson comments: "Integrity is the true writer's determination not to buckle under market forces, not to strangle her own voice for the sake of a public who prefers its words in whispers. The pressures on young writers to produce to order and to produce more of the same, if they have had a success, is now at overload, and the media act viciously in either ignoring or pillorying any voice that is not their kind of journalese." When I choose to write an essay book that includes work that may have been published first in magazines, reviewers will often write about the work as though it is stale, nothing new. A book of mine might include ten new essays (which alone could be a book) and four or five pieces that were published elsewhere and a reviewer might insist that there is no new work in the collection. Men can produce collections in which every piece has been published elsewhere and this will not even be mentioned in reviews. This critical generosity cuts across race. Two books that come to mind are Cornel West's collection *Race Matters* and Henry Louis Gates Jr.'s book *Thirteen Ways of Looking at a Black Man*. While feminist intervention altered the nature of contemporary women's writing, it has had little impact on critical evaluations of that work in the mainstream press.

Dissident writing is always more likely to be trashed in mainstream reviews. Rarely do mainstream critiques of my work talk about the content of the writing—the ideas. It took years of writing books that were published by alternative presses for this work to be acknowledged by the mainstream publishing world. Had I stopped writing early on it is unlikely that my books would ever have received any notice in mainstream culture. Ironically, producing a body of work has been one of the reasons it has not been easy for critics to overlook my writing even as they often imply in written critique and conversation that I should write less. Usually these critics are other women. While contemporary feminism highlighted difficulties women writers face by challenging and intervening on institutionalized barriers, it also opened up new possibilities (i.e., women's presses, more women entering the field of publishing). The incredible success of feminist and/or women's writing in the marketplace certainly compelled mainstream publishers to reconsider old approaches to writing by and about women. It is simply easier for women writers to write and sell work than ever before. As a consequence it has become more difficult for women to attribute failure to write or sustain creativity solely to sexist biases. These changes have led to conflict and competition between women who write a lot and those who do not, especially when the latter attribute nonproduction to sexist barriers. The harshest critics of my work have been less well-known black women writers and/or individuals who have had difficulty producing new work.

Like other women writers, who face barriers but surmount them to do the work they feel called to do, I find it disheartening when our literary triumphs however grand or small are not seen as part of a significant advance for all women writers. Until the prolific female writer, and more specifically the black female writer, is no longer seen as an anomaly we cannot rest assured that the degree of gender equity that exists currently in the writing and publishing world is here to stay. And while women writers should not be in any way fixated on the notion of quantity, we all should feel utterly free to write as much as time, grace, and the imagination allow.

Time remains a central concern for all women writers. It is not simply a question of finding time to write—one also writes against time, knowing that life is short. Like the poet Donald Hall I was enchanted by the Scripture that admonishes us to "work while it is day for the night cometh when no man can work." Even as a child these words made an impression. They haunted my own search for discipline as a writer. In his memoir *Life Work* Hall contemplates the relation between writing and dying, stating that "if work is no antidote to death, nor a denial of it, death is a powerful stimulus to work. Get done what you can." Annie Dillard urges us to "write as if you were dying." A large number of black women writers both past and present have gone to early graves. To know their life stories is to be made aware of how death hovers. When I was a young girl I studied the lives of writers I admired hoping to find guidance for my work. One of my favorite literary mentors was the playwright and critical thinker Lorraine Hansberry, who died in her mid-thirties. Her essay "The Negro Writer and His Roots" posed challenging questions for a young writer and intellectual. Hansberry declared: "The foremost enemy of the Negro intelligentsia of the past has been and remains—isolation. No more than can the Negro people afford to imagine themselves removed from the most pressing world issues of our time—war and peace, colonialism, capitalism vs. socialism—can I believe that the Negro writer imagines that he will be exempt from artistic examination of questions which plague the intellect and spirit of man." Of course, I often pondered the paths Hansberry might have taken had she lived longer. Her death and the early deaths of Pat Parker, Audre Lorde, Toni Cade Bambara, to name only a few, stand as constant reminders that life is not promised—that it is crucial for a writer to respect time. Without urgency or panic, a writer can use this recognition to both make the necessary time for writing and make much of that time.

Like many writers, I am protective of the time I spend writing. Even though women write more today than ever before, most women writers still grapple with the issue of time. Often writing is the task saved for the end of the day. Not just because it is hard to value writing time, to place it above other demands, but because writing is hard. Oftentimes the writer seeks to avoid the difficulties that must be faced when we work with words. Although I have written many books, writing is still not easy. Writing so much has changed me. I no longer stand in awe of the difficulties faced when working with words, overwhelmed by the feeling of being lost in a strange place unable to find my way or crushed to silence. Now I accept that facing the difficult is part of the heroic journey of writing, a preparation, a ritual of sanctification—that it is through this arduous process of grappling with words that writing becomes my true home, a place of solace and comfort.

Meena Alexander

■

Lyric in a Time of Violence

When Meena Alexander's memoir *Fault Lines* first appeared in 1993, prominent literary scholar Catharine R. Stimpson noted her as "a leading member of a very special generation of women writers." *Fault Lines* brilliantly evokes a life lived—and rendered—at the crossroads of multiple exiles, languages, and worlds. Ten years later, this internationally-celebrated poet, novelist, and critic brought out a startling new edition (2003) that may permanently change how we read and write lives. In "Book of Childhood," a new hundred-page coda, Alexander explores with equal parts delicacy and rage the nature of traumatic memory and recovery. Born in Allahabad shortly after India regained its independence, she would move with her family to Sudan when she was five years old. Annual transoceanic voyages between south India and a civil war–stricken Sudan would be the stuff of her adolescence—and of her works to come. Writing poetry by age ten, often secretly, her first published poem appeared in a Khartoum newspaper when she was just fifteen. That same year she would also change her name from Mary Elizabeth to Meena, a name "stripped free of the colonial burden." In her life and work as a transnational writer, this would be the first of many acts of artistic and political self-determination.

In this selection from "Book of Childhood," Alexander's project to (re)member the violence from her past is radically altered by the September 11, 2001, attacks on the World Trade Center, just a few miles from her home in Upper Manhattan. Here she depicts her daily struggle to respond–as writer, woman, mother, New Yorker, South Asian, educator, survivor, and public poet—to this day's violence and its ceaseless aftershocks around the world. What we are left with is a powerful meditation on the creative process in a violent world—and the necessity of art in that world.

■

The girl who eats stones, swallows them so that she can live. She comes to me at a time of difficulty.

She comes as if to say, so long as one lives there is no escape.

Time has touched her. She is a woman now, just as I am.

There is a slight shimmer of grey at her temples. She has grown wings, large wings, but she keeps them folded.

In dreams I see her, wings folded, as she crouches by the stones at Liberty Street, at the foot of the burning towers.

She is dressed in a blood red sari, and at times she tears apart the sari, tears the blouse and strips to her skin to show me the heart beating underneath.

Noke, noke, she flaps her wings so that I can learn to look and see, so I can write elegies for those who died the day the towers burst into flames, and for those who were killed in another country, in the aftermath.

Sometimes I think inside me is a girl child who refuses to die. She has become a dark metamorphic creature.

She has grown wings, wears bloody clothing, and keeps pace with me.

The sky is very blue on the morning of September 11, utterly bright and clear, one of the those September mornings when it feels as if light might flow through your body.

I wake up early, as I often do to write. Just returned from Lavigny, I am getting back into my New York skin, learning the sounds and smells of the apartment again. The bits of prose I wrote in Lavigny have come to nothing. I set them away in a drawer and try to settle into preparing for class.

A little after 8 A.M., I pick up the phone and call amma. Sometimes it feels as if my life is punctuated by these phone calls. When I listen to her, space is stitched together, migration turns true. Her voice at the other end restores, abrades.

For the first time in so many years, she has gone on a journey. During the time that appa was ill, it was impossible for her to leave him and travel away. She has boarded a plane, flying north from Kochi, into the city of Chennai to visit my younger sister.

Amma asks how I am settling back in, how the children are doing. I feel a sense of fulfilment, sipping my morning tea. For months now I have helped her, step by step. Asking her to buy a new suitcase, set our family documents in a neighbour's safe, get another chowkidar for the house she is leaving behind for a short while.

I put the phone down, stretch out my legs, and imagine my mother in my sister's garden in Tambaram, the deer that saunter in, the aging peacock that struts in through the tangled vines.

Then the phone rings sharply. Once, twice.

"Turn on the TV, Mom. Right now."

Adam's voice is pitched with some emotion I cannot identify. At his insistence, I turn on the TV.

The twin towers fill the screen. They are something I have taken for granted, those twin towers I see from Fifth Avenue when I go to work. I have often wondered what it would be like to live in such a tall building of steel and glass, though I know people only work there. Once when I went I had to have my photo ID taken, and I held tight onto it, as a marker of something, what I could not tell.

Now on the screen I see a tower with a ball of fire exploding through it.

First a streak of fire that a plane made as it rammed through, then flames and smoke and the slow black implosion of the building. I keep watching till it collapses on the screen. I cannot bear it anymore. There are thousands of all-too-ordinary people working in those towers. Down below is the plaza where my daughter, Svati, now a teenager, went for a dance performance just two nights ago, and close by is the pier where Adam hung out when he was at Stuyvesant High School. I think of the pier and the blue waters of the estuary, which now on TV look as if they are on fire too.

I force myself to leave the apartment, to walk outside. I feel as if I am walking outside of my own body.

Fort Washington Avenue is so very still. I walk toward the park.

I see two women who are cleaning up, leaves, debris, odds and ends. They wear blue T-shirts. The sky is very clear, the leaves on this northern end of Manhattan, a deep green. A perfect fall day.

One woman says: "I saw the slip of a moon, tiny, like that."

She points at the sky.

"It was a sign, surely. I have never seen a moon like that so early. In the afternoon for sure, but in the morning? Never."

The other woman nods. We are all searching for signs.

A man stands by a huge truck that has a parrot sign on it, Parrot

Hauling. He has a parrot on his arm, plume perfect as if it flew off the side of the truck. He is listening to the radio.

"Do you know what today is?" he asks.

I shake my head.

"Nine eleven," he says. "Nine one one. Get it? What other day could it be? September 11, 2001."

I keep walking till I reach the stone parapets by the highway and the river. I have never seen George Washington Bridge like this, no traffic, absolutely nothing except a police car, its lights flashing in the clear light of day.

Approaching I see a man with a dog. He works in the Bronx court-house, he tells me, and has walked over the bridge. All the traffic over bridges is stopped, he says, all the subways are closed.

I start to worry for Svati, who goes to the Bronx High School of Science. I return home but cannot reach her on the phone. The lines are overloaded. Cell phones are dead. Finally I reach her and she tells me that she is at the home of a friend near the school and that she will walk back, over the 181st Street Bridge. I call up my cousin who lives nearby so he and his wife will come with me to pick her up. I am shaking inside and feel faint.

Ella, a friend who lives on Bleecker Street, calls.

"I saw both towers fall," she says. "It was a terrible thing, Meena. I saw them burst and fall from my balcony. And I saw them on my TV screen. One and the other, at the very same time. What is happening to us? What?" As I listen to her, I hold tight to the phone for fear I will drop it.

In the afternoon I wait by the bridge with other anxious people. The city uptown is in an odd state of disarray. There are police, people milling about not knowing what to do. I run forward, seeing my child walk slowly, tired from her trek, over the bridge. I rush to embrace her and tears fill my eyes. She is a little awkward seeing me like that. Her friends, all girls of fifteen, are laughing, trying to make sense of the day. Laughter covers over their fear. They had thought they might have to bed down in the school but then finally were allowed to leave.

Walking back with Svati on Overlook Terrace we meet the super's son, who has walked home from Wall Street. His white shirt is stained with sweat.

"I saw a man leap as I was running," he says. "And another. A woman too. Yes, a woman jumped. She was filled with fire."

My child is with me as she hears this; she has walked safely over the bridge. She listens, her eyes moist.

In the evening as she is drinking warm milk, Svati tells me of announcements that were made over the public address system in the school to inform the children of the events. Children who had parents at the World Trade Center were encouraged to call them. Some of the children were weeping.

"There was such a long line at the phone, Mama," she said. "I couldn't have reached you just then, and in any case I knew you were at home. You told me you were going to stay home and write."

Then she tells me about her drama class. The semester has just begun and they are all new in class. It is composed mainly of white Jewish children. A girl leans over to her and says, "So are you Middle Eastern?"

"No," my daughter says. "Why would you ask me that?"

"Because you have that olive color."

"My skin was screaming at me, Mama," my beautiful girl child says, her face puckering up, tears prickling her eyes.

"They were all staring at me. All the kids in class."

There is rage in her and grief. Together we sit on the couch and watch the details of the devastation in this island city we love. Those in flight and those dead. The mounds of burning wood and plaster and glass and steel.

Students send me emails. Zohra from Afghanistan, who has spent bits and pieces of her childhood in other countries.

"Like typical New Yorkers," she says, "we tried to be brave."

But after hearing that the Pentagon was hit there was panic at the Graduate Center. Zohra tells me all this, two days later, with great calm. In the company of others she decided to walk home to Brooklyn.

At night I speak to Adam again. I tell him that Stuyvesant has been turned into a triage center for the wounded. One of Svati's friends tells her that as they were fleeing the school, the wounded were being borne in on stretchers. This stays in my mind, makes a mark there.

Adam wants to return home immediately. He is in his senior year at Brown University and wants to catch the train back from Providence. I tell him to be careful, to wait a few days. Just the other day three Indians were taken off the Boston train in handcuffs. They were utterly innocent, but they were taken for terrorists. Adam is six foot two. A handsome young man, he has cultivated a mop of dark curly hair. I tell him to get a haircut, to be safe. I do not want him to be picked up. Then suddenly I catch myself short, anxious that my maternal fears will puncture the fabric of our lives. But that fabric has darkened, shrunk a little. It has shredded in places.

Two days later it is Thursday. At the end of spring a friend and I had dreamt up a course we wanted to call Translated Lives: Postcolonial Texts. But Francesca is still in Paris, for her father is ill. Our course is on migration, crossing borders, what it means to make a habitation with words. In preparation I was reading some trauma theory and post-colonial texts, performances as well as poetry.

I pick up my papers and prepare to go to the university. I need to make a space to think and feel and grieve with my students. The timing of this week's reading seems uncanny: the topics are trauma, memory, war. I pack Theresa Cha's *Dictée,* a text that has enormous resonance for me, into my bag, also Cathy Caruth's *Unclaimed Experience,* which I had brought home to read again. As well as the thin Xerox of that fierce, lovely essay by Toni Morrison, "The Site of Memory," a defense of fragments.

What does it mean to fashion a self in the face of a violent world? I try to pack the truth of my life into what I will tell my students. Slowly I make my way to work.

On Broadway, as I make for the university, an acquaintance says, "Be careful."

"Why?" I ask.

"Because you have dark skin, they might think you are an Arab," she says. I laugh this off, but my skin starts to feel tight and parched.

The university is next to the Empire State Building, which was evacuated. There were ninety bomb scares in Manhattan, all of them false.

A smoke haze covers the far downtown end of Fifth Avenue, where the twin towers used to be. I think I see twisted metal sticking up. Smoke drifts uptown. The underground parking garages are filled with acrid smoke, the sweet scent of burning flesh and twisted metal and wood.

At the university, one of my students breaks out weeping and I try to comfort her. Another says she has been weeping off and on and doesn't know why. Why? Why, she asks.

Everyone looks dazed. A colleague comes up, his eyes red. "I was there," he says, "and saw the towers explode. I was in divorce court at the time. I ran for my life."

Yesterday they handed out smoke masks to people in our building. Today the wind from the site of devastation is milder. We have a community meeting to discuss evacuation procedures. A man says: "I know that patriotism is in short supply at the Graduate Center, but isn't this the moment to put up an American flag?" All the flags that were there have blown into the barbed wire of the scaffolding. The perpetual scaffolding we have for building improvement.

At night on Fort Washington Avenue, when I return home the leaves are black in the trees. The street lamps burn outside the shrine of Mother Cabrini.

Now there is a mountain in my dreams. Not Mont Blanc. This is a mountain of twisted metal parts and rubble and human bodies. Fire pours out of it. In my dream I see body parts, a hand, a thigh, a torn lip, twisted in. I wake up in the middle of the night to try to call amma, to reassure her that we are alive, but the phone lines are still dead.

The next night it rains. The rain mixed with mud makes the rescue work very hard. There is a mountain of metal, the debris of the towers. Fearful that lightning would strike, the rescue workers had to be very careful. My girl child wants to stay at home on the weekend. In this green bowl at the northern edge of the island.

I do not know what else to say just now, I write in my journal.

I write to myself so that time will not stop short.

The devastation is enormous, mounds of rubble and metal and glass and innocent lives blown to tiny bits. It rains and the leaves are very green. Elsewhere by Ground Zero rain mixes with ash and makes the rescue work very difficult. This is our floating life, this peril, this sweet island with its southern tip burning.

When I was a child I saw the sea burn.

How often I have thought that sentence but with no page to set it on, no place to make it mine. As I sit and write, my words fly off the page. I think of geese lumbering into the wind. Or paper kites grown men have held in their hands, stretched taut over wind, over water, lit by the half darkness. But the darkness turns into barbed wire. In reaching for the past I am forced to crawl through it.

Barbed wire grips fences, scaffoldings, beams. You cannot toss barbed wire into the skies and have it hold. Who would have thought that you could have jets holding innocent passengers hurled into tall towers that flame?

What did Nagarjuna mean when he wrote: "If fire is lit in water, who can extinguish it?" At the time he was living on an island, and he wrote his aphorisms on rock.

There was rock under the tall towers that flamed on this island where I live. After the planes hit the towers on that terrible day in September and the towers burst into flames and fell, rock started to burn in all its crevices too, a slow burn through the veins of the earth where gases leaked out and caught fire, and wires and fuselage and plastics and metal and bone and hair started to mass and fuse in a sortilege that this island of Manhattan had never seen before.

Tor of destruction that made even the clouds weep. Two days after September 11, clouds amassed in the sky in New York City and then it started to rain.

The leaves were very green outside my window. Leaves of linden and birch and, in the distance, across a stone wall, the Hudson River. The garden between the two apartment blocks was still sweet, at the edge of autumn, overgrown, plants gone to seed.

At night I dreamt of a flash of fire, a plane with fire from its wings, bursting apart the bricks, then vanishing in a puff of smoke. This keeps repeating. The plane is not coming through our building yet, but rather through the one next to ours, a building exactly like this, with which we share a garden. In the dream I am floating, above my own body. I wake up, sit bolt upright in shock as I start to remember.

I cannot keep up prose anymore. I turn to my first love, poetry. I do not want to write about childhood. I do not want to be swallowed up in the past with so much molten and flowing. I need to bear witness to what is now, and the poem will allow me to do what I can.

I make tiny notes on scraps of paper. I feel the lyric poem will allow me to catch the edginess of things, the sharp nervosity, the flaming, falling buildings.

I must work back from the pressure of the present into the past, for that is the only way I will reach into the real. And when someone questions me about this I say: In all my work, place is layered on place to make a palimpsest of sense. That is the kind of art I make. Yet the very indices of place have been altered by traumatic awareness.

It seems to me that the lyric poem is a form of extreme silence, which is protected from the world. To make a lyric poem I have to enter into a dream state. But at the same time, almost by virtue of that disconnect, it becomes a very intense location to reflect on the world.

The day I went to the university to teach my class, I started the first of a cycle of three elegies for the dead. I called them "Aftermath," "Invisible City," and, the last, "Pitfire." I used couplets making twelve lines for each poem, and somehow the form helped me to crystallize and think through without fear. Here are the first two poems; they need to stand side by side:

Aftermath

There is an uncommon light in the sky
Pale petals are scored into stone.

I want to write of the linden tree
That stoops at the edge of the river

But its leaves are filled with insects
With wings the color of dry blood.

At the far side of the river Hudson
By the southern tip of our island

A mountain soars, a torrent of sentences
Syllables of flame stitch the rubble

An eye, a lip, a cut hand blooms
Sweet and bitter smoke stains the sky.

New York City, September 13–18, 2001

Invisible City

Sweet and bitter smoke stains the air
The verb *stains,* has a thread torn out

I step out to the linden grove
Bruised trees are the color of sand.

Something uncoils and blows at my feet
Sliver of mist? Bolt of beatitude?

A scrap of what was once called sky?
I murmur words that come to me

Tall towers, twin towers I used to see.
A bloody seam of sense drops free.

By Liberty Street, on a knot of rubble
In altered light, I see a bird cry.

New York City, October 17–November 3, 2001

While making my poems I kept walking down to Ground Zero, as close as I could get, making returns, a pilgrimage, the site a graveyard for thousands, filled with the stench of burning flesh and wires.

On one trip, as I walked past Liberty Street I was struck by the extreme youth of the soldier guarding the perimeter, a young lad freckled, fresh faced. Behind him the shell of Tower 2, against which an ancient patriarch was getting photographed. Small children screaming in delight at pigeons, a rescue worker holding his hands to this own throat, face sunk with exhaustion, his gas mask at his hip.

I made a third poem as part of this cycle and called it "Pitfire." Nine months later I was invited to read my elegies at the Hunter College graduation. In Radio City Music Hall, a place I had never set foot in before, I stood at a lectern and read my poems. The bagpipers of the New York City Fire Department had just played their haunting notes for the dead. My voice was clear but I could feel the waves of suffering in their music.

I turned to face the bagpipers, who were still on stage as I read "Pitfire," a poem I had written in such loneliness, never dreaming that I would one day read it aloud, return it in sound and breath to the part of the world it came from.

Pitfire

In altered light I hear a bird cry.
By the pit, tor of metal, strut of death.

Bird song yet. *Liturgie de cristal.*
Flesh in fiery pieces, mute sediments of love.

Shall a soul visit her mutilated parts?
How much shall a body be home?

Under these burnt balconies of air,
Autumnal duty that greets us.

At night, a clarinet solo I put on:
Bird song pitched to a gorge, a net of cries.

Later a voice caught on a line:
"See we've touched the bird's throat."

New York City, November 20–December 5, 2001

The poem needs to be sharp, as clear and facetted as broken glass. It must pick up the multitudinous cries of the world that we are.

Later in the month of September, I started another poem. I called it "Kabir Sings in the City of Burning Towers." I need to tell the story behind it.

There was a meeting of the newly established Asian/Asian-American Research Institute. I had been asked to serve on the governing board, and the board members were to meet at the Graduate Center. As I recall it, the first meeting was set for barely a week after September 11, but that was postponed and we met in October.

It was the sort of gathering to which I would wear a sari without thinking twice, but now something nagged at me. Two of my South Asian students had encountered trouble wearing salwar kameez, men yelling, one throwing a paper bag with an empty bottle inside. A friend of mine called from Boston. She told me how a man had yelled and spat at her. There was a pall of suspicion extending over Arabs and beyond to South Asians, brown people who looked like they could be Arabs.

I wanted to pick my battles. In all the grief and torment of a city under seige I wanted some control over the small things of life. With what it was like on the street, it made no sense to deliberately stick out. My daughter told me that the cousin of an Irani friend of hers, a young woman with long black hair, had endured a man in the subway who brandished scissors and cut off some of her hair. Immigrants were being swept up and put in detention with no charges lodged against them.

I decided to save my energies for writing, and I was writing a great deal of poetry.

I rolled up my sari in a manner that would not crease it, set it carefully in a plastic bag that I lodged in the center of my bookbag. In the fourth floor ladies' room I slipped out of my slacks and put on my sari. I watched the silk fall to the tiled floor and stared at my face in the mirror.

How dark I looked, unmistakably Indian. I needed to think through my fear. Later when I reentered that fourth floor ladies' room and looked in the mirror, I heard Kabir, the medieval poet saint who I love, singing to me in secret. He was giving me courage to live my life.

Kabir Sings in a City of Burning Towers

What a shame
they scared you so
you plucked your sari off,
crushed it into a ball

then spread it
on the toilet floor.
Sparks from the towers
fled through the weave of silk.

With your black hair
and sun dark skin
you're just a child of earth.
Kabir the weaver sings:

O men and dogs
in times of grief
our rolling earth
grows small.

I had written my poems quickly, to survive. But after writing there came
a time of fragmentation, being torn apart in so many directions: the fear
on this island, the condition of our lives, not knowing what could strike
next, fire, pestilence—that bitty white powder filled with anthrax spores. A
floor of the building where I teach was shut down for awhile. Meanwhile,
on the other side of the globe in Afghanistan, the terrible bombardment by
the United States, stones ground down, children starving, women in
burkhas fleeing. Both are places real. I live in one, I reach out to the other.
Disjoined in space, they coexist in time, in a molten present.

As a child I had lived at the borders of war. Moving back and forth
across the Indian Ocean, between Kerala and Khartoum in the Sudan.
In Sudan there was a civil war raging. On the way to India we often
stopped in Aden, in what is now Yemen. There were British Tommies
on the rocks and Yemeni freedom fighters hidden by the broken walls.
More recently in India, in the last few years there has been the rise of a
fascist Hindu movement, and terrible ethnic violence has scarred
Gujarat. Then too there has been the escalation on the border with
Pakistan and the fear of war. All this has been part of my personal history and has left a mark on my writing.

How can these violent versions of the real that cut into memory be
translated into art?

Art in a time of trauma, a necessary translation, "fragments of a ves-
sel," writes Walter Benjamin, "to be glued together."

But what if the paste shows, the seams, the fractures?

In a city blown up at its southern tip, the work of art must use the
frame of the real, translating a script almost illegible, a code of traumatic recovery.

It seems to me that in its rhythms the poem, the artwork, can incorporate scansion of the actual, the broken steps, the pauses, the blunt silences, the brutal explosions. So that what is pieced together is a work that exists as an object in the world but also, in its fearful consonance, its shimmering stretch, allows the world entry.

I think of it as a recasting that permits our lives to be given back to us, fragile, precarious.

Alia Mamdouh

■

Baghdad: These Cities Dying in Our Arms

In a recent conversation with Mona Chollet, Alia Mamdouh turns the tables on her interviewer with a question of her own: "What weight do all the books on Earth have compared to the groans of the people of Iraq, Palestine, and Bosnia?" But in her own work as a fearless writer and thinker, Mamdouh consistently brings art's power to subvert tyranny and repression to bear. Born in Baghdad in 1944, this seasoned journalist, essayist, short story writer, and novelist began her career as a reporter and editor in the 1970s. Shortly after the publication of her first novel in 1981, the government listed her among the country's "deceitful and seditious" writers for tackling themes such as sex, institutional power, and human rights. While never banned from writing in Iraq, she was effectively forced to publish her works abroad to avoid heavy censorship. In exile since 1982, Mamdouh continues to write fiercely against the politics of fear, homegrown totalitarianisms, and Western imperialisms. She has also lived and reported from Beirut and London, and has been in residence at the Centre Georges Pompidou in Paris since 2001.

"Baghdad: These Cities Dying in Our Arms" (2001) first appeared in English translation on Autodafe.org, the international library of censored writers. Commanding her talents as storyteller and commentator, here Mamdouh unfurls less obvious connections between state tyranny and violence at home; the body and the text; the ideologue and women's sexual repression; the exiled writer and her dying nation. She also casts in high relief the troubling, even damaging reception of Arab literature by the West. Here again she invokes the capacity of art to alter radically the worlds we live in: "I am rebuilding my country before you. It is a construction of anger, vast beauty, and identity, and I submit it to the act of writing—that will give it a finality."

■

1. The Region of Hell

In the fifth century B.C., legend tells us, Hiero, tyrant of Syracuse, forbade his subjects the use of speech; his cruelty was that extreme. Had I remained in the first City of B, Baghdad, I would have perished at an early age. In my heavy clothes, I could not imagine being able to walk. Thin and pale, I seemed to others a creature condemned to die of its own internal wars. Yet, no sooner would they draw near than my bearing would assault them. I would not allow them to look upon my suffering. Everything seemed headed for ruin, under the force of oppression. The cruelty was so extreme that I could only respond to injustice with joking, sarcasm, and irony.

At home we lived like the sightless. In my family there were no commander types—no chiefs, fighters, heroes, nor even politicians. The men were ordinary, just men you would encounter in the side streets and alleys. Simple employees they were, living out their lives amidst sleeplessness, illness, and deprivation. They had entered no prisons, inherited no sharp class divisions. They were ordinary folk, so utterly ordinary that they seemed masquerades of themselves.

My family maintained its public face by means of its own secret fear, a calculation that left out nothing. It was a fear that moved in ever-widening circles, rippling outward from living room to shared bedrooms, to school and the street, and even to the bathroom.

This fear might carry various labels: chivalry, friendliness, the bond of the womb and of an exclusive disdain. To this very moment I do not know how to name it, but I am certain that it will appear as I write. For it lurks in the experiences of many years; it is there on the blank, white pages that wait for the contents of emptied suitcases, even should the inscription remain muddled. I can still envision those individuals, as if we never did leave the region of hell. If, like them, I draw on my sense of touch to feel their warmth then, I will hear it said—now, here, in the West—that I still suffer from a measure of the primitive in my behavior.

Fine: I am a writer of the sensual. I trust my senses. I listen, I taste, and I take in smells, and that is the way I know how people and cities work. Creative writing must order things; it must repair and rebuild homelands, the nations we have left behind for places of exile, as we set ourselves to refurnish them anew. There must always be confrontations over what lies between us, not in the guise of enemies and plunderers, but as an attempt to cleanse our associations of any tendency to write revenge. I have tried as best I could to move beyond the expected roles—heroine, martyr, victim. For these are merely masks through which we prevaricate.

2. The Question of Writing

The most stirring—and the most cheerful—image of what I can call my first exile, a scene in black and white, takes place in my hometown. I hold the rock in my hand as I run after all of those who threaten me, those of this gang or that group, men or women, teachers, maternal aunts, paternal uncles, men of the grim neighborhood where I live.

First there was my father, the first policeman I ever stood up to in my life, since that was his line of work. He renounced his uniform and whip only in death, as I was about to turn sixteen. I was determined to keep him in a state of confusion; meek at home, I was ferocious in the street. And, because I felt so unattractive next to my handsome brother, I could not hold myself straight when I walked.

I held one thing in reserve: transgressing the limits of the forbidden in my mind and imagination. Waiting for the storm to rise and break over me, I conserved my power there. My body was my primary refuge and sole place of residence. That was where I placed my reliance as I moved toward maturity, even if my body had trapped me in its mines and riddles on the way. We were together, yet not bound to any specific place; no heroisms, no losses that left their mark on us. I would recount my stories, and tell of things that had left lumps in my throat, and my weight would begin to drop. We would sit together; but my body wanted to return alone—my body, the written and the writing simultaneously; the author that would ultimately fix the persona of the legacy left at the time of death, my death. From here and from there, the questions of writing show up. I stammer, because I am not the eloquent speaker that I should be; I attribute this to my difference; and I am branded as contradictory, accused of taking interest in matters of the body, openly, incessantly. Perhaps that is so—indeed, it is definitely so; but these are merely the ruses through which I work to erect contraries. I do this that I may merit this world, the only world permitted to me. In this I am no different from all the world's sinners, who know that nothing can be certain, that nothing is decisive, and that nothing is sufficient.

For writing is not salvation. Rather, in the best of circumstances it is a predicament that impels us to descend into the secret water of poetry's essence, in which the swimmer is cursed, while the one who comes out is tattooed with pleasure and delight. Is writing exile?

3. The Magic of the Kill

I was standing in front of my aunt as she ripped pages from my notebook, in which I had recorded some of my hunting expeditions. It seems that my case interested her in some way; but it was not me she was concerned about. She was not clever at sniffing out the fragrance of game, and was not an experienced or trained hunter. Frivolous and anxious, she was uncomfortable with the lost and love-mad souls around me, who wanted to fly from my phalanx. Only this aunt helped me to discover the censorship of the crude. She did not feign her harshness; like me, she dreamed of transgressing the boundaries of the forbidden, but for her this meant the taboos forbidden to me. Yet I had already offered my possessions to be trampled on with a vengefulness that did not wait for any executioner.

It would have been idiotic to attempt a rejoinder to the injustice, or to seek help, for everyone seemed to turn into one and the same person—invisible but nonetheless present, like the tyrant Hiero. The rooms had no keys; and I beheld my own words buried in dust and obduracy. That was when I turned my back upon them, all of them, every one, and took my life into my own hands. Only I would help myself. For severe and contradictory situations, consciously or not, allow some talents to flourish in a criminal fashion, if their fiber is already weakened by flaws and they lack the habitudes of personal strength. I was talking to myself as I turned the coals that smoldered inside me; and my manner of expression grew more deranged after the plundering of my secret little paradise. I transformed myself into a text—my own impossible, isolated text. I was alone, as people rarely are, and the blow was as extreme as it was valuable and enticing.

For the literary work, whatever its worth as creative literature, derives its power in some measure from that element of extreme cruelty or hardness. Venturing out into the streets and new cities, rubbing up against the shoulders of the people I encountered, I collected faces, lineaments, complicated relationships, and intertwined lives. I did not look behind me, except to gather the fragments of those creatures and to reunite the residues remaining in the depths of things, at the bottom of drinking glasses, and the sediments people carry. These residues might not spark much interest among some of us, but as we give the glass a shake, suddenly they cause us to see the project of our bloodlines clearly before us. It is my assertion that such a harsh solitude causes the characters to overwhelm the writer and to impose their existence.

In cold sympathy I killed the members of my family, one by one. Yes indeed, there are stages in life when we must learn the arts of killing. We must possess the boldness of the killer in order to deserve the honor of being cursed. Thereby I granted to my grandmother a space of unalterable faith, as if that sphere were at once the antidote and the dictator-like regime. Thereby, I dressed my father in ruffled peacock feathers. When I increased the pressure, there flitted upward before me the ringing tones of vanity, leaving the bones bare. What, then, can you do with the dead and the living around you, if it is your duty to move the story forward once again, from behind new masks, so that it will remain in harmony with your intended goal: to approach the self, and to undo the pledge that binds you in obligation to the other?

4. The First-Person Pronoun

Starting out from those simple but valuable truths, I tracked the footsteps of the characters in my novels, short stories, and other texts; starting out from the voices that stand in the middle of the road, halfway between the gods and the devils, halfway between the free circulation of faults, failure, deficiencies, errors, the private passions buried deep within us, that some of us do not dare to approach and acknowledge, neither before our own selves nor across the table. This was one of my justifications for using the first-person pronoun in most of my writings, that pronoun that the critics do not favor. It was a manner of putting myself in opposition to all, in the face of unjust ideas and iniquitous laws that were threatening my individuality—and my very existence—first and foremost as a female who was trying to undo and redo her relationship to the self, and then pushing it to the ultimate end-point, to exercise a will that still has not diminished, the will to rebel. And since I did not agree with any political faction, and as events and disasters revealed, I was that individual who, not seeking the cloak of a joint existence and program, appears nervously sensitive, for that person has no protection but the spiritual bruises incurred on the path in search of the truths of existence and the self.

The transformations in the world outside were so rapid that we could not keep up with them. What remained at the end of it all were not the grand mirages, but, to the contrary, the inner light that gives the spirit radiance. The imagination fissured, one fruit of those forbidden dreams, life's most wondrous means of defense, adversaries of foolishness and monstrosity, even if we are the victim; but rather that than being the victim of fanaticism, extremism, and terrorism. This is what allows me to confirm that such a choice was a kind of provocation against various kinds of coercion and restraint, for most of our Arabic writings remain subject to the didactic. There is always there, before them, the professorial chair, the pulpit, and the examination booklet of the greatest of inks, the West. First, then, we should have tried to originate, or invent, or discover a language to block the aggression, to split the ranks, to repel the humiliation and abasement that grew stronger day after day. From my own observations, it seems to me that across the passage of the last thirty years, a secret language has formed inside of our Arabic language; I can describe it as a furtive language. It is a language that lies between the spaces of all colors, even if they appear blunt, violent, stumbling. All we have to do is to write ourselves, to be Us, to present our own experiences and to extend what lies inside of us, so that the places, the people, and the existences that surround and abut us will expand as well.

At this point, there intrudes the problematic of translating our contemporary Arabic literature and culture. What the West does—especially France, with its gratifying efforts at providing information and acquaintance, organizing conferences and educational series, and so forth—I admit to thinking of as relations of consolation. Such activities construct a gaze that remains characterized by simplification, abridgement, and condescension. It is as if they are saying to us, or to themselves: Come, now, let us read or listen to the wailing, the muttering, of those writers, men and women, for that is all we hear. This is why a writer or a book may "explode" here in the West, because the writer or the book pleased and delighted the westerner with an exotic quality. For the West is the giver of blessings and medals, and the strict arbiter of pleasures and titles. We must say "I" in all simplicity, with a refined simplicity if we are truly to be the masters of our own words.

5. The Pleasure of Divulging Secrets

The women I used to see in the marketplace hammam[1] resembled a forgotten continent, replete with chaos and lack of expectation. I did not write about them in order to cast abuse on them, because the hammam also mirrored a sort of hell, but rather out of the imperative to craft those bodies with a character of mirth, liveliness, and sensitivity. As the bodies made their sweat and sent it off in front of me, they formed a vast free matter. Without trying to design or observe, I found myself watching bodies coming into their fullness and others on the verge of death. In the end, all that remained in my head—and fortunately so—were words, the writer's only consolation.

In that small space, the hammam was subject to the body's authority—it was the body's space—and it constituted the perplexity of instinctual desires. The rights to divulge secrets became preeminent. I was in a state of bewilderment. I did not neglect or ignore those secrets, nor did I try to recuperate the situation by seeing it as a case of adopting a desperate moral stance. It was one of the points where the thunderbolt had struck. There my breathing stopped, and there I began to see, in mid-formation, the arts of my games of the imagination—storytelling, narrative, the slyness of writing among ceremonies of water, food, and excessive expenditure. I was enamored of ordinary women, educated through their own efforts and not by means of blueprints for refinement; it was a greater and truer penchant than I could have had for intellectuals and militants, traitorous as they so often are. For I did not belong to any party. For me, the matter was not one of maneuvers; the question was how I could become a true writer. Across on the other bank, the image of the nationalist and Marxist parties in my country was esteemed by all, but the image I had formed of most men was of bureaucratic functionaries who jammed the ranks of the parties. As a result, the parties were nothing more than sites where lives, and people who dreamed of freedom and liberation, were buried or dissolved. If this was so for the men, then what of the women?

That was my generation, the sixties generation, whose list of teachers doubled and changed from one month to the next. They would line up behind Mao, Guevara, Marx of course, Bakunin, Trotsky, Gamal Abd al-Nasir, the Baath Party theorist Michel Aflaq, and so forth. They took up their posts beneath the era's banners, schools, and intellectual trends, with no emotion, neither awe nor alarm. They would contemplate their ample bellies for hours at a time, sitting day and night among their cigarette smoke and coughs, in dialogue and dispute. The Iraqi, it seems, is one of those human creatures who has been taught well that ideology stands alone in its importance; only ideology counts, and only ideology can supply all of the answers; these were people who had had blood ties, who could be united only by blood, and torn asunder only by blood. Ink and writing were under severe constraint, so that the blood, thickening, would allow us to see everything directly, not by means of an intermediary or delegate. Indeed, I do not give preference to those who work by delegation, for we all know that "the closets were full of corpses" both before and after the magic of that steel order, the Soviet Union, unraveled.

As I wrote in an essay published after the second Gulf War, "That was one of the richest cultural and political stages that Iraq passed through; the plantings of that era are still the most beautiful and the tallest-growing, a generation whose martyrs, vagabonds, and victims of hunger number more that those who sit behind elegant desks in air-conditioned rooms. This was a generation whose destruction was greater than those who caused that destruction."[2] This is what I focus on in my novel published a few months ago, *al-Ghulama* (The Girl),[3] what I call the culture of emptiness, the Iraqi tragedy that has rarely ever had its match. What we call the ideologue I envision as a scarecrow: elegant, perfumed, and stuffed with theories. He is the latest product to be given distinction by contemporary Arab ideologies. An ignoble product he is, adorned with and adulterated by that European self-importance that time has excused, and equally he is a product of the earliest period of Arabic decline and decadence. And perhaps the most glaring, and the most painful, image of that ideologue emerges in connection with women's status. For he still erupts in anger if she takes pleasure in being his partner in the marital bed. He simply brands her with prostitution.

6. The Bitterness of Departure

And so what do transitory ones like me do with freedom? What shall I do in Paris—"Baris" in Arabic, my second "City of B"—after the seductive, fancy gowns have disappeared? The idle fantasies, the consequences of lovely sins, are all gone. The intensities of love, the extreme thinness, all are things of the past. There is no doubt that the slyness that inheres in this age that I am remains an unexpected gift in all circumstances. Every ten years, I attempt to integrate myself into a new city, and I fail. All of them: Baghdad, Beirut, Rabat, London, and now Paris. Beirut, to the same extent, and Paris before Baghdad—the cities that begin with the letter B—are the ones that have compelled me to echo what was said by the prince of Vienna: "I love my situation, a stranger wherever I am. I am a Frenchman in Austria, an Austrian in France, and both in Russia. It is the most successful way to placate the self in all places, and to not be dependent on any one place." But I am dependent on my own country. For when we leave the nation, the nation begins to live anew. It is not merely a pile of rocks, a communications network, and a history. It is us—human beings who live within it or adjacent to it, or far from it such that every second it pierces us. Some nations might push one to madness or suicide, or remain a conduit of blood transfusions in order that one accept one's life. Why do we imagine that nations are immune to error? We must liberate ourselves from the consequences of holding the nation sacred, and from its tyranny. Yet Paris will not become my nation. Here, I find a state of anonymity that enraptures me: it prevents me from achieving any true integration. This integration, which most French governments have focused on as necessary, I see as a personal aggression against me. It is true that I am not in my own place because, in all simplicity, I do not know where my place is. I am a writer who chose to be on the margin, yet not marginalized, to remain unconcerned about being part of any groups, about cultural militias, or the light. If anyone should think about integrating me when I am at this age, I imagine him experiencing the highest degree of trouble.

Let's say that I am like the lover who flees from the one she has before her, though she might return to the same lover wearing different masks. For memory betrays, yet it is one of the artist's most important spurs. My memory attacks me among the cities, the places of exile, every one, resembling a flowing river that the mud and the wild plants enter, and the sediments from different rivers, as it runs across the territories of others.

Yes, I am Iraqi, in every vein of mine, and every day that my country is exposed to tyranny I know what I can do. I take hold of my nation and my culture, not out of a principle of chauvinism, but by expanding my own sojourn there as I transform it into the main character of every novel I have written, as I observe, and analyze, and bear witness to the humbug, the ideological stupidities, the baseness, and the ugliness of international politics, which has made my country and my people pay very dearly. To write of Iraq in this sense, is to protect myself to the highest degree, to protect the collectivity of cultural values of a country that is one of the most ancient civilized parts of the world. In consequence, to write this way is to confront how, as writer and as citizen of Iraq, I am plundered and alienated by others. The perceptive reader will elicit the bitterness that is Iraq in the language and the acts of characters. For this is a moral position and is the only path to freedom.

I longed to write of a passion that is Arab, that transforms body and spirit into a wafting fragrance, unrolling the forty words of Arab love across the pages, and recording the most radiant periods of the art of love in Arabic culture. For love is all that can persist in the face of the culture of the void. It is what makes places sympathetic and gives people nobility.

But who, I wonder, cares about love these days, about women, about men indeed? For whom is life the primary concern? Who thinks about learning French, when American has become the duke and the duchess, the lord, the count, and the cowboy? This is all I need, to start me cursing as I see the skulls extending the length of our bald globe. No, I do not need a new language. My eyes have already been pierced by the viper's sting—that is what they call it, "the blue waters"—the glaucoma that afflicted me during the war of '91, as I stared straight into the lens, contrary to the principle that says no actor must look directly at the camera. With a close-up shot, I am rebuilding my country before you. It is a construction of anger, vast beauty, and identity, and I submit it to the act of writing—that will give it a finality. I will not magnify it in order to turn it into an elegy, nor will I hide it and leave it to moan alone.

There are many cities that die in our arms, more quickly than we can anticipate. Some dead cities—those that are in the process of dying—

are more intensely alive than those we label as living. For the conflict between the dead is more violent than the struggle of the living. The dead are many, very many. What is the importance, then, of stories, novels, words of witness, texts, of all places of exile, if they are unable to see or hear the screams of eighteen million Iraqi men and women, boys and girls? What do the bombs equal—those from before history and those that have followed Americanization—if the world can close peaceful eyes to the moaning of human beings?

Face to face before Baghdad, as it whispers. Come, just to pluck out the first words, and to take the measure of the first virgin to whom the people have given the first kiss, the kiss that kills.

As writers and artists, must we suffer and go into exile so that the nation does not die? Why do nations appear more valuable and beautiful than their citizens, in the eyes of certain leaders and chiefs? Here, writing takes on one of its finest pretexts: we must change the futures of the characters in our novels, as long as we cannot change our own futures as writers, even if despair lies at the end of the road. But death is not what we hope for, either, departing our countries—orphans, sick and alone, having suffered all harms, as they made their way and entered their phantom existences, leaving us the story, all the stories, all the places, and the indifferences of the lands of exile.

Translated from the Arabic by Marilyn Booth

NOTES

1. See Alia Mamdouh's novel *al-Naftalin,* translated into French as *La naphtaline* (Paris: Actes sud, 1996) and into English as *Mothballs* (London: Garnet, 1997; New York: Feminist Press, forthcoming 2005), as well as into five other languages.

2. I wrote this personal essay on the generation of the 1960s in Baghdad for *Faradis* magazine; it was published in Paris. The Iraqi poet 'Abd al-Qadir al-Jinabi was its publisher.

3. London and Beirut: Dar al-Saqi lil-nashr, 2000. This has not appeared in translation.

Eva Johnson

■

On the Line *and* The Black Pen

Born in northern Australia, Eva Johnson is an award-winning playwright and poet. She began writing plays about her community's history, culture, land rights, and brutal subjugation by white settlers in the 1970s, shortly after "Aborigines were honoured with citizenship rights in their own country." Johnson's long career as a writer, lecturer, and Indigenous rights activist has significantly influenced Australia's literary, black consciousness, and women's movements. She writes frequently about slavery, sexism, homophobia, cultural identity, and other themes "that are crucial to Aboriginal people and our experiences." Johnson's "outstanding contributions to Aboriginal and Torres Strait Islander arts culture" were honored in 1993 with the Australia Council's first Red Ochre Award. Her plays have been staged at venues around the world, including the Hiroshoma Arts Festival and the Second World Indigenous Youth Conference. *What Do They Call Me,* her most recent play, was produced to acclaim in Melbourne. As critic Jennifer Tannoch-Bland notes in her review of the 1999 production, Johnson's "amazing use of language" brings the struggles and resistance of Indigenous Australian women—and the world of non-Indigenous/white Australia—into sharp critical focus.

In the 1994 essay "On the Line," Johnson observes the gravity of writing as an Aboriginal woman. Powerfully aware of history and the literary ground beneath her feet, she closes with "The Black Pen," a poem she dedicates to "Aboriginal writers who have forged the way for writers such as I, writers whom I acknowledge as our heroes of the pen." As the poem's title suggests, here Johnson urges black writers to dip into the history of so much blood spilt, of so many lost, of all that was stolen—and write the world anew.

■

On the Line

The biggest question that lies important in my life at the moment is, what is my role in this country, as a writer, a woman, a mother and most importantly, as an Aborigine?

My sense of responsibility comes from a place where, as a writer, the knowledge that I have acquired is the tool that connects both traditional and contemporary Aboriginal concepts. Aboriginal writing includes society as the focus of our Art.

My writing is specifically Aboriginal because it deals with my life experiences as an Aborigine and those of other Aborigines. Writing for me, as an Indigenous Australian, is about the will to survive. I try to work towards the accomplishment of the ideal of freedom through writing plays which seek to eliminate the many confusions that hinder Aboriginal people and I deal with questions that are crucial to Aboriginal people and our experiences.

Aboriginality is a major part of the texture and meaning of all important works by Aboriginal writers. Writings of protest, resistance and cultural revolution have typified Aboriginal literature.

My writing allows me to speak. The characters in my plays are real; they are living a life on stage, perhaps their lives, perhaps that of another Aborigine and their experiences. I write about people who have been under prescribed treatment for over two hundred years, who have endured the harshness, the traumas, of a hostile racial history in their own country. These historical events are different configurations of racism but these are lived experiences. My writing exemplifies these experiences. My writing is often triggered by childhood memories...

I remember my mother running through the bushes
with me on her back,
her screams deafened my ears.
Other women were running too.
She placed me in the bushes on the ground,
covered me with leaves.
The sound of hooves galloping
pounded my heart
my screams of fear burst my lungs
exposed by camouflage.

Strange hands brushed away the leaves
picked me up, placed something sweet in my mouth
I spat it out
put me on the back of a horse.
The bush became deadly silent.
That was the last time I saw my mother.

from the play Tjindarella, 1984

I began writing in the late 1970's when Aboriginal people were no longer content to remain invisible. From 1967 when Aborigines were honoured with citizenship rights in their own country, when we were no longer seen as part of the flora and fauna, the first moves began towards constituting a black consciousness, a black social force in this country.

Writing became one of the most powerful tools of protest. Thus began the resurrection of a new kind of writer, beginning with such well-respected Aboriginal writers as Kevin Gilbert, Oodgeroo Noonuccal and Hyllus Maris. These writers are part of Aboriginal history and indeed the history of establishing Aboriginal Literature within the context of Australian literature.

My whole focus as a writer is to deal with history. The Land Rights struggle brought to light a particular political concept for me. I began to write poetry about the land, the people and the living spirits that are part of Aboriginal culture. Through the genre of land, black consciousness, I sieved through the events of history, especially the treatment of Aborigines, and drew a clear conclusion of how immense the future struggle for Aborigines would be. My initial response was that of anger.

The realisation for me was that while struggling for acceptance in this country, the enemy seen by those in power was in fact my own Aboriginality, my own blackness. It was used against me by a manipulative structure that would inevitably use as its tool restrictive policies, with a view to destroying any sense of self-worth and most importantly, cultural identity.

So initially, anger became a catalyst for my writing. Anger became a valuable political tool for analysis, confrontation, redress, and in fact acted as a neon repellant against any notion of serving the government in the very institutions that moulds Aboriginality into useless captive tokens.

Writing became my partner in the war against injustice. Writing became a therapeutic balm, using works of creative expression to expel negative thought, writing words of self-affirmation, love and wisdom. Writing became a part of my spirit, the very core of my being. Writing brought me to understanding the true concepts of Aboriginality, Identity and most importantly, a sense of humour. Writing about our oppression through humour is for me one of the most poignant interactions with reality.

> Weavilly porrige I'm going insane
> weavilly porrige gonna wreck my brain
> H,mmm, mission food
> send'm from heaben
> must be good
> bless'em little weavill
> bless'em little me
> I been lungga trick'em
> just you see
> catch'em little weavill
> put'em in the tea
> only fulla drink'em up
> MISSIONARY!!!!!

I am often asked if my work is autobiographical. For the most part it is. So many things have happened to me in my lifetime that it is important for me to retrace, to record some of the events. My children grew up in an era that had no relation to any of the childhood experiences that I had. They want to learn of my past, our past, Australia's history in the past.

I also have an inherent interest in all that is Aboriginal. Thus anything that hinders or threatens the progress of Aboriginal survival forces me to respond. Every day I deal with the notion of superiority/inferiority and that is unsettling to me as it brings with it the sense of imbalance in this society. Does my writing sabotage the notion of white racial superiority and bring to reality the power of my existence?

Writing has the power to unveil almost any conscious or unconscious thought. I write to that consciousness, the conscious demon that arrived in this country two hundred years ago.

I'm not sure whether I take my writing seriously enough. The process of my writing is erratic and at most times steered by time deadlines. Procrastination is my greatest enemy. I detest being 'organised' and much prefer to do things in my own time. But I am no longer afraid of what I write, nor do I allow any room for self-censoring. MY writing has to be attuned to my philosophical and spiritual beliefs, in that whatever I write, the contents must come from that part of me which is the conscious source of my being.

Writing is the most daring thing I have ever done and the most rewarding. The rewards of my writing are reflected by those who acknowledge my work, particularly Aboriginal people. For me this acknowledgement is an affirmation that the audience for whom I specifically write endorses the worth of my work.

There are other Aboriginal writers who have forged the way for writers such as I, writers whom I acknowledge as our heroes of the pen. To them I dedicate this poem. As someone once said . . . Speak loud, speak unsettling things and be dangerous.

The Black Pen

The Black Pen that traced our history,
the unspoken words silenced by fear
that brought to life the power of truths,
coloured red,
carved indelibly in blood along journeys
that knew the anguish of the land.
The Black Pen that witnessed the tortures of slavery
and abduction of a people hurled against the face of 'civilization'
their flesh throbbing with the winds and the waters.

The Black Pen that fights against injustice,
coloured red,
carved indelibly in blood on walls
of prison cells, in words that resist the silence of genocide,
that expose the curse of the ignorant, the sentences of death.
The Black Pen echoes the cries of Women,

whose children were captured tokens of servility,
their future sabotaged by institutions,
fractured by displaced identity.

The Black Pen that speaks with courage,
coloured red,
carved indelibly in blood,
searches for new visions along the paths of our Ancestors,
that return us to the meeting places
of the winds and the undrained beds of the waters.
The Black Pen celebrates our defiance,
our resistance, our survival, our unity,
sets our spirits free,
and honours the memory of those
read on pages
where blood red flows no more,
where indelible black ink vanishes,
No More . . . .

II.

Blood and Ink

Grannies, where are you? Little girls, where are you? Who tells about
the mysteries? And who tells you about what's happening?
—*Sheila Masote*

Yvonne Vera

∎

Writing Near the Bone

In her review of *Sign and Taboo: Perspectives on the Poetic Fiction of Yvonne Vera* (2002), literary scholar Eva Hunter observes that "recognition of Vera's voice as one of the most exciting to have emerged . . . in the last decade spreads far beyond Africa." Among southern Africa's most widely celebrated authors, Vera is often noted for her supple lyricism and powerful subject matter. Since her literary debut in 1992, she has been been writing complex, innovative novels that wrestle with Zimbabwe's lingering colonial legacy and offer radical alternatives for a liberated Africa's future. Born in Zimbabwe (then under British occupation) in 1964, Vera came of age during the black majority's liberation struggle, which ended ninety years of British and white minority rule in 1980. In her most recent novel, *The Stone Virgins* (2002), she takes an unflinching look at the oppression and resistance of women within the liberation movement and in the years of civil war that followed. Shortlisted twice for the Commonwealth Writers Prize, she won the award in 1997 for her novel *Under the Tongue*. Her novels have been translated into nearly ten languages.

In "Writing Near the Bone" (1997), Vera reflects on her childhood initiation into the world of writing. Immersed by her mother and grandmother in the community's rich oral and literary traditions, she would come to know writing as a force entirely organic and sensual, one of great power and daily importance: "Our bodies, our earth, the smell of rain, beetles and our noses, this was writing."

∎

There is no essential truth about being a female writer. The best writing comes from the boundaries, the ungendered spaces between male and female. I am talking of writing itself, not the story or theme. Knowing a story is one thing, writing it quite another.

I like to think of writing in limitless terms, with no particular contract with the reader, especially that of gender. When I have discovered that unmarked and fearless territory then I am free to write, even more free to be a woman writing. Sometimes the light coming through my window has been much more important than the fact that I am a woman writing.

There must be a serious purpose to my work, that is all. I must be in touch with the earth. I can never mistake that source of inspiration and energy to be gender, it is something we all share. It is true, however, that one writes best on themes, feelings, actions and sentiments one is more closely connected with. In this regard I like to think that I am writing. I am a woman. I am writing.

The woman I am is inside the writing, embraced and freed by it. For me writing is light, a radiance that captures everything in a fine profile. This light searches and illuminates, it is a safe place from which to uncover the emotional havoc of our experience. Light is a bright warmth which heals. Writing can be this kind of light. Within it I do not hide. I travel bravely beyond that light, into the shadows that this light creates, and in that darkness it is also possible to be free, to write, to be a woman.

I like the peasant shoes which Van Gogh painted for example, their lack of light. They are a lot darker than the reprints suggest, no light at all except an almost clear patch of ground behind them and that is hardly light, really. You feel the absence of light in these pictures and that really draws your head closer and your emotion and you really want to look and you feel heavy with a new delight. You look at these shoes and wonder where they have been and who has been and what has been and did these shoes ever grow anything that held some life in it, that breathed perhaps, that threw some kind of light into the world. When I went to the gallery shop in Amsterdam I looked for a postcard with the shoes: the reproduction was so bright, I said this is terrible I will not buy this card even though I want so much to do so. I went back into the gallery and looked at the shoes again and found a large evocative canvas, thrilling in its sadness. I knew this had been written not without light but beyond light.

I found the same immaculate transcription of image and emotion with "'The Potato Eaters." It was a lot darker than the "Peasant Shoes." There were four or five little cups and something properly muddy was being poured into them. The cups were white but free of light. And figures in the foreground, possibly a child, had her back to the viewer.

It was difficult standing and watching the back of this child who some-how was a potato eater and was about to drink something so muddy from a cup that was nearly white. There was a lantern of some kind hanging above the group but its presence created shadows, not warmth or recognition. The picture was very imposing in its emotion, but beautiful, harmful.

I learnt to write when I was almost six and at the same time also dis-covered the magic of my own body as a writing surface, I lived with my grandmother for some years while my mother was pursuing her stud-ies. Many other children lived with my grandmother. The house was very small and most afternoons we were kept outside where we woke with some cousins and sat on large metal garbage cans, our legs hardly long enough to touch the ground.

The skin over my legs would be dry, taut, even heavy. It carried the cold of our winter. Using the edges of my fingernails or pieces of dry grass broken from my grandmother's broom I would start to write on my legs. I would write on my small thighs but this surface was soft and the words would vanish and not stay for long, but it felt different to write there, a sharp and ticklish sensation which made us laugh and feel as though we had placed the words in a hidden place.

Our hope increased we travelled downward to the legs where the skin broke like black clay, and we wrote our names to all eternity. Here we wrote near the bone and spread the words all the way to the ankles. We wrote deep into the skin and under skin where the words could not escape. Here, the skin was thirsty, it seemed, and we liked it. The words formed light grey intermingling paths that meant something to our imagination and freed us and made us forget the missing laughters of our mothers. We felt the words in gradual bursts of pain, the first words we had written would become less felt, the pain of that scratch-ing now faded, and the last words where we had dug too deep would be pulsating still, unable to be quiet.

We looked up and laughed and drew figures of our bodies there, and the bodies of our grandmothers which we squeezed among the letters. It was possible, when you had used a small piece dry bark for your pen, to be bleeding in small dots. Such words could never depart or be for-gotten. This was bleeding, not writing. It was important to write. Then, before running indoors to my grandmother who would have been distressed at the changed shades of our bodies, we would use handfuls of saliva to wipe our bodies clean. This saliva spread a warm and calming feeling over us.

I learnt to write if not on the body then on the ground. We would spread the loamy soil into a smooth surface with the palm of our hands using loving and careful motions, then we would write with the tips of our fingers. Bending over that earth, touching it with our noses, we would learn to write large words which led us into another realm of feeling and of understanding our place in the world. Proud of our accomplishment we would then stand back to see what we had written. We had burrowed the earth like certain kinds of beetles and we were immensely satisfied. We left these letters there, on the ground, and ran off to do our chores. I always liked writing after the rains when the soil held to our naked feet and claimed us entirely. Then we drew shapes on the ground which could be seen for distances. Our bodies and our earth, the smell of rain, beetles and our noses, this was writing.

Jennifer DiMarco

■

Word Warrior

Seattle native Jennifer DiMarco wrote her first book at the tender age of ten. Over the next eight years, she would write a dozen novels and several plays. After several years of self-publishing, she sold her first novel to a commercial press. Within weeks, *Escape to the Wind* (1993) had bumped *Jurassic Park* on the *Seattle Times* best-seller list and exhausted its first printing. At the time, the novel's author was nineteen years old. Now thirty, this "writer of brilliance and personal integrity" is also CEO of Windstorm Creative, one of the world's largest independent presses. An award-winning poet and biographer, DiMarco is also a commited social justice activist. She lectures frequently on creative arts and queer youth empowerment. While critics often categorize her novels as "lesbian sci fi," DiMarco's explicit project as a writer is broader: "My goal is to write quality stories that are lesbian and gay fiction and that deal with diversity through sexuality, camaraderie, truth."

There is, however, a painful underside to DiMarco's prolific career. In "Word Warrior" (1995), DiMarco offers a frank portrait of her traumatic beginnings as a young writer. She openly discusses the childhood violence that nearly cost her life—and how the love of her mothers helped her decide to save it. As DiMarco testifies, the power of words would arm both her struggle to heal herself and, ultimately, her lifelong battle against injustice everywhere.

■

"I reclaimed my power, my energy and my life with a passion. I wrote until I cried, until I laughed out loud. I wrote about dispelling pain, darkness, hate."

When I was three years old, my father was killed. His body was never found. I learned very quickly that living is harder than dying. Two years later, my mother married a woman and taught me what the word *survivor* meant.

Mama says, *My daughter was born during an incredible thunderstorm. She was energized at birth by the Goddess's electrical light show.*

I remember the studio apartment. The wallpaper had tiny flowers beneath the dark stains. The carpet was worn thin and scratchy on bare feet. There were four of us: Mama, Mumu, baby Angel and me. Life was overalls from the Salvation Army, parents who worked more for less pay, and an elder daughter with long, wild hair and eyes full of dreams. Full of pride.

Mumu says, *Remember: As a woman, nothing is ever handed to you. You have to fight for everything. And a fighter faces the world head on.*

We had nothing so we took nothing for granted. I never expected more, didn't know what more was, but was taught to always reach for it. To always demand better. And we did have love. I knew what love was: the power behind holding hands as readily as you could make a fist. Strength through protection.

Mama says, *My daughter told me something today. She said, "Mama, only a coward hates, so I'm going to be brave." And I told her, "You don't ever hate anyone, except a bigot."*

I never knew what school-shopping was, and new clothes meant Mumu's old ones. Everything was shared, from toys to tea to time. Even working double shifts, one of my parents always seemed to be home to tuck me in, kiss me good night. And when exhaustion found them asleep on the couch, I would be the one to bring in the blanket and wish them sweet dreams.

True, at dinnertime there wasn't always food on the table, but we still gathered together.

Mumu says, *Dear Goddess, thank you for this time together and for our strong girls. Bless and guide them with courage, strength, faith and love. Walk with them as they grow and face the world.*

Courage, strength, faith and *love.* These are the things that made my soul. These are the things that my parents gave me. I knew they were important. I felt them and lived them. But I never knew that they could be weapons and armor as well, until I was ten years old.

I went away for the summer. I had always dreamed of traveling. My parents wanted the world for me. The trip seemed perfect. I would stay with family, and family meant safety. I felt perfect. I stood an inch over four feet, my eyes perpetually wide, taking in everything about me—a young owl, ready to try out her wings for the first time. I flew from

Seattle in a huge plane to the huger New York City, and into the arms of my great-uncle, who had offered and paid for it all.

She'll learn culture, he had told my parents with a wide grin that showed his teeth. But his idea of culture had nothing to do with Broadway plays or art galleries. *She'll see all of New York.* But all I saw were the three rooms of his house, drawn blinds, locked doors, hard walls and harder floors.

He never had any intention of showing me New York. No intention of showing me anything outside the darkness of his home. He had lied to my parents. They had no idea the danger their daughter was in. He was the first person I ever knew who lied.

Mama says, *God lets bad things happen to good people to test their faith, but the Goddess knows the faithful and knows that bad things make people stronger. And there's nothing wrong with stronger.*

And so it was with *courage* that I held my head high, even when my chin trembled. With *courage* that I kept breathing, living, even when I was terrified.

You feel free to call your parents whenever you want. The phone is right here. He sneers as he speaks. His eyes gleam shadows. He stands so close to the phone that his shoulder touches it. He watches me. He is always, forever watching me. Whenever my parents call me, he stands with his hands on my neck, locking our eyes. He knows I'm too afraid to even touch the phone. With his sneer he pounds a slice of beef for dinner.

Blood splatters on the phone . . .

the wall . . .

the floor . . .

the sheets . . .

all summer long. . . .

Once more, there is a shadow blocking the doorway, sucking the safety from my borrowed room. The shadow says, *I pray to God every day and light candles, so that I'll never do this again.* But every night "again" happened, and so it was with *strength* that I lived, even when I was too scared to open my mouth and scream, *no.* . . .

During the night, my blue eyes would stare into the darkness for hours. I would measure my breathing, slow it down so it made barely a whisper. My body ached, but I did not move from my tight, curled position. I worried that my thundering heart was making too much noise. I knew I mustn't make a sound. Never must the blankets rustle or the headboard creak, because that would tell him I was awake. That would bring him to my room, to me.

And then it would begin again . . .

his hard hands . . .

his crushing weight . . .

his thick breath . . .

all night long. . . .

During the day, his deep-set eyes watched me. To say he watched me constantly would be an understatement. He was never more than one or two feet away. I was always where he could reach me. Eating, bathing, walking aimlessly from room to room, using the toilet. I was never without his stare.

Never without his presence . . .

his snarls . . .

his glare . . .

his ugliness . . .

all day long. . . .

I was not allowed out of his house. I was not allowed to open the blinds or unlock the doors. Day was not safe. Night was not safe. I was not safe. But I fought despair and fear to stay alive. I fought the living, breathing horrors my life was suddenly made of. I fought by living. By opening my eyes each morning. By continuing to breathe.

And it was *faith* and *love* that brought me, scrambling, sobbing with joy, to the phone, after he finally went out, finally left me alone, nearly sixty days after it all began. *Faith* that even after so long, the sun still shone beyond those dark shutters, and that beyond the locked doors, the world still existed. *Love* that told me I would have enough time before he returned with his threats and violence, that there would be enough time for Mama and Mumu to answer my phone call, to hear in my voice everything, to believe me, and bring me home.

And they did.

Mumu says, *Everyday heroes go unnoticed. They look darkness in the eye and still shine their light. Everyday someone goes without recognition. My daughter will never be overlooked.*

There were long nights after that summer. Too much fear to explain and a lot of denial. I questioned life, *Why?* and death, *Why not?* There were night-terrors instead of nightmares, skin memories instead of safe memories. I wondered if there would ever be an end to the hurt, to the haunting darkness. I wondered if I would ever find myself again, if I still knew who I was.

Mama says, *This is for you. A real book, but with blank pages, for you to fill with anything you want. And you can keep it all to yourself . . . or you can share it with the world. Because I love you.*

Words. Words had become more and more sparse for me. Words were truth, and the truth was hard. So hard. There are a lot of ways to deal with darkness: Ignore it, lie about it, scream at it, cry . . . or talk about it. I wanted so badly to tell my story, to tell my parents everything that had happened, everything I had thought, felt, seen. I knew that if I could just speak, just say the words, then the three of us would share the horror, face it, kill it. But I couldn't. My own voice terrified me. My own life had become my worst fear. I loved my parents, but I hated the darkness in my past. I was scared that if I spoke about it, it would return. I was still very afraid.

But when Mama gave me that special book with the clean, ready pages, she gave me a safe place. A place where the truth could be my own. My parents did not ask me to forget my experience or stop me from realizing that others felt pain as well. They let me see the world as it really was. No, it wasn't all safe, but safety still existed. They didn't ask me to pour out the pain and wash it away, they simply asked me to show it, to reveal the darkness, perhaps make room for some light. They knew healing would come at its own pace, in its own space. And it did. My space was that book, my pace was the turning of the pages that I wrote upon.

So, it was words. My parents had taught me with their own lives: the way they stood strong but knew how to cry, the way their pride shone even when they were afraid. And their principles: the never-ending courage to live, strength to face fear and faith in love. Their understanding of themselves, of women, of me, had been the reason for my survival. They gave me, from the day I first saw them, the skills to survive. And now, surrounded by all this that they were, words became my healing. Words became my expression, my voice, my activism, joy, rage, and release. Mama and Mumu said to me, *Write, share it all.* And I did.

By the time I was eighteen, I had filled up dozens of journals and notebooks. I had written twelve novels and four stage plays. First I would write, face my emotions on paper, and then I could share them, talk about them, I reclaimed my power, my energy and my life with a passion. I wrote until I cried, until I laughed out loud. I wrote about dispelling pain, darkness, hate. I was suddenly looking at the world, looking at fear and prejudice with an overwhelming need for justice. *Without fear,* I decided, *there could be no hate.* And hate was what I had found in my great-uncle, hate was the root I wanted to destroy.

So I wrote. I wrote books about strong women, and men, facing the world head on, demanding that it do better. I created characters from real people, and told their stories of battling darkness, their stories of triumph. I wrote stories that never got told, the true ones. Stories that reflected life, that weren't always safe, because life wasn't always safe. I wrote for me. I wrote for others. I wrote to make a difference.

With words I battled abuse, challenged bigotry. Issues that so many people brushed aside or refused to see. People chose to be blind to struggle. I chose to open their eyes. The more open eyes we have, the less darkness will be allowed to exist. If you ignore abuse and bigotry, they do not go away. They grow. I wanted to stunt that growth. I wrote so others wouldn't be swallowed by horror as I had been. Words allowed me to deal with the world around me, to make sense of it all, to put it in perspective. I wrote to continue living my life, instead of reliving my past. I told my parents, *I write to bring light to the shadows and voice to the silence. To shed light on misconceptions, bring light into the darkness. To speak for those not spoken for, to speak the truth.* They held me tight. They told me I was brave and bold, that I was their warrior.

I said, *I'm not afraid.* And my truth was bright.

Mumu says, *Healing comes from inside. From within. Healing is a constant, shining, powerful process.*

And when my written words became spoken words, when chapters became speeches, my parents stood with me, encouraged me. They continued to light my path of verse and phrase. I went on to speak at high schools, conferences and community centers. I spoke about crossing over the boundaries of prejudice to embrace each other, about the power of challenging the world, reaching for your dreams and accepting only the best. In a strong, steady voice I talked about hate and how it is a force that must be stopped, here, now. I made the connections that so many turned away from: Prejudice is fear of the unknown, child abuse is the fear of innocence, and fear creates hatred. I shared with everyone the courage and faith I had grown up with, the fear I had fought with strength and love, and the words I had used, and still use, to reach out and touch the world.

I said, *Open your eyes. By doing nothing to stop hate, we are condoning it. Stand up against the horrors. Segregation is wrong. Battery is wrong. Oppression is wrong. Abuse is wrong. there is no time to choose blindness. Do not run, do not hide. Stop it from happening again.*

Mama says, *From the fires my daughter has risen. She was born in lightning, she fought with lightning, and now she will live like lightning: bright and brilliant.*

And when I fell in love, I fell with all my heart and soul. Uncondition-ally, loyally, completely. Just like I had been surrounded with, just like I felt inside my whole life.

My Love, she turned to me with pride in her eyes, beneath her silver curls, and told me she was dying of cancer. She waited for me to run away. She said, *It's a risk to love me.* I took her hands in my own and returned, *It's a bigger risk not to.* And I ran nowhere.

In my twenty years, I have learned that there are forces in the world that can take away women's rights. They can invalidate our love, beat us down, rape us, make up our minds for us. These forces insist that all strong women undermine men, and that all lesbians hate men alto-gether. They insist if we're beautiful, we must be stupid, and if we don't take extreme measures to stop their rape, then we are to blame.

A lot can be taken away from a woman. A lot can be done to break her. Fear is a disease, and hatred and violence are the symptoms. There are those who wish to crush us, defeat us. But we must not, we will not, grant their wishes. Together, all women must rise up. We must take our stand in unity and power. Raise our voices against the dark-ness. Then, instead of being crushed, we will stand strong. Instead of being defeated, we will be victorious. We will conquer hate. I will never forget these facts. I will never for an instant doubt. Because through the fear, the hatred and the violence, we are indeed standing strong in our victory. We are surviving.

I was raised by two women. I was raised in a feminist household. I am very proud of my family and my herstory. My parents taught me more than I could ever tell in one story, perhaps more than I could tell in one hundred. But my soul is still made of courage, strength, faith and love, even as it is tested by fire, by pain and by struggle. My parents gave me these tools of survival, and someday I will pass them on to a child of my own. I will continue the fight.

Even if I could, I would never change anything about my life. My life has made me who I am today.

I was raised to survive. And I will.

Taslima Nasrin

■

The World of Poetry

Taslima Nasrin is an outspoken journalist, novelist, poet, and doctor. She was born in 1962 in Bangladesh (then Bengali East Pakistan), where she began her medical career working among the country's poorest women. Alarmed by the conditions of women living under religious fundamentalism, she soon began registering protest through writing. With the 1993 publication of *Lajja* (Shame), Nasrin's struggle against intensifying attacks by Islamic militants was launched onto the international stage. Quickly banned by the government, *Lajja* depicts the December 1992 massacre of thousands of Hindu Bangladeshis by Muslim compatriots following the destruction of the Babri Masjid, a mosque in Ayodhya, India. Fundamentalist groups accused her of blasphemy, organizing massive demonstrations where thousands demanded her execution. In fear for her life, in 1994 she fled to Sweden a wanted fugitive. Four years later, she secretly returned home to care for her dying mother and surrendered to the government. But the death threats continued, forcing her to seek asylum once more. Nasrin continues to fight tirelessly against fundamentalism, calling out the dangerous hypocrisy of "powerful Western states [that] have declared protecting human rights to be one of their supreme objectives and then patronized fundamentalism, overtly or covertly."

The following selection first appeared in Nasrin's memoir *Amar Meyebela* (My Girlhood). As part of her project to break the silence around the lives of girls and women, Nasrin decided to invent a new Bengali word—*meyebela,* or "girlhood." First published in 1999, this award-winning book was also banned in Bangladesh for blasphemy. Here she recalls how a friendship with a gifted young writer awakened her to the power of words—those that wound and those that set us free.

■

In this hungry world, the earth is harsh,
the full moon like a burned bun.

Uncle Siddique had uttered these words while standing in Grandma's moonlit courtyard. At the time, Uncle Kana, seated on a low stool, was telling us the story of the two warriors, Sohrab and Rustam. Uncle Siddique's words made him stop and smile. "Who wants to eat a bun? Who's that hungry?" he asked.

"Thousands of poor people starve to death!" Uncle Siddique replied, his wooden clogs striking on the floor as he walked.

I said softly, so that no one could hear me:

> Get me that moon-bun
> Someone, do.
> Some I shall eat,
> The rest I'll give the slum dwellers, too.

Uncle Kana heard me. His ears were very sharp. "What is this? Has everyone here turned into a poet? Who just mentioned the slum dwellers?"

I didn't reply. Silently, I covered my face with my hands.

This was one of my many bad habits. I often made up little rhymes that were parodies of popular and well-known poems. If I were asked to recite a poem in school, I forgot the real one. Instead, what sprang to my lips were the funny ones I'd made up. There was one that began:

> Busy bee, busy bee, are you on a buzzing spree?
> Stop a while and chat with me.
>
> I'm off collecting nectar, my friend,
> Time's slipping by,
> Cannot stop and chat,
> I have got to fly.

One evening, as I was sitting in Grandma's house, reading aloud from a book of rhymes, I spotted Uncle Kana crossing the courtyard. Instead of "Busy bee, busy bee," I said to him:

> Uncle Kana, Uncle Kana, where are you off to?
> Stop a while and chat with me, oh please do.
>
> I'm off looking for all the kids,
> Got no time to chat.
> I have lovely tales to tell
> Both of this and of that.

Ma heard me from inside and shouted, "Oy, what's all this? You're getting into a very bad habit. Stop making fun of old rhymes!"

On New Year's Day, naughty and impertinent girls in my school hung up on the notice board a list of nicknames given to certain students. No one could ever figure out who thought up the names or who put them up, but everyone crowded around to read the list. On one occasion, I found the words "a burst melon" next to my own name. In fact, there was more than one list. On a different wall, someone wrote of me, "butter wouldn't melt in her mouth."

The most beautiful girl in my class, Dilruba, had "slut" next to her name. "What does it mean?" I asked her. Tears sprang to Dilruba's eyes. She didn't reply. I felt very sorry for her. So I sat beside her, gently placing my hand on her back. I had heard the word before because Ma used that word when she lost her temper with any of our maids and began abusing them. But no one had ever told me its meaning. We were not close friends, but from the time I reached out to her, we were drawn to each other. Slowly, just as the first rays of dawn wipe out the darkness of night, Dilruba began to influence me, and I blossomed like a lotus.

Once our friendship was formed, Dilruba began telling me stories. She told me about her brothers and sisters, Lata, Pata, Tona, and Tuni. Based on her stories, my imagination took flight and they began living in my mind. Later, I met them in Dilruba's house, even exchanged a few words with them; but somehow, the people in Dilruba's stories seemed more real to me than those in real life. When I met Lata after her illness, I didn't ask her how she was. Instead, I asked Dilruba when we were alone, "What happened to her?" She replied, "Lata didn't recover. A number of doctors saw her, a number of medicines were given to her, but Lata kept shrinking until she became as thin as a thread. That thread simply hung in her room. Some said it should be dropped into a river; some said it should be held in a close embrace. Then someone did come along, held her close, kissed her, and Lata opened her eyes. She smiled, and we all thought she would live again."

When Dilruba told me these stories, she seemed to inhabit a different world. Even when she looked at me, it was as if she was looking at something else. Once my anxiety about Lata's health was over, Dilruba showed me a notebook. It was full of her poetry. I began reading, then stopped suddenly at a page:

> Grassflower,
> will you take me? Will you?
> All my days I have spent here and there.
> Finally, to you—my haven—I say,
> take everything I have;
> take me in your arms;
> touch me;
> touch me softly.
> I have come to you so late,
> if you reject me,
> then make me drown in nowhere,
> I will struggle up the bank
> to return to you once more.
> If you throw me nowhere again,
> still I will try to reach you.
> Grassflower, take me, will you?

"Dilruba, will you teach me how to write poetry" I asked, bending over the page.

Her lips were soft and pink, flawless as the rest of her face. She had masses of thick curly hair tied into a knot behind her head. A few unruly strands escaped from it and hung over her forehead and neck, some touching her chin. Looking at her, I suddenly had a strong feeling of déjà vu. This whole scene had taken place before—I, asking to be taught to write poetry, Dilruba, saying nothing in reply. I had sat beside another girl, who had looked exactly like Dilruba. We were before an open notebook, by an open window, beyond which was an open field. The sky rolled down to meet the field where it ended.

Dilruba was even quieter and shyer than me. When all the other girls ran and skipped all over the playing field, she sat quietly by a window, staring at the distant sky.

"No one can be taught to write poetry. If you look at the sky, you will be moved to tears. If you can cry, really cry with all your heart, you will be able to write," Dilruba told me. Her voice held a gentle warmth.

Quite often she was punished for not paying attention in class, and she was made to stand holding her ears with both hands. Sometimes she was even told to leave the classroom. She did not seem to mind at all. She remained outside the door, standing on one leg, her eyes fixed on the sky, with which she seemed to have a strange rapport. When I looked at her, I felt as if someone had cast a spell on me. I walked by her side, talked to her, placed a hand on her shoulder, all in a sort of trance.

I tried looking at the sky as well, but, unlike Dilruba, my eyes did not fill with tears. However, one day I found a torn, empty paper bag in our courtyard and, thinking of Dilruba, found myself writing a poem on it:

> Let's play, Dilruba.
> Do you know how to play gollachhut?
> Let's get lost.
> Let's go somewhere,
> far away,
> across seven seas,
> thirteen rivers;
> Dilruba, let's go.

Dilruba smiled sweetly when she read the poem. I had never seen such a sweet smile. Runi's smile had been like this . . . but no, it wasn't wholly like Dilruba's; it was slightly different. "Anyone who has an attractive smile has no need to talk," Rabindranath had once said, and he was right. I had felt very shy in Runi's presence, but not in Dilruba's. We built a different world together, one in which we simply played with words. Dilruba wrote in her notebook:

> Wherever you want me to go, I will.
> I will melt into you, I promise.

In return, you must come close to me
And say only, "I love you."
Nothing else.
Wherever you want me to go, I will!

That was all I had learned to do: love. Our love grew deeper. We left home and traveled to distant lands, like princes did in fairy tales, across seven seas and thirteen rivers. Only in our imagination of course. Neither of us could do anything to step out of the real world.

I thought Dilruba was very much like the poetry she wrote—quiet, like a still, deep pool in a forest, its water the same shade of blue as the sky. Just occasionally, one or two leaves dropped into it and floated on its surface, like rafts. They were rafts Dilruba had made just for herself, to sail away on.

One day, the same Dilruba shocked me profoundly by announcing that she was about to get married. Her father had made all the arrangements.

"No!" I exclaimed, gazing at her pale face and gray eyes. "You must refuse. Tell your father you won't do it."

Dilruba gave me a wan smile. Only someone burning with a high fever, ailing for many days, would smile like that. The very next day she stopped coming to school. I was totally alone. Even after the school day was over, I sat by the window for a long time, starting at the sky, feeling intensely her absence. Where was she? Had she turned her face away from everyone in hurt and pain and vanished into the sky? I tried very hard to find her there. Now, for the first time, looking at the sky brought tears to my eyes.

Two days before her wedding Dilruba came to our house, to San Souci. This time she came to run away from home, to escape to a dense, lonely forest, to a land of dreams far, far away from this cruel world, where girls whose hearts were sad could fly up to the sky and play hide-and-seek with the fairies hidden in the clouds. She opened our black front gate and stepped in. I happened to be standing at a window from which the gate was visible. Mesmerized, I looked at her beautiful face and saw her move toward the house. It seemed to me as if she was not walking, but floating.

She didn't get very far. Through the same window I watched her leave. Baba had refused to let her enter. She was turned away from the front door. Baba had asked her who she was, where she lived, why she was at our house, and then decided that there was no reason for a young girl to ignore her studies in the late afternoon to visit anyone. He had simply looked furious and pointed at the gate. "Get out. You've come just to a chat? Wasting everyone's time! Bad girl! Get out at once!"

The "bad girl," the "slut," had left without a word. I didn't know it then but I would never see her again. I didn't know that she would be married off to a total stranger, a much older man. Her notebook of poems would be burned, and she would be forced into a life of peeling, cleaning, grinding, cooking, and serving, as well as bearing a child almost every year.

And what would happen to me? Would I continue to watch the sky on her behalf and feel tears welling up in my eyes? Would I go on writing poetry? I would hate our society and the rules it imposed; would feel the invisible shackles placed on my hands and feet, realize that my wings had been chopped off, and that I was to be thrust into a strong cage where I would remain for eternity.

Or—perhaps—it was the other way around. Perhaps there was a cage inside my own being that confined me and pulled me back into its depths each time I wanted to spread my wings and soar in the sky.

Joy Harjo

■

Finding the Groove

Poet and musician Joy Harjo was born in Tulsa, "the northern border of the Creek Nation," in 1951. Trained as a painter at the Institute of American Indian Arts, she began writing in the 1970s. In the wake of surging political agitation for Native sovereignty (and mounting pressure on marginal artists, from both mainstream reviewers and community dissidents, to create works-to-fit), Harjo cultivated her artistic voice as a powerful mode of survival, resistance, and self-expression. Her first major publication, *The Last Song* (1975), appeared just two years following the AIM-led takeover of Wounded Knee— a site of bitter resonance in Native America–United States history. Nearly thirty years later, readers like fellow poet Adrienne Rich still "turn and return to Harjo's poetry for her breathtaking complex witness and for her world-remaking language." The award-winning author of seven poetry volumes, including *How We Became Human: New and Selected Poems 1975–2001,* Harjo is also coeditor of the groundbreaking collection *Reinventing the Enemy's Language: Contemporary Native American Women's Writings of North America* (1997). In 2003 she received the Arrell Gibson Award for Lifetime Achievement. She is also a recipient of the Lifetime Achivement Award from the Native Writers Circle of The Americas.

With Joy Harjo and Poetic Justice, and now as a solo artist, Harjo blends poetry with rock, jazz, and traditional music, mapping new paths toward knowledge, justice, and liberation. In "Finding the Groove," she traces the origins of this lifelong project back to an early encounter with the world between sound and language—music. With customary grace and subtlety, Harjo recounts how jazz transformed an ordinary drive with her parents through "Indian Territory. . . . [and] the energy thrown off by the struggle there," awakening her to the extraordinary grief, strength, and tenderness of being human.

■

Once I was so small I could barely peer over the top of the backseat of the black Cadillac my father polished and tuned daily; I wanted to see everything. It was around the time I acquired language, or even before that time, when something happened that changed my relationship to the spin of the world. My concept of language, of what was possible with music, was charged by this revelatory moment. It changed even the way I looked at the sun. This suspended integer of time probably escaped ordinary notice in my parents' universe, which informed most of my vision of the ordinary world. They were still omnipresent gods.

We were driving somewhere in Tulsa, the northern border of the Creek Nation. I don't know where we were going or where we had been, but I do know the sun was boiling the asphalt, the car windows open for any breeze as I stood on tiptoes on the floorboard behind my father, a handsome god who smelled of Old Spice, whose slick black hair was always impeccably groomed, his clothes perfectly creased and ironed. The radio was on. I loved the radio, jukeboxes, or any magic thing containing music, even then.

I wonder now what signaled this moment of revelation, a loop of time that at first glance could be any place in time. I became acutely aware of the line the jazz saxophonist was playing, a sound that could only have been John Coltrane. I didn't know the words *jazz* and *saxophone*—or the concepts. At that age I was in a world that did not depend on humans for naming. I was slowly fitting myself to this configuration, as do all children in this constellation.

I don't know how to say it, with what sounds or words, but in that confluence of hot southern afternoon, in the breeze of aftershave and humidity, I followed the improvised horn line of Coltrane to the beginning, to the place of the birth of sound. I was suspended in whirling stars, a moon to which I'd traveled often by then. I grieved my parents' failing, my own life, which I saw stretched the length of that rhapsody. We were a small but crucial point in the construction, every thought, every flick of an eyelash, every dragonfly wing, every word mattered. We were nothing, yet we were everything. We were present at each angle of existence, poised at the center of the world as we drove together in my father's prized black Cadillac, through that humid summer day.

My rite of passage into the world of humanity occurred then, via jazz. Coltrane's horn had made a startling bridge between familiar and strange lands, between mystery and the need to breathe. Molecular structure is shifted according to tone and grace, reshapes the DNA spiral. Coltrane was not the first explorer, but he was one of the most gifted, could find new configurations of tones where there had been none discovered or known and bring them back to earth.

As that child I sensed this music had to do with me, the journey of my family as the soul made its way through lungs and blood, from Alabama to Indian Territory. We were there when jazz was born, for though the music is predominately West African in concept with European harmonic structures, jazz could not have happened without the influence of the Muskogee people, without the shape of the particular lands marking the southeast corner of this continent, without the energy thrown off from the struggle there.

On that humid afternoon as I began my own particular journey, I found a way toward the realization of knowledge in this world, a way to hear beyond the ordinary waves of language. A love supreme. A love supreme.

I am still on that journey. The stuff I need for singing by whatever means is garnered from every thought, every heart that ever pounded the earth, the intelligence that directs the stars. The shapes of mountains, cities, a whistle leaf of grass, or a human bent with loss will revise the pattern of the story, the song. I take it from there, write or play through the heartbreak of the tenderness of being until I am the sky, the earth, the song and the singer.

Sandra Cisneros

■

Only Daughter

Sandra Cisneros is an award-winning novelist, poet, essayist, and short story writer. Lauded in the *New York Times* "not only as a gifted writer, but an absolutely essential one," she emerged as a prominent literary voice during the Latina renaissance of the 1990s. Now the best-selling author of two major novels and several poetry volumes, Cisneros continues to transform the landscape of American literature. Although born in Chicago's Latin quarter, she and her family were frequently uprooted by her father's periodic homesickness for his native Mexico City. To escape her loneliness and the miseries of poverty, she turned to books and writing poetry. In the late 1970s she studied at the largely white Iowa Writers' Workshop. Intensely alienated when class discussion turned to "universal" markers of home and identity, Cisneros gradually realized the invisibility of Chicana experience in U.S. society, culture, and literature. Determined to "write the stories that haven't been written," she began work on her first novel. A true break-through in 1984, *The House on Mango Street* was a critical sleeper for nearly a decade; in fact, the first few years after its initial publication were among the worst, economically and emotionally, of Cisneros's life. *Mango Street* is now a modern classic with over 2 million copies sold, and Esperanza Cordero stands among American literature's most celebrated young protag-onists. Cisneros's most recent work is the sweeping multigenerational epic *Caramelo* (2002).

Cisneros credits growing up "the only daughter" in a family of six sons as paramount to her strong female characters and the frank exploration of women's sexuality in her writing. In "Only Daughter" (1990), Cisneros also grapples with her father's troubling perspective on daughterhood and its ambivalent impact on her writing career—and the woman she would become. Here she admits, "My father represents, then, the public majority. A public who is disinterested in reading, and yet one who I am writing about and for, and privately trying to woo."

Once, several years ago, when I was just starting out my writing career, I was asked to write my own contributor's note for an anthology I was part of. I wrote: "I am the only daughter in a family of six sons. *That* explains everything."

Well, I've thought about that ever since, and yes, it explains a lot to me, but for the reader's sake I should have written: "I am the only daughter of a *Mexican* family of six sons." Or even: "I am the only daughter of a Mexican father and a Mexican-American mother." Or: "I am the only daughter of a working-class family of nine." All of these had everything to do with who I am today.

I was/am the only daughter and *only* a daughter. Being an only daughter in a family of six sons forced me by circumstance to spend a lot of time by myself because my brothers felt it beneath them to play with a *girl* in public. But that aloneness, that loneliness, was good for a would-be writer—it allowed me time to think and think, to imagine, to read and prepare myself.

Being only a daughter for my father meant my destiny would lead me to become someone's wife. That's what he believed. But when I was in fifth grade and shared my plans for college with him, I was sure he understood. I remember my father saying, *"Que bueno, mi'ja, that's good."* That meant a lot to me, especially since my brothers thought the idea hilarious. What I didn't realize was that my father thought college was good for girls—good for finding a husband. After four years in college and two more in graduate school, and still no husband, my father shakes his head even now and says I wasted all that education.

In retrospect, I'm lucky my father believed daughters were meant for husbands. It meant it didn't matter if I majored in something silly like English. After all, I'd find a nice professional eventually, right? This allowed me the liberty to putter about embroidering my little poems and stories without my father interrupting with so much as a "What's that you're writing?"

But the truth is, I wanted him to interrupt. I wanted my father to understand what it was I was scribbling, to introduce me as "My only daughter, the writer." Not as "This is only my daughter. She teaches." *Es maestra*—teacher. Not even *profesora*.

In a sense, everything I have ever written has been for him, to win his approval even though I know my father can't read English words, even though my father's only reading includes the brown-ink *Esto* sports magazines from Mexico City and the bloody *¡Alarma!* magazines that feature yet another sighting of *La Virgen de Guadalupe* on a tortilla or a wife's revenge on her philandering husband by bashing his skull in with a *molcajete* (a kitchen mortar made of volcanic rock.) Or the *fotonovelas,* the little picture paperbacks with tragedy and trauma erupting from the characters' mouths in bubbles.

My father represents, then, the public majority. A public who is disinterested in reading, and yet one whom I am writing about and for, and privately trying to woo.

When we were growing up in Chicago, we moved a lot because of my father. He suffered bouts of nostalgia. Then we'd have to let go of our flat, store the furniture with mother's relatives, load the station wagon with baggage and bologna sandwiches and head south. To Mexico City.

We came back, of course. To yet another Chicago flat, another Chicago neighborhood, another Catholic school. Each time, my father would seek out the parish priest in order to get a tuition break, and complain or boast: "I have seven sons."

He meant *siete hijos,* seven children, but he translated it as "sons." "I have seven sons." To anyone who would listen. The Sears Roebuck employee who sold us the washing machine. The short-order cook where my father ate his ham-and-eggs breakfasts. "I have seven sons." As if he deserved a medal from the state.

My papa. He didn't mean anything by that mistranslation, I'm sure. But somehow I could feel myself being erased. I'd tug my father's sleeve and whisper: "Not seven sons. Six! and *one daughter.*"

When my oldest brother graduated from medical school, he fulfilled my father's dream that we study hard and use this—our heads, instead of this—our hands. Even now my father's hands are thick and yellow, stubbed by a history of hammer and nails and twine and coils and springs. "Use this," my father said, tapping his head, "and not this," showing us those hands. He always looked tired when he said it.

Wasn't college an investment? And hadn't I spent all those years in college? And if I didn't marry, what was it all for? Why would anyone go to college and then choose to be poor? Especially someone who had always been poor.

Last year, after ten years of writing professionally, the financial rewards started to trickle in. My second National Endowment for the Arts Fellowship. A guest professorship at the University of California, Berkeley. My book, which sold to a major New York publishing house.

At Christmas, I flew home to Chicago. The house was throbbing, same as always: hot tamales and sweet tamales hissing in my mother's pressure cooker, and everybody—my mother, six brothers, wives, babies, aunts, cousins—talking too loud and at the same time. Like in a Fellini film, because that's just how we are.

I went upstairs to my father's room. One of my stories had just been translated into Spanish and published in an anthology of Chicano writing and I wanted to show it to him. Ever since he recovered from a stroke two years ago, my father likes to spend his leisure hours horizontally. And that's how I found him, watching a Pedro Infante movie Galavisión and eating rice pudding.

There was a glass filled with milk on the bedside table. There were several vials of pills and balled Kleenex. And on the floor, one black sock and a plastic urinal that I didn't want to look at but looked at anyway. Pedro Infante was about to burst into song, and my father was laughing.

I'm not sure if it was because my story was translated into Spanish, or because it was published in Mexico, or perhaps because the story dealt with Tepeyac, the *colonia* my father was raised in and the house he grew up in, but at any rate, my father punched the mute button on his remote control and read my story.

I sat on the bed next to my father and waited. He read it very slowly. As if he were reading each line over and over. He laughed at all the right places and read lines he liked out loud. He pointed and asked questions: "Is this So-and-so?" "Yes," I said. He kept reading.

When he was finally finished, after what seemed like hours, my father looked up and asked: "Where can we get more copies of this for the relatives?"

Of all the wonderful things that happened to me last year, that was the most wonderful.

Amy Ling

■

Why Write?

A founding mother of Asian American studies, the late Amy Ling (1939–1999) was an internationally renowned critic and scholar. The literary world was deeply saddened by her untimely death following a long struggle with breast cancer. But Ling's pioneering work in Asian American studies leaves behind a legacy that will endure. *The Journal of Asian American Studies* applauded her ambitious multigenre anthology *Yellow Light: The Flowering of Asian American Arts* (2000) as "an important marker of the state of Asian American creativity at the end of the twentieth century." Critic Stewart David Ikeda also notes the lasting signficance of Ling's final work, "one that shows just how far we APAs [Asian Pacific Americans] have come and how far we will yet go to profoundly affect American culture in the next century." Born in Beijing, Ling and her family immigrated to the United States when she was six. In the 1980s she was among the brave first to study Chinese American women writers, a commitment that nearly ended her academic career. After a protracted battle at Rutgers University over the "significance" of this burgeoning field, Ling went on to become founding director of the Asian American studies program at the University of Wisconsin, Madison. And it was while writing *Between Worlds: Women Writers of Chinese Ancestry* (1990) that Ling rediscovered the late-nineteenth century works of Edith and Winnifred Eaton, now considered the foremothers of Asian American literature. With *Mrs. Spring Fragrance and Other Writings* (1995), the first edited collection of Edith Eaton/Sui Sin Far's work, Ling showed the world what she had known all along to be true: "Despite Chinese custom that left wives back in China to care for their husband's parents, despite U.S. immigration laws that tried to keep them out of this country, women writers of Chinese ancestry managed to have a history one hundred years in length. . . . Each writer I uncovered affirmed me, made me less of an anomaly; each seemed a gift."

Writing poetry, Ling would discover yet another precious gift of connection. In "Why Write?" she discusses how poetry helped her unlearn damaging lessons studied as a "good student" in all-white schools—and as her mother's daughter. Here Ling testifies to poetry's power to distill hidden truths from our everyday hurts, transforming the ways we view those closest to us and even ourselves.

■

As a girl in the pretelevision era, I always loved to read but never gave much thought to writing. From the Victorian novels I devoured, I had learned that girls could only aspire to be the inspiration for male authors and artists, never themselves be authors or artists. But one day, when I was in the ninth grade, in Brooklyn, my English teacher gave me an A+ on a paragraph I had dashed off in class, "The Joys of Spring," which reveled in daffodils, tulips, robins, and the welcome warmth. I'd recycled certain phrases I'd read or heard elsewhere, but I'd also plumbed, and slightly exaggerated, my pleasure at earth's return to life. After reading my paper to the class, the teacher returned it with a smile and a new look of admiration. I was astounded but also delighted because my father gave me a dollar for A's in those days. Busy in the kitchen, my mother, the English major, made no comment.

From ages six through ten, I was the only Chinese girl in Allentown, Pennsylvania, and Mexico, Missouri. When we moved to East New York, I became one of a handful in my junior high and high school; and even at Queens College, there were very few Asians. We did not seek each other out, as though for us to be more than one would call too much attention to our alien presence. Not only did I live in a world that idolized long-legged, blue-eyed blondes, but, having skipped two grades, I was two years younger than everyone else and socially immature. Thus, feeling isolated and estranged, I became a diligent student with a painfully insecure sense of self.

Never seeing myself reflected in anything I ever read was another reason that writing never occurred to me. Writing seemed to require confidence, imagination, and experience—none of which I had in any appreciable quantity. So I gazed with awe and envy at my classmate and friend Toni Cade (Bambara), who had lots of all three of these qualities and who later became justly famous. Her mother encouraged her; my mother silenced me: "If you don't have something nice to say, don't say anything." My father only picked out the flaws in my drawings, never mentioned the good points.

Several decades later, after the Civil Rights and Feminist movements, after Maxine Hong Kingston, Mitsuye Yamada, and Nellie Wong had blazoned the way, and after I had been invited to join a supportive women's writing group, I explored my own self-censorship and self-suppression in a poem:

Questions

Of what am I compounded that I simmer,
do not boil; lid clamped tight against the light,
smolder but never erupt to cast rivers
of scorching, hellish red making new lands,
sputter but never soar to explode ruby
emerald magic against night skies
to craning necks and gasping ohs? What
element too much, what too little or in fatal
combination so that nothing has been,
ever is the catalyst? Why like the caterpillar
do I crawl, dragging butterfly's wings?
And worst of all, if ignorance be bliss
why am I punished by consciousness of this?

Finding the right imagery and polishing this poem with the help of others in the group were pleasures so delicious that I couldn't believe it was not forbidden fruit. I had discovered a cool, clear, crystal spring bubbling up inside me—a secret and wonderful source.

After writing a series of poems exploring my between-worlds identity, I moved outward to other members of my family—other sources of deep love and deep pain. Like most daughters, I had/have a difficult relationship with my mother. Nothing I do pleases her, and yet, because she is my mother, I keep trying. She once had me drive her back to Allentown because there were no trustworthy dentists in New York, only to have the dentist tell her that she should find someone closer to home. I told her that, but would she listen to me? A concert pianist in China, she hinted strongly, after I began to bring home a salary, that she would like a grand piano. Unable to afford a new one, I looked in Buy Lines and drove her from Queens to Brooklyn to look at a used baby grand. She liked it; I paid for it and had it sent to her house. There it sat for years, untouched. She refused to play and would make lame excuses. Her rejection of my gift hurt and angered me for years until I sat down and wrote:

Mother's Piano

One Christmas mother asked for a grand piano.
She would have studied at Julliard,
been a concert pianist had it not been for
his daily letters flying visions of love around
the world to entice her back from
America, its golden gate wonders,
satin and lace underwear, new sights all
across the continent, and being a sight herself
at church meetings. "My foster daughter,
everyone, a Chinese orphan, whom I took in
when she was two, now a college graduate,
product of our mission schools, a living
example of the fine use we've made of your
generous dollars, faithful friends, cheerful givers."

Back she went to her own country,
into the arms of a husband, ten months later
in her arms, a child, crying, needing, developing
sores all over its body, running
sores that had to be bathed one by one, raw
sores that came from the bad combination of
their blood, she said; back to a land cratered
by bombs, raped by gun-bearing Japanese; a land
where an egg was a luxury, an orange a celebration.
She had to cut up her chiffon dresses
to make clothes for her daughter.
There was no money for a piano;
this was no time for music.

Thirty years later, with her own house in Queens,
her husband ejected for the accumulated bad blood
between them, her children grown, unnested,

she asked her daughter for a concert grand,
would not hear her house was too small, grands too dear.
The daughter took her all over town for a used baby grand;
mother chose one with a good tone, a Christman.
A tuner checked it over, a mover moved it in,
her friend admired it, but mother said,
"Oh, that thing? It takes up too much room.
Do you know anyone who wants a third-hand piano?"
would not touch it for years,
"I am too tired after work; my fingers will not
move as they used to; they are too old."

One day last summer, she received a letter
from her teacher of fifty years ago.
Rose Waldron, now eighty-three, wanted to bus from Seattle
to see New York and her favorite piano student.
Then mother opened the Christman and began to play.

In writing this poem, I realized more than the usual exhilaration of
transforming an experience into shapeable words and images on a page.
Unexpectedly, I had arrived at a deeper understanding of my mother
and the quality of her life.

The foster daughter of an unmarried missionary nurse to China
from Pennsylvania, Mother, too, had been brought up between worlds.
For the missionary children, she was always "that Chinese girl," while
the Chinese referred to her as "that missionary child." Being shown off
as a curiosity in the United States had to have been alienating. So she
married for love but returned after a year of material luxuries to a
China in the throes of war. After we immigrated to the United States,
Father, despite his prestigious ceramic engineering degree, was always
the last hired and first fired. Her teaching credentials from China dismissed in New York, Mother took up secretarial work. In China she
had had servants; here, she had to make coffee for her boss—a task that
was, for her, a daily humiliation. I had been the baby with all the sores
that she had to bathe one by one; no wonder she was demanding,
resentful, and bitter.

In the process of reviewing her story and setting it down, I was able
to step outside my own emotions and to regard her through a different

perspective. No longer was I the hurt daughter angered by my mother's selfish demands. Instead, I was a woman feeling the justifiable disappoint-ment and anguish of another woman. I was happy that the right catalyst had come back into her life to galvanize her to making music, delighted the piano was being used. She was like a child again, eager to please her teacher. Suddenly, I understood that all her life, she too has been seeking praise from a mother-figure. How much alike we are!

From this experience, I learned that writing can be a great catharsis, a means of untangling knots of gut-deep emotion, sometimes buried for years. The process begins with an inner Geiger counter, surveying my emotional landscape until it discovers a particularly profound knot. I take it out and examine it. It then becomes a subject that poses an intellectual and aesthetic challenge as I work to craft it into a finished object: poem, story, essay. And if I am lucky, the careful word-smithing magically transmutes this personal tangle of emotion into something that moves others. There can be no more satisfying alchemy than this.

However, life goes on. Yesterday, I asked my eighty-four-year-old mother if she liked the intricately beaded garnet necklace I sent her for her birthday. She seemed annoyed: "I don't wear costume jewelry any-more. It's too much trouble to put on and take off." She left the blooming gardenia I gave her for Mother's Day at my sister's house: "Too difficult to care for." And as for the sewing box I gave her at Christmas: "I don't sew much these days."

It's time to write more poems.

Judith Clark

The Girl Behind the Smile

Judith Clark is a poet, independent scholar, peer-educator, and lifelong activist. Since 1983 she has been serving a sentence of seventy-five years to life at Bedford Hills Correctional Facility. Born in Brooklyn to a politically radical family, at age fourteen Clark began her activist work in the civil rights movement. As Clark notes, working "in the radical social movements of that era defined my life before prison. But my own unacknowledged needs and psychological issues drove me further and further into the extreme margins of those movements." In 1981 Clark was arrested as the get-away driver in an armed robbery, "during which three people were killed." Although she declared herself a political prisoner during her trial and moved herself to a basement holding cell, Clark's later two-year lockup in solitary confinement nearly broke her. During this difficult time she turned to books, "particularly women writers." It was also while in lockup that Clark began writing daily. Initially a record of the deep resonance she felt when reading writers like Joan Nestle, Alice Walker, and Grace Paley, her journal soon evolved into a space for exploring, through poetry and memoir, her own voice and world. Clark's poetry has appeared in the *New Yorker, Ikon, Bridges,* and *Global City Review.* She is also a contributor to *Aliens at the Border* and *More In Than Out,* two volumes that came out of Hettie Jones's writing workshops at Bedford, and Bell Gale Chevigny's *Doing Time,* the anthology of PEN prison writing contest winners. Her short memoir essays have appeared in *Red Diaper Babies: Children of the Left* and *A Wretch Like Me.* Clark also continues her activist work through writing. She is coauthor of *Breaking the Walls of Silence,* a book about the AIDS peer-education, counseling, and support program she codeveloped in response to the growing epidemic at Bedford. After completing her bachelor's and master's degrees in psychology, she published several articles from her thesis on long-termer mothers and their relationships with their children. She is part of the writing group with writer/activist Eve Ensler featured in the recent PBS documentary *What I Want My Words to Do to You.*

Writing has proven not only crucial to Clark's survival while in prison; it "has been a central part of my evolution" there. In "The Girl Behind the Smile" (2003), Clark opens a window onto her journey as a woman writer. Now "the mother of a young woman writer," here again she is reminded—this time by reading the words of her daughter—of the power in being not one or the other, but both.

It is my journal that keeps me above the surface of the waters. On the days when I feel close to drowning. Drowning in anger that wells up, like a tidal wave, from the pit of the stomach, burning my heart, choking my throat. . . . The walls are closing in, closer and closer. My cell window faces a brick wall, and I wonder if they are sending me a message. . . . But I can't let "them" invade my mind. I don't want to write about "them." I want to write my stories, *my* poems, *my* words. My words.

(Writing exercise, 10/13/93)

Although I have published numerous poems, essays, and articles, I still hesitate to call myself "a writer." How many women writers share that fear of making a fraudulent claim? But I have no problem joining the words *woman* and *writer.* My journey toward being a writer has been a woman's journey, which like so many women's journeys began in silence.

from "Panic"

Papa, driving the family car
  debates politics with Saul
Mama, next to him
   navigates
in the back seat
  Brother pinches
  me scrunched
   between him and Saul

Papa's voice rises
as he turns

The Girl Behind the Smile

> *red faced*
> *jabbing his finger at Saul*
> *his bullet words*
> *flying*
> *scatter-shot*

My family deified the Word. The books that lined every wall of our home represented the ultimate truth that my parents believed in. Ours was a family of talkers and debaters. Meals, car trips, poker games were all occasions for political discussion and debate. But in this atmosphere saturated with the language of ideas, there were many silences.

I had trouble with my speech as a young child. When I was an infant, my family traveled to the Soviet Union, where we lived for three years. I came to speech in two languages, always knowing which language to use with whom. When we came back to the U.S., I intuited the unspoken message to stop speaking in Russian—that it was somehow dangerous. But the echo of that first language left a residue on my tongue. I slurred my r's and l's to the point of being unintelligible. My parents were told by school authorities to send me to a speech therapist. I can't remember how long I went to him; only that I hated it. His musty, smoke-filled office choked me, and my words got stuck in my throat every time he sat, too close, and commanded me to speak into his tape recorder. *The red bird went round the corner, whirled up onto the blue window ledge.* Somehow, he succeeded in retraining my tongue. Cured of my "speech defect," I emerged with a strong Brooklyn accent unlike anyone else's in my family–and just like that cigar smoking therapist's! His would not be the last embodied voice I would adopt to comply with the expectations of one higher authority or another.

from "there is the girl"

there is the girl/shouting slogans/there is the girl blindly/smiling/there is the girl/rocking/herself to sleep/there is the girl smiling . . . there is the girl behind the smile/yearning to be known . . .

No one who knew me in my younger years as a "movement militant"—before the crime, before prison—would have suspected that I was lost in silence, least of all myself. I masked my silence with the strident cacophony of slogans and rhetoric. I disdained words as empty promises. "Put your money where your mouth is" was my motto. I was a woman of action. That rejection of a language and communication represented a fundamental disconnect, a nihilism that degenerated into and justified violence.

from "these hands"
. . . these hands clenched
into defiant, upraised fists
pointed accusing fingers
punched, ripped and drew blood
   gripped the careening wheels of delusions
     trembling with fear and fury

and when child, home, lifework
and freedom
   were lost
these hands kept on
   writing, gesturing
desperately drawing
   words in air

until one day
these hands
stopped . . .

In my fifth year of incarceration, I was locked up in solitary confinement for two years. Everything in me wound down to a halt. I lost all energy to write letters and articles filled with hopeful revolutionary rhetoric, felt no desire for visits with political comrades seeking to show their solidarity. I lived from week to week for visits with my father and daughter, and from a professor with whom I'd begun to look at myself. I stopped being "a public political prisoner" and went into a seclusion of silence. My day-to-day company came from reading books, particularly women's writings: Joan Nestle, Audre Lorde, Jo Sinclair, Dorothy Allison, Cherríe Moraga, Barbara Smith, June Jordan, Minnie Bruce Pratt, Maya Angelou, Grace Paley, and many others. I was drawn to writers who defined themselves and their work in the context of community. Their words triggered memories and images, fomented deep longings, drew me into new ways of posing questions, challenged me to see things from different angles. I had begun to keep a journal, and while I was writing to and for myself, it often felt like I was in conversations with these women writers.

The words of these women helped me feel less isolated—that despite our differences and how very far out on the limb of humanity I had taken myself, the challenges I faced and the emotions they evoked were not unknown to others. Soon I realized that in order to face myself and do some serious psychological work, I had to "shelve" my political assumptions and identity. Reading Alice Walker's poem "On Stripping Bark from Myself," I was reassured that there was another person who felt as raw and naked as I did. Months later, after a hard holiday season, I wrote in a poem,

> *Everyone has her nightmares*
> *her prison cell*
> > *solitary box*
> *that she alone can enter*
> > *hesitantly*
> *fearful*
> > *of getting trapped*
> > > *without the key*

Exploring the many truths revealed by women writers opened in my mind the sheer possibility of multiple truths. I began writing narratives to explore the varied dimensions of my own experience. Writing about our voyage to the Soviet Union in my mother's harried voice, I felt her intense loneliness and her anger at living in the shadow of my father. And for the first time, the Gordian knot of our conflict was loosened.

Viscerally aware of how these women's words nurtured and challenged me, and how different my journal writing felt from my previous "political writing," I contemplated the power of words and my relationship to "the word." I began to appreciate how my attitude that words were only legitimate if acted on actually eviscerated the power of words to express feelings and desires we would never want to act on. Such literalness robbed me of fantasy and imagination, through which we grow to relate to a world full of conflict, injustice, and possibility. Words could either illuminate deeply experienced truths, or mask and distort reality. Words could either connect or disconnect. I thought about my relationship to words. I had come to prison cloaked in the mantles of "freedom fighter" and "political prisoner." Words spun from whole cloth, a flimsy fabric that began to fray quickly. In those early years inside, I had written speeches, arguments, and political tracts—a torrent of words that had begun to feel illusory and dishonest. They were words meant to stave off questions and doubt; pat phrases, like "to be a mother is to care about the children of the world," meant to stanch the hemorrhaging of shame and guilt about my own child.

My search for a new language was central to the choices I wanted to make. I wrote out in bold letters some lines from Adrienne Rich's "Transcendental Etude":

> *But there come times—perhaps this is one of them—*
> *[. . .]*
> *when we have to*
> *pull back from the incantations,*
> *rhythms we've moved to thoughtlessly,*
> *and disenthrall ourselves, bestow*
> *ourselves to silence, or a severer listening, cleansed*
> *of oratory, formulas, choruses, laments, static*
> *crowding the wires.*

And I let Adrienne's words light my way through the beautiful darkness.

When I call myself "a woman writer," I am giving homage to all those women writers who kept me alive and hopeful, whose words were like kindling, stoking my own creative embers. I am a writer, able to face harsh realities and tell my truth because of these women. The "woman" attached to my "writer" is really "women." It is an affirmation of my sense of community, inside and outside of prison.

There are women whose *words* reached me, and then there are the women who went beyond their own lives to enter into *this* world and our lives. I learned the craft of poetry writing in a workshop taught by Hettie Jones. For over a decade, until the doors were closed to her, she came weekly to conduct a poetry workshop. Many women passed through Hettie's workshop. But a core of us stayed and wrote and read our work aloud and grew into writers. Ours was an emboldened sisterhood, and we were in love with each other's words. The sacred energy of our circle and our communal silence of concentration generated the beginnings of most of my best poems. Their enthusiastic responses led me to believe that my work had potential. Hettie taught me the physical pleasure of working on a poem, of carving away words, changing and reshaping until the poem emerges.

> *. . . what I want*
> *is to sink into my heart*
> *   for   words that*
> *take us to a different plane*
>
> *where lines dividing and defining*
> *melt into rivers,*
> *   oceans that carry us to a*
> *unravaged continent*
> *   of understanding*

In recent years, Eve Ensler has facilitated a workshop where we write narratives from our lives as a means to explore those parts of ourselves we had disavowed and disowned. We've written about our crimes, struggling to own and understand ourselves and take responsibility. We've pushed each other to find the words to express remorse and seek reconciliation. Our work together helped me to write what may be the most important words I have published—a letter of apology for my crime.

> *. . . It's that place–that miserable, weak, isolated, muzzled part of me–that strangely, I want you to know. . . . It is that part of me that makes me a kindred soul to every lost, desperate creature on the Earth. That part of me has known fear and therefore would never want to engender fear in another. . . . She has been alone and voiceless too long. Let me let her speak, to call out her desire for love. Let her be heard.*
>
> (Writing exercise, 1999)

I do not think I could have made the shift of consciousness, thinking, feeling, and personality necessary to emerge into an honest sense of remorse without my search for a language to express what I was feeling and discovering.

> *flesh*
> *overflowing waistbands*
> *jiggling under tee shirts*
>
> *slack chin   heavy breasts*
> *loose, sticky thigh meat*
>
> *I dreamed of taking a sharp knife,*
> *slicing it away*
> *believing that*
>   *smaller, I would be*
>
> *quieter*
>   *my tongue tamed*
>   *as in clitorodectomy*
>   *that other hungry organ*

Writing has been central in my repossessing those aspects of myself that I had disavowed, dispossessed, and denied, beginning with my female-ness. When I was young, being female meant feeling puny and afraid. Later, it was about hating my flesh and the longings of my flesh. I grew up into a literature dominated by the male voice, from Tolstoy to Bellow, and by the notion that great literature separated the word from the body. Great ideas emerged from great minds, and to think great thoughts, one had to become liberated from the subjectivity of the body. While I welcomed and enjoyed the explosion of literature and poetry by women in the 1970s, it did not seep into my own soul. It could not change me until I was ready to face all that I was throwing overboard.

> *. . . there is the girl who turns*
>   *into her stillness to*
> *create worlds*
>   *teeming with sound and surprise*

Today, my words emerge from my body. While I write in various modes, I feel most at home writing poetry because it is a language of rhythm, of senses. Poetry is about breath. It flows from the heartbeat, the cadence of my natural rhythms, the sounds that emerge from my vocal chords through my wide open mouth–all that is okay in poetry. Poetry forgets shoulds and leaps beyond literal, dualist meaning. This is not to say that poetry lacks discipline. One must hold true to the structure of a poem, its shape, and let go of the excess. Writing poetry is like labor: hard as hell, also incredibly satisfying.

I am a mother, and more to the point, the mother of a young woman writer. I did not know that she would choose a writer's life. But when she was very young, I knew that I wanted her to have the power of the word, to be able to speak and write her own truth and be heard. Watching her grow up and contend with all the negative messages that threatened to deny her a sense of her own potential was at times enraging and disheartening. But she truly has that writer's way of observing and knowing, a capacity to reflect as she experiences life and use a complicated language encompassing self and other, and embracing diversity. Recently, she helped edit a collection of politically inspired short fiction; in her bio, she gave me a most precious gift in thanking me for teaching her "all that words can do."

I am a lesbian, a Jew, a prisoner; but if in describing me you paired any of those words with *writer,* I would add the words *more than.* Not so with the word *woman.* Being a woman encompasses all the potential I can imagine. It also bears the experience of being Other, of being an observer, of having to reclaim that potential—and therefore loving it, and valuing it all the more.

III.

On Writing Herself

To write is to become.
—Trinh T. Minh-ha

Jeanette Winterson

∎

The Semiotics of Sex

Born in Manchester, England, Jeanette Winterson is a prize-winning novelist. Her work has gained an international audience for its dazzling language
and wickedly subversive play on traditional narrative forms (gender, most
famously, but also the presumed boundaries between myth, history, and
imagination). At age twenty-six she took the literary world by storm with her
stunning debut, *Oranges Are Not the Only Fruit* (1985). Since, she has written seven novels, a comic book, an essay collection, a short story volume, two
screenplays, and a children's book. She is also a regular contributor to *The
Guardian* and *The Times* of London, writing sharply observed essays on body
politics, art in a global marketplace, and more. The *San Francisco Chronicle*
called her "one of our most brilliant, visionary storytellers," while the
Evening Standard noted that "many consider her to be the best living writer
in [English]." Wild critical and commercial success notwithstanding,
Winterson is no stranger to controversy or bitter fame. As noted in a recent
Guardian profile (2000), in the 1990s she was the subject of intense critical
backlash, with her personal life and especially "her sexuality, her unfeminine
choices, [and] her humourless determination to take her work seriously"
bearing the brunt. Considered by some a "literary outlaw," Winterson also
openly defies the "confines implied in the rubber stamps of 'feminist,' 'lesbian,' and 'postmodern'"—whether imposed by those seeking blood or common ground.

   At once a passionate inquiry into art's complexities and a fiery indictment
of identity politics, "The Semiotics of Sex" first appeared in her essay collection *Art Objects* (1995). Here she turns her discomfiting gaze to the paradox
of artistic self-determination and (sexual) difference in the creation and
appraisal of art. Unsurprisingly, her position on the matter is bold and
unequivocal: "Judge the writer by the work."

▪

I was in a bookshop recently when a young woman approached me. She told me she was writing an essay on my work and that of Radclyffe Hall. Could I help?

'Yes,' I said. 'Our work has nothing in common.'

'I thought you were a lesbian,' she said.

I have become aware that the chosen sexual difference of one writer is, in itself, thought sufficient to bind her in semiotic sisterhood with any other writer, also lesbian, dead or alive.

I am, after all, a pervert, so I will not mind sharing a bed with a dead body. This bed in the shape of a book, this book in the shape of a bed, must accommodate us every one, because, whatever our style, philosophy, class, age, preoccupations and talent, we are lesbians and isn't that the golden key to the single door of our work?

In any discussion of art and the artist, heterosexuality is back-grounded, whilst homosexuality is foregrounded. What you fuck is much more important than how you write. This may be because reading takes more effort than sex. It may be because the word 'sex' is more exciting than the word 'book'. Or is it? Surely that depends on what kind of sex and what kind of book? I can only assume that straight sex is so dull that even a book makes better reportage. No-one asks Iris Murdoch about her sex life. Every interviewer I meet asks me about mine and what they do not ask they invent. I am a writer who happens to love women. I am not a lesbian who happens to write.

What is it about? Prurience? Stupidity? And as Descartes didn't say, 'I fuck therefore I am.'? The straight world is willful in its pursuit of queers and it seems to me that to continually ask someone about their homosexuality, when the reason to talk is a book, a picture, a play, is harassment by the back door.

The Queer world has colluded in the misreading of art as sexuality. Art is difference, but not necessarily sexual difference, and while to be outside of the mainstream of imposed choice is likely to make someone more conscious, it does not automatically make that someone an artist. A great deal of gay writing, especially gay writing around the AIDS crisis, is therapy, is release, is not art. It is its subject matter and no more and I hope by now that I have convinced my readers in these essays, that all art, including literature, is much more than its subject matter. It is true that a number of gay and lesbian writers have attracted an audience and some attention simply because they are queer. Lesbians and gays do need their own culture, as any subgroup does, including the sub-group of heterosexuality, but the problems start when we assume that the fact of our queerness bestows on us special powers. It might make for certain advantages (it is helpful for a woman artist not to have a husband) but it cannot, of itself, guarantee art. Lesbians and gay men, who have to examine so much of what the straight world takes for granted, must keep on examining their own standards in all things, and especially the standards we set for our own work.

I think this is particularly urgent where fiction and poetry are concerned and where it is most tempting to assume that the autobiography of Difference will be enough.

Let me put it another way: if I am in love with Peggy and I am a composer I can express that love in an ensemble or a symphony. If I am in love with Peggy and I am a painter, I need not paint her portrait, I am free to express my passion in splendid harmonies of colour and line. If I am a writer, I will have to be careful, I must not fall into the trap of believing that my passion, of itself, is art. As a composer or a painter I know that it is not. I know that I shall have to find a translation of form to make myself clear. I know that the language of my passion and the language of my art are not the same thing.

Of course there is a paradox here; the most powerful written work often masquerades as autobiography. It offers itself as raw when in fact it is sophisticated. It presents itself as a kind of diary when really it is an oration. The best work speaks intimately to you even though it has been consciously made to speak intimately to thousands of others. The bad writer believes that sincerity of feeling will be enough, and pins her faith on the power of experience. The true writer knows that feeling must give way to form. It is through the form, not in spite of, or accidental to it, that the most powerful emotions are let loose over the greatest number of people.

Art must resist autobiography if it hopes to cross boundaries of class, culture . . . and . . . sexuality. Literature is not a lecture delivered to a special interest group, it is a force that unites its audience. The sub-groups are broken down.

How each artist learns to translate autobiography into art is a problem that each artist solves for themselves. When solved, unpicking is impossible, we cannot work backwards from the finished text into its raw material. The commonest mistake of critics and biographers is to assume that what holds significance for them necessarily held significance for the writer. Forcing the work back into autobiography is a way of trying to contain it, of making what has become unlike anything else into what is just like everything else. It may be that in the modern world, afraid of feeling, it is more comfortable to turn the critical gaze away from a fully realised piece of work. It is always easier to focus on sex. The sexuality of the writer is a wonderful diversion.

If Queer culture is now working against assumptions of identity as sexuality, art gets there first, by implicitly or explicitly creating emotion around the forbidden. Some of the early feminist arguments surrounding the wrongfulness of men painting provocative female nudes seem to me to have overlooked the possibility or the fact of another female as the viewer. Why should she identify with the nude? What deep taboos make her unable to desire the nude?

Opera, before and after the nineteenth century, but not during, enjoyed serious games of sexual ambiguity, and opera fans will know the delicious and disturbing pleasure of watching a woman disguised as a man and hearing her woo another woman with a voice unmistakably female. Our opera ancestors knew the now forbidden pleasure of listening to a man sing as a woman; in his diary, Casanova writes of the fascination and desire felt for these compromising creatures by otherwise heterosexual men. Music is androgynously sexy and with the same sensuous determination penetrates male and female alike. Unless of course one resists it, and how much sex-resistance goes on under the lie of 'I don't like opera.'?

Similarly, I am sure that a lot of the coyness and silliness that accompanies productions of Shakespeare that include cross-dressing roles, is an attempt to steer them clear of Queer. As long as we all know that a pretence is happening; the pretence of Principal Boy or music-hall camp, we are safe in our het-suits. Too many directors overlook the obvious fact that in Shakespeare, the disguises are meant to convince. They are not a comedian's joke. We too must fall in love. We too must know what it is to find that we have desired another woman, desired another man. And should we really take at face value those fifth acts where everyone simply swops their partner to the proper sex and goes home to live happily ever after?

I am not suggesting that we should all part with our husbands and live Queer.

I am not suggesting that a lesbian who recognises desire for a man sleep with him. We need not be so crude. What we do need is to accept in ourselves, with pleasure, the subtle and various emotions that are in the infinity of a human being. More, not less, is the capacity of the heart. More not less is the capacity of art.

Art coaxes out of us emotions we normally do not feel. It is not that art sets out to shock (that is rare), it is rather that art occupies ground unconquered by social niceties. Seeking neither to please nor to displease, art works to enlarge emotional possibility. In a dead society that inevitably puts it on the side of the rebels. Do not mistake me, I am not of the voting party of bohemians and bad boys, and the rebelliousness of art does not make every rebel an artist. The rebellion of art is a daily rebellion against the state of living death routinely called real life.

> Where every public decision has to be justified in the scale of corporate profit, poetry unsettles these apparently self-evident propositions, not through ideology, but by its very presence and ways of being, its embodiment of states of longing and desire.
>
> Adrienne Rich, *What is Found There: Notebooks on Poetry and Politics* (1993)

And not only public decisions but also private compromises. Calculations of the heart that should never be made. It is through the acceptance of breakdown; breakdown of fellowship, of trust, of community, of communication, of language, of love, that we begin to break down ourselves, a fragmented society afraid of feeling.

Against this fear, art is fresh healing and fresh pain. The rebel writer who brings healing and pain, need not be a Marxist or a Socialist, need not be political in the journalistic sense and may fail the shifting tests of Correctness, while standing as a rebuke to the hollowed out days and as a refuge for our stray hearts. Communist and People's Man, Stephen Spender, had the right credentials, but Catholic and cultural reactionary T. S. Eliot made the poetry. It is not always so paradoxical but it can be, and the above example should be reason enough not to judge the work by the writer. Judge the writer by the work.

When I read Adrienne Rich or Oscar Wilde, rebels of very different types, the fact of their homosexuality should not be uppermost. I am not reading their work to get at their private lives, I am reading their work because I need the depth-charge it carries.

Their formal significance, the strength of their images, their fidelity to language makes it possible for them to reach me across distance and time. If each were not an exceptional writer, neither would be able to reach beyond the interests of their own sub-group. The truth is that both have an audience who do not share the sexuality or the subversiveness of playwright and poet but who cannot fail to be affected by those elements when they read Rich and Wilde. Art succeeds where polemic fails.

Nevertheless, there are plenty of heterosexual readers who won't touch books by Queers and plenty of Queer readers who are only out to scan a bent kiss. We all know of men who won't read books by women and in spite of the backlash that dresses this up in high sounding notions of creativity, it is ordinary terror of difference. Men do not feel comfortable looking at the world through eyes that are not male. It has nothing to do with sentences or syntax, it is sexism by any other name. It would be a pity if lesbians and gay men retreated into the same kind of cultural separatism. We learn early how to live in two worlds; our own and that of the dominant model, why not learn how to live in multiple worlds? The strange prismatic worlds that art offers? I do not want to read only books by women, only books by Queers, I want all that there is, so long as it is genuine and it seems to me that to choose our reading matter according to the sex and/or sexuality of the writer is a dismal way to read. For lesbians and gay men it has been vital to create our own counter-culture but that does not mean that there is nothing in straight culture that we can use. We are more sophisticated that that and it is worth remembering that the conventional mind is its own prison.

The man who won't read Virginia Woolf, the lesbian who won't touch T. S. Eliot, are both putting subjective concerns in between themselves and the work. Literature, whether made by heterosexuals or homosexuals, whether to do with lives gay or straight, packs in it supplies of energy and emotion that all of us need. Obviously if a thing is not art, we will not get any artistic pleasure out of it and we will find it void of the kind of energy and emotion we can draw on indefinitely. It is difficult, when we are surrounded by trivia makers and trivia merchants, all claiming for themselves the power of art, not to fall for the lie that there is no such thing or that it is anything. The smallness of it all is depressing and it is inevitable that we will have to whip out the magnifying glass of our own interests to bring the thing up to size: 'Is it about me?' 'Is it amusing?' 'Is it dirty?' 'What about the sex?' are not aesthetic questions but they are the questions asked by most reviewers and by most readers most of the time. Unless we set up criteria of judgement that are relevant to literature, and not to sociology, entertainment, topicality etc., we are going to find it harder and harder to know what it is that separates art from everything else.

Learning to read is more than learning to group the letters on a page. Learning to read is a skill that marshals the entire resources of body and mind. I do not mean the endless dross-skimming that passes for literacy, I mean the ability to engage with a text as you would another human being. To recognise it in its own right, separate, particular, to let it speak in its own voice, not in a ventriloquism of yours. To find its relationship to you that is not its relationship to anyone else. To recognise, at the same time, that you are neither the means nor the method of its existence and that the love between you is not a mutual suicide. The love between you offers an alternative paradigm; a complete and fully realised vision in a chaotic unrealised world. Art is not amnesia, and the popular idea of books as escapism or diversion, misses altogether what art is. There is plenty of escapism and diversion to be had, but it cannot be had from real books, real pictures, real music, real theatre. Art is the realization of complex emotion.

We value sensitive machines. We spend billions of pounds to make them more sensitive yet, so that they detect minerals deep in the earth's crust, radioactivity thousands of miles away. We don't value sensitive human beings and we spend no money on their priority. As machines become more delicate and human beings coarser, will antennae and fibre-optic claim for themselves what was uniquely human? Not rationality, not logic, but that strange network of fragile perception, that means I can imagine, that teaches me to love, a lodging of recognition and tenderness where I sometimes know the essential beat that rhythms life.

The artist as radar can help me. The artist who combines an exceptional sensibility with an exceptional control over her material. This equipment, unfunded, unregarded, gift and discipline kept tuned to untapped frequencies, will bring home signals otherwise lost to me. Will make for my ears and eyes what was the property of the hawk. This sharpness and stretch of wings has not in it the comfort of escape. It has in it warnings and chances and painful beauty. It is not what I know and it is not what I am. The mirror turns out to be a thorough looking-glass, and beyond are places I have never reached. Once reached there is no need to leave them again. Art is not tourism, it is an ever-expanding territory. Art is not Capitalism, what I find in it, I may keep. The title takes my name.

The realisation of complex emotion.

Complex emotion is pivoted around the forbidden. When I feel the complexities of a situation I am feeling the many-sidedness of it, not the obvious smooth shape, grasped at once and easily forgotten. Complexity leads to perplexity. I do not know my place. There is a clash between what I feel and what I had expected to feel. My logical self fails me, and no matter how I try to pace it out, there is still something left over that will not be accounted for. All of us have felt like this, all of us have tried to make the rough places smooth; to reason our way out of a gathering storm. Usually dishonesty is our best guide. We call inner turbulence 'blowing things up out of all proportion'. We call it 'seven-year itch'. We call it 'over-tiredness'. Like Adam we name our beasts, but not well, and we find they do not come when called.

Complex emotion often follows some major event in our lives; sex, falling in love, birth, death, are the commonest and in each of these potencies are strong taboos. The striking loneliness of the individual when confronted with these large happenings that we all share, is a loneliness of displacement. The person is thrown out of the normal groove of their life and whilst they stumble, they also have to carry a new weight of feeling, feeling that threatens to overwhelm them. Consequences of misery and breakdown are typical and in a repressive society that pretends to be liberal, misery and breakdown can be used as subtle punishments for what we no longer dare legislate against. Inability to cope is defined as a serious weakness in a macho culture like ours, but what is inability to cope, except a spasmodic, faint and fainter protest against a closed-in drugged-up life where suburban values are touted as the greatest good? A newborn child, the moment of falling in love, can cause in us seismic shocks that will, if we let them, help to re-evaluate what things matter, what things we take for granted. This is frightening, and as we get older it is harder to face such risks to the deadness that we are. Art offers the challenge we desire but also the shape we need when our own world seems most shapeless. The formal beauty of art is threat and relief to the formless neutrality of unrealised life.

'Ah' you will say, 'She means Art as Consolation. The lonely romantic who reads Jane Eyre. The computer misfit wandering with Wordsworth.'

I do not think of art as Consolation. I think of it as Creation. I think of it as an energetic space that begets energetic space. Works of art do not reproduce themselves, they re-create themselves and have at the same time sufficient permanent power to create rooms for us, the dispossessed. In other words, art makes it possible to live in energetic space.

When I talk about creating emotion around the forbidden, I do not mean disgust around the well known. Forget the lowlife, tourist, squeaky clean middle-class bad boys who call their sex-depravity in blunt prose, fine writing. Forget the copycat girls who wouldn't know the end of a dildo from a vacuum rod. They are only chintz dipped in mud and we are after real material. What is forbidden is scarier, sexier, unnightmared by the white-collar cataloguers of crap. 'Don't do that' makes for easy revolt. What is forbidden is hidden. To worm into the heart and mind until what one truly desires has been encased in dark walls of what one ought to desire, is the success of the serpent. Serpents of state, serpents of religion, serpents in the service of education, monied serpents, mythic serpents, weaving their lies backwards into history. Two myths out of many: the first, Hebrew: Eve in the garden persuaded to eat that which she has never desired to eat ('The serpent bade me to eat'). The second, Greek: Medusa, the Gorgon, whose serpent hair turns all who look on her to stone.

There are many ways of reading these myths, that is the way with myths, but for the purposes of this argument, I want us to be wary of bodies insinuated to desire what they do not desire and of hearts turned to stone.

How can I know what I feel? When a writer asks herself that question she will have to find the words to answer it, even if the answer is another question. The writer will have to make her words into a true equivalent of her heart. If she cannot, if she can only hazard at the heart, arbitrarily, temporarily she may be a psychologist but she will not be a poet.

It is the poet who goes further than any human scientist. The poet who with her dredging net must haul up difficult things and return them to the present. As she does this, the reader will begin to recognise parts of herself so neatly buried that they seem to have been buried from birth. She will be able to hear clearly the voices that have whispered at her for so many years. Some of those voices will prove false, she will perhaps learn to fear her own fears. The attendant personalities that are clinically labelled as schizophrenia, can be brought into a harmonious balance. It is not necessary to be shut up in one self, to grind through life like an ox at a mill, always treading the same ground. Human beings are capable of powered flight; we can travel across ourselves and find that self multiple and vast. The artist knows this; at the same time that art is prising away old dead structures that have rusted almost unnoticed into our flesh, art is pushing at the boundaries we thought were fixed. The convenient lies fall; the only boundaries are the boundaries of our imagination.

How much can we imagine? The artist is an imaginer. The artist imagines the forbidden because to her it is not forbidden. If she is freer than other people it is the freedom of her single allegiance to her work. Most of us have divided loyalties, most of us have sold ourselves. The artist is not divided and she is not for sale. Her clarity of purpose protects her although it is her clarity of purpose that is most likely to irritate most people. We are not happy with obsessives, visionaries, which means, in effect, that we are not happy with artists. Why do we flee from feeling? Why do we celebrate those who lower us in the mire of their own making while we hound those who come to us with hands full of difficult beauty?

If we could imagine ourselves out of despair?

If we could imagine ourselves out of helplessness?

What would happen if we could imagine in ourselves authentic desire?

> What would happen if one woman told the truth about her-self? The world would split open.
>
> Muriel Rukeyser

In search of this truth, beyond the fear of the consequences of this truth, are the flight-maps of art. When truth is at stake, and in a society that desperately needs truth, we have to be wary of those side-tracks to nowhere that mislead us from the journey we need to make. There are plenty of Last Days signposts to persuade us that nothing is worth doing and that each one of us lives in a private nightmare occasionally relieved by temporary pleasure.

Art is not a private nightmare, not even a private dream, it is a shared human connection that traces the possibilities of past and future in the whorl of now. It is a construct, like science, like religion, like the world itself. It is as artificial as you and me and as natural too. We have never been able to live without it, we have never been able to live with it. We claim it makes no difference whilst nervously barring it out of our lives. Part of this barring is to gender it, to sex it, to find ways of containing and reducing this fascinating fear. But to what are our efforts directed? What is it that we seek to mock and discourage? It is the human spirit free.

I was in a bookshop recently and a young man came up to me and said 'Is *Sexing the Cherry* a reading of *Four Quartets?*'
'Yes,' I said, and he kissed me.

Assia Djebar

■

Writing in the Language of the Other

Assia Djebar is a prolific novelist, poet, translator, scholar, playwright, and film-maker. She is considered among today's most defiant and influential Francophone writers. Born Fatima-Zohra Imalayène in Cherchell, she adopted the pen name Assia Djebar with the publication of her first novel in 1957. *La soif* (Thirst) appeared at the beginning of Algeria's long struggle for independence, when Djebar was twenty-one. She wrote the novel in two months while participating in the national student strike of 1956. The story of a half-Algerian, half-French young woman's coming of age amid the complexities of Westernization, *La soif* was acclaimed in Europe but dismissed by many Algerian critics as politically irrelevant. But Djebar remained steadfast in reimagining Algerian history through the eyes of its women, publishing several novels in the 1960s that critiqued French colonialism and Islamic patriarchy in equal measure. In the immediate years following independence, Djebar experienced tremendous pressure to abandon French. Unwilling to compromise her voice, she opted instead to enter a ten-year literary silence. While "living in voluntary muteness," Djebar studied classical Arabic and continued her study of Algerian history through film. The 1980 appearance of *Les femmes d'Alger dans leur appartement* (Women of Algiers in Their Apartment) announced Djebar's decisive return to the literary world—and a major watershed in the evolution of a singular artistic voice. Bending French to the rhythms and allusions of Arabic, with *Women of Algiers* Djebar emerged as a writer determined to define herself. Nevertheless, she remains clear-eyed to her ambivalent positioning as a "woman novelist in the French language"—a language freighted with a century of occupation, yet the only one in which her work, "in its original text," can appear. Here she pointedly observes how the very decision to write in a language of her own choosing helped transform "writing that could historically signify my extra-territoriality into my only true territory."

In 1996 Djebar won the Neustadt Prize for Contributions to World Literature "for perceptively crossing borders of culture, language, and history in her fiction and poetry." She made history at the 2000 Frankfurt Book Fair as the first Arab woman writer to receive the Fair's prestigious Peace Prize.

A woman novelist in the French language, that is how I might present myself today, my hands held out in a gesture of offering. And what do I have to offer after entering literature, more than forty-five years ago, if not ten novels, two collections of short stories, two plays, and a short collection of poems, an example of these works in one hand (let's say the right hand since, while I write, I am not a "left-handed woman,"[1] and in the left hand two rolls of 16 mm color film (1,500 meters and 800 meters) corresponding to two full-length films that I wrote and directed.

Such is my small harvest at my womanly age, which is the age of maturity. Where would the difference be between me and any other woman my age who would introduce herself with, for example, four adult children and two or three younger ones, perhaps even with one or two grandchildren in front of this group, and in this case it would be her human oeuvre?

But now, this is my speech *(parole)*: and my speech is in the French language. I am a woman and a "French speaker." Certainly this speech might have been deployed in another register—in Arabic, or eventually in another language. Nevertheless, my literary writing, in its original text, can only be French.

Thus, my speech, capable of doubling and trebling, participates in many cultures, even though I have but one manner of writing: the French one.

In the past, one would say: "I am a man (or a woman) of my word" and assert: "I keep my word,"[2] and the meaning was understood almost in terms of honor. Well, I choose to present myself before you with this assertion: "I am a woman of my wording," in a tone of seriousness and love.

I have but one manner of writing: that of the French language; with it I trace each page of each book, whether fiction or reflections.

I am an Algerian woman, but rather than referring to my native land, I should refer to the language of my male and female ancestors; "I am an Arabo-Berber woman" and add "writing in French."

Since my first novel, forty-five years have elapsed, changing nothing of my identity whether it involves papers, passport, the fact of belonging, by blood and soil.

Nonetheless, forty-five years later, I acknowledge this: I present myself first as a writer, a novelist, as if the act of writing, when it is daily, solitary to the point of asceticism, might come to modify the weight of belonging. Because identity is not made up only of paper or blood but also of *language*. And if it seems that language, as is frequently said, is a "means of communication," it is above all for me as a writer, a "means of transformation," insofar as I practice writing as an *adventure*.

In May 1982, in Ottawa, during my first stay in Canada, I was to speak at a conference on French literature. I remember I had been thinking about it very early in the morning, a little before the time specified for my talk.

Rushed by having to make a public speech, I suddenly discovered this obvious fact: Up to now I have used the French language as a *veil*. A veil over my individual self, a veil over my woman's body; I could almost say a veil over my own voice.

And I recalled my experience as a young girl going out into the street with a lady (my mother), a city woman enveloped in her white silk veil, a smaller veil of embroidered gauze over her face, and I, a little girl with my hand clinging to the rough edge of immaculate silk, conscious of the villagers' voyeuristic glances at this veiled city woman who went every Thursday to the bathhouse.

A veil neither of dissimulation nor of masking, but of suggestion and ambiguity, a barrier-veil to desires certainly, but also a veil subsuming the desire of men.

Thus it was for me a first stage in my journey as a writer. This writing, I wanted it far from me, as if in its hollows, in its thin and thick cursive script, I could hide myself somewhat, conscious of the extraliterary curiosity that my writings would raise before I even began—in a way, a little like my mother's city-woman silhouette marching through the village center in front of the peasants.

I tried to explain to those men and women in Ottawa who had read my most recent texts (notably at the time, *Women of Algiers in Their Apartment*) to what degree I had paid the price for this ambiguity: about the ten years of nonpublication, living in voluntary muteness, I would almost say with sudden aphasia. As if I were trying, entangled in this silk veil symbolically evoked, to pull away from the French language without altogether leaving it! To go around it, then choose to reenter it.

To repossess it like a landlady, not as an occupant with hereditary rights. Thus, French was truly becoming for me as welcoming home, maybe even a permanent place where each day the ephemeral nature of dwelling is sensed. Finally I crossed the threshold freely, no longer submitting to a colonized situation.

So well did I do that this language seems to me a house that I will inhabit henceforth and that I will try to put my mark on every day—knowing all the while that over the soil that supports it I have no direct rights. But if I do not pretend to *jus soli* (birthright by soil), at least, at the risk of an easy wordplay, I can pursue not my right to the *sol* (soil) but to the *soleil* (sun)!

Because my characters, both in *Women of Algiers* as well as in my novel (*A Sister to Scheherezade*) struggle against the traditional veil, attempting to remove it yet becoming caught again, I, as author, have found my space in this writing.

A woman's space that willingly inscribes at the same time her inside and her outside, her intimacy and her unveiling, as much her anchor as its opposite, her navigation. Writing that could historically signify my extraterritoriality yet is becoming, gradually, my only true territory.

"The language of the 'other,'" I announced. After 1982, having written for over two years *Fantasia: An Algerian Cavalcade*, the first volume of a four-novel series that is a "quest for identity" and admittedly semi-autobiographical, I asked myself: This language of the other, what does it represent for me? By what means did it enter so deeply within me? Am I at the point that I might seize my portion of "otherness," of the foreignness that is inevitably included in a group of origin? I, who, barely twenty years old, entered into literature almost blindfolded, yet feeling as though drowned in light?

The first sentence in the book *Fantasia* answers, I would say directly and certainly, fundamental question, with its multiple answers that come to die, like successive waves on the sand of the shore, without exhausting such questioning. Yes, my first answer was clearly my father's hand:

A little Arab girl going to school for the first time, one autumn morning, walking hand in hand with her father.

As for me, need I remind you of the situation of any emigrant child today, in Europe or in Canada, who goes to school and is socialized little by little in the host country's language, in the "outside language," I would say. This child comes home every day and usually he finds his mother there, sometimes his father as well, speaking in *the language of elsewhere,* the language of rupture and separation. It is in this language that he hears his mother, the sound of his origins, and he is sometimes unable to respond. As if absence, like the absence within himself, were calling out to him. For he was too rapidly thrown into *the language of here*—the language of the other, the outside language, and, in intimate contrast, one that has become the language of "here and now."

We can only imagine what fragile wavering, what imperceptible imbalance, what insidious risk of vertigo—if not of schizophrenia—penetrates this precocious identity.

My childhood, as I have wanted to tell it, was split equally between two languages, my inner partition reflecting a parallel division between the world of cloistered women and the world of men, native ones as well as foreigners. For me, the nubile girl who would never be cloistered, French—for an entire century the language of the conquerors, of the colonizers, of the new possessors—this language had changed for me into *the father's language.*

Father had held out his hand to lead me to school. He would never become the future jailer: He was becoming the mediator. A profound change began then. Because he was a French teacher, he had assimilated an initial hybridity of which I would be the beneficiary.

> After more than a century of French occupation, which ended not so long ago in a flaying, a territory of languages still remains between two peoples, two memories; the French language, body and voice, is installed within me like a proud fortress, whereas the mother tongue, all orality, made up of rags, tatters and shreds, resists and attacks, between two tired breaths. (Djebar, *Fantasia*)

"A territory of languages between two peoples," I noted. This common language was shared with other migrants, from other cultures and other tongues. How—whether one chooses or is pushed to write—yes, how does the language thus appropriated "function," as it were, when it is put to use, in the hands of the professional scribe?

I would answer by putting forth the idea that, when one is a writer but has only recently come to a language—let us say without the cultural heritage that is carried with it—to write in the language of the other often means to make the "other" perceptible, the other in all languages, and the other's power of alterity.

Let me explain. In 1982 I was finishing a second film project, a unique one: through film archival images reconstituting a recent Maghrebi past. No longer as a simple historical illustration or as an aural commentary about images placed within a chronological continuity—no.

I felt quite quickly that those who photographed, who took pictures of yesterday, had an "other" gaze (the gaze, I might say, "of a tourist"). They took pictures of everything, that is, of nothing really essential. Because what was essential was clandestine, hidden, outside of the frame.

To reconstitute on the screen several decades of a colonized people's life had to make you feel to what degree reality, in each image, was in the margins; how everything, once, a long time ago, barely seen, became emptied of meaning. In short, these images hid the past, by proposing a sort of deforming, illusory screen.

How, then, to approach this "identity" of a past that is finished? The sound *beneath* the images could not be a commentary; it had to fill a void, to make us feel this emptiness. It should "denounce" and alert, without being polemical, or even "engagé." I then understood that, through the sound, I must bring back, suggest, perhaps even resuscitate *invisible voices*, the voices of those who had not been photographed because they were crouching in the shadow because they were held in scorn.

> Memory is a woman's voice,
> Night after night
> We strangle it
> Under the bed
> With leaden sleep!

sang an actress, beneath the body of the first Maghrebi women photographed in color, at the beginning of the 1920s.

So I return to this "other" of all writing.

Through this work on visual memory (nine months in the editing booth, working with rolls of film but also with musicians made to sing, made to take up fragments of anonymous folks songs), understood that, in the same way, in literature, the hidden, the forgotten ones of my group of origin should be brought to light, but specifically in the French language.

Throughout the entire Algerian nineteenth century, a century of confrontations, of violence, of effervescence, no painter of battles had followed those ancestors who struggled, who pranced on horseback under the sun in order to defy and to die. I felt within me the urgency of bringing up these images but to do so with French words.

Hence, in the language known as the language of the other, I found myself possessed by the need to reminisce about an elsewhere, about a dead Arabo-Berger past, my own. As if the heredity of blood was to be transmuted into a welcoming language, and in fact this is the true welcome, rather than merely stepping over the threshold of the other's home.

Thus my Ariadne's thread became my ear. Yes I heard Arabic and Berber (the wails, cries, ululations of my ancestors of the nineteenth century); I could truly hear them and thereby resuscitate them, those barbarians, in the French language.

So much so that to write becomes to inscribe, to transcribe, to write from the depths *("en creux"),* to bring back to the text, to the paper, to the manuscript, to the hand, to bring back at the same time the funereal chants and the buried bodies: yes to bring back the other (once considered the enemy, unable to assimilate) through language.

Was I able to convey what was, for me, this work of exhumation, of unearthing the "other" of languages? Perhaps this is what a writer primarily does: always bring back what is buried, locked up, the shadow so long engulfed by the words of language. To bring darkness to light.

In conclusion, I might ask myself: Living in two cultures, straddling two memories, two languages, bringing together in one writing the dark aspect, the repressed—in the end, what difference does this make to me?

Am I doomed to be a woman in transition, a passing writer, to deliver the message in stereo, so that instead of double loyalty it is double betrayal that awaits me?[3] Not to write anymore, fearing the risk, bit by bit, of never again speaking the *"words of the tribe"* (according to the beautiful Italian novel by Natalia Ginsburg,[4] this would mean to never again be part of any tribe, of any group, without being able, in fact, to add up two pasts, to treasures).

A gradual displacement, slow and infinite deracination, no doubt, as if it were necessary to wrench out one's roots. Wrenching out while discovering yourself, discovering yourself because of wrenching out.

Who am I? I answered at the beginning: first and foremost a woman novelist in the French language. Why not end by asking myself this question once more: Who am I? A woman whose culture of origin is Arab and Islam. So let's underline it: In Islam, the woman is the hostess, that is *passagère*[5]; risking, at each moment, unilateral repudiation, she cannot truly claim a permanent place.

Thus, in a religion that begins with an almost sacred emigration, the woman becomes a constant emigrant, without a destination and, because of this, a creature that deserves both the best and the worst. The best symbolically, the worst historically.

As for me, even though writing every day in the French language, or indeed because I write this way, I am in fact only one of the women in this multitude. Simply a *migrant*. The most beautiful label, I believe, in Islamic culture.

Translated by Isabelle de Courtivron and Susan Slyomovics

NOTES

1. Refers to the novel by Peter Handke, *The Left-Handed Woman* (Farrar, Straus and Giroux, 1978)

2. French literally: "I have only one word" means "I keep my word."

3. Djebar plays with the juxtaposition and double meaning of "double fidélité" (which also means stereo) and "double dérive" (to be cut adrift).

4. French translation of Natalia Ginsburg's novel *Lessico Famigliara* (Torino: Einaudi, 1963[?]; 1985).

5. "Passagère" means both "a passenger" and "passing through."

REFERENCES

Djebar, Assia. *Fantasia: An Algerian Cavalcade*. New York: Seven Stories Press, 1993.

Liza Fiol-Matta

■

Beyond Survival: A Politics/Poetics of Puerto Rican Consciousness

Now Dean of the College of Arts and Sciences at New Jersey City University, Liza Fiol-Matta is a veteran scholar and educator in women's studies. Her pioneering work in the field is considered instrumental in changing the ways we think, teach, and learn about women of color in North America, particularly the history, culture, and literature of Puerto Rican women. In 1994, she and coeditor Mariam K. Chamberlain started a small revolution—in women's studies and beyond—with the publication of *Women of Color and the Multicultural Curriculum*. An indispensable handbook in the movement to center women of color's experiences and perspectives in college curricula, *WCMC* was named 1995 Outstanding Book on the Subject of Human Rights in North America by the Gustavus Myers Center. Fiol-Matta has written extensively on feminism, nationalism, and identity in Latina literature. As a poet, she has contributed work to many U.S. and Puerto Rican publications, including *Callaloo, Diálogo,* and *The Peace Review.*

Born in Puerto Rico, Fiol-Matta was six years old when her father moved their family to a military base in "segregated Arkansas." In this selection from *Telling to Live: Latina Feminist Testimonios* (2001), she plumbs childhood memories of her displaced mother's long departure into silence, and of her own early life as a "girl child sacrificed to the act of translating." In the poetry of fellow Latina writers, she finds words to locate these and other "results of systemic political and colonial oppression." Within this community of writers, Fiol-Matta discovers that she is not alone in her permanent exile between two cultures and two languages. Here she articulates a quiet resistance against the everyday ravages of colonialism on the Puerto Rican diaspora: "In the process of exploring how a bilingual and bicultural writer comes to consciousness . . , I have discovered that, writing at the beginning of the second century of colonization by the United States, I must still struggle to reappropriate my history and take back the power to define myself."

■

dedicarse al rescate de un poeta
de las garras del bilingüismo colonial
no es cosa fácil.

es rescatar a la vez memoria, escribir historia,
inventarse imágines que llenen las lagunas,
inventarse a uno mismo como hecho innegable,

es dejar dicho: fui, así que fuimos;
soy, así que somos; y seguiremos siendo.

es agacharse en las estaciones del subway
y documentarse, escribiendo obsesivamente en libretas,
en cualquier hoja de papel: estoy y escribo.

Rescuing a poet
from the claws of colonial bilingualism
is not an easy thing.

It means rescuing memory, writing history,
inventing images to fill in the blanks,
inventing oneself as an undeniable fact,

leave having said: I was, therefore we were;
I am, therefore we are; and we will continue being.

It means squatting in subway stations
and documenting oneself, writing obsessively in notebooks,
or on any piece of paper: I am here and I write.

In this essay I attempt to define the cultural space I occupy as a middle-class, college-educated, bilingual, lesbian, white Puerto Rican woman. In the process of exploring how a bilingual and bicultural writer comes to consciousness about her languages and her identity, I have discovered that, writing at the beginning of the century of colonization by the United States, I must still struggle to reappropriate my history and take back the power to define myself.

Puerto Rican lives have been codified by a series of articles of war and legislative acts. Puerto Rican history, however, is made up by more than these. We also have the examples of resistance of the Grito de Lares uprising against the Spanish in 1868, the ceding by Spain of a short-lived but hard-fought autonomy in 1898, the internationalism of Luisa Capetillo and the early feminist and labor movements, Pedro Albízu Campos and the Nationalist Party, the brave march of Nationalists in Ponce in 1937 that ended in their massacre, the revolutionary actions of Lolita Lebrón and others in the attack on the House of Representatives in Washington in 1953, the draft resistance movement during the Vietnam War, the Young Lords Party, the continued struggle of Puerto Ricans in various independence movements, and the renewed mobilization against the U.S. Navy's presence on the island of Vieques.

So it should come as no surprise that, given the complex history of Puerto Rican colonialism, I make for an uneasy American citizen. My imposed U.S. passport erases my real nationality; my accentless American English betrays no regional affect. However, one aspect of the recovery from the indignities of colonialism is to have survived the sojourn identity recovery and returned to tell the tale. Thus my trajectory in defining my Puerto Rican consciousness is a story of recovery of/from language, of/from dislocation and exile, of/from displacement and marginalization. It is a story of surviving disruption and invalidation, and of putting into words the possibility of wholeness despite continuous interruption. More importantly, though, it is a story that goes beyond survival.

Because I am a product of a colonial history, I find myself situated in what Homi Bhabha calls "the *in-between* spaces." Just as Puerto Rican history has not been (to use Bhabha's words) "a continuous narrative of national progress," Puerto Rican consciousness reflects a narrative fragmented by/in "the meanwhile." We are located in an in-between space created by colonialism: in-between languages, in-between geographies, in-between racial discourses.

It is never far from my mind that I have been forced by historical forces into a cycle of migration that has felt at times like an overwhelming reciprocal betrayal, a doubled geographic dislocation. Like many Puerto Ricans, I struggle to inhabit a place that can hold the contradictions of nationalism, *patria,* migration, exile, and diaspora. But there is no place for me on my island, nor am I totally comfortable in the United States. The geography of my world is as much conceptual as territorial. It is as much Northeastern United States as it is

Caribbean, as much Army bases as island, as much the subway as ocean and horizon. Chicana poet Lorna Dee Cervantes' words resonate for me when she writes: "Every day I am deluged with reminders / that this is not / my land / and this is my land." But sometimes I mean both my island and this land.

Like so many immigrants, I have been engaged in a lifelong tug-of-war of language, which mimics the back-and-forth between the island and the misnomered "mainland." Neither Spanish nor English is my second language. When I was younger, I struggled thinking that one or the other made me more authentic. But I now accept that my bilingualism and biculturalism are my inheritance. Or, as Guillermo Gómez-Peña puts it: "The border-crosser develops two or more voices. . . . We develop different speaking selves that speak for different aspects of our identity."

The New York Puerto Rican poet Sandra María Esteves writes of this simultaneously double-voiced identity in her poem "Not Neither":

> Bring Puertorriqueña Americana
> Born in the Bronx, not really *jíbara*
> Not really *hablando bien*
> But yet not *gringa* either,
> *Pero ni portorra, pero sí portorra* too
> *Pero ni que* what am I? . . .

In 1958 I was six years old and recently arrived to the United States from Puerto Rico. My father, a career Army officer, had been stationed in Fort Chaffee, Arkansas. As a member of a local Brownie troop in Fort Smith, Arkansas, I was selected to represent my troop onstage during a ceremony in which we handed over what I remember as a jar full of coins as part of a fundraising drive for the town. I did not really know English yet, but for several days I practiced saying the name and number of my troop and the amount we had collected. This was my first public performance in the United States, the first time my "public" voice was heard; maybe it was the first time I realized I had a public voice. I remember being called up to the stage and the microphone brushing my lips. My recollection is that I bowed my head and shyly mumbled the required words in this new and foreign language. I vaguely remember going back to my seat.

I have always felt a twinge of unease for the little Puerto Rican girl, who, speaking her accented English, was such a novelty in her Brownie troop in that segregated Arkansas town. On the other hand, I would not be surprised at all to learn that I probably volunteered to get on that stage and speak. Two years later, at Loretto Academy in El Paso (with my father posted at Fort Bliss), I was onstage again, this time playing the piano in the school talent show. Just as I hadn't known English two years before, I had never played the piano either. Nevertheless, I performed my spontaneously composed piece, "The Happy Clowns." I think there was already something of the survivor in that child, uprooted as she was every year and a half as her father was transferred from posting to posting. There was something in her that wouldn't be silenced, that forced others to take notice of her.

While I am wary of employing the language of recovery and abuse to name the results of systemic political and colonial oppression, I nevertheless have found it useful to think in these terms. I am not saying that individual recovery can take the place of political action, but that this recovery is an important part of political activism. The literature of Latinos/as is full of references to the ways that bilingual or "Spanish-surnamed" children are subject in the classroom and playground to the kinds of sudden disapproval that confuse the "good" children they are trying to be. This abuse begins early in the educational process of Latino/a children and continues as we take survival strategies into the workplace and the world at large. Theorizing colonialism as abuse can yield insight into why we feel that no matter how much we modify our actions and attempt to measure up to norms imposed from outside, we do not seem to be able to develop satisfactory strategies to protect the self. No matter how well we speak English, or how light or dark our skin is, or how well we do in school and work, there is always the lingering doubt that we are not "loved for who we really are" but for the facsimile of the dominant culture that we can, with varying success, represent. Perhaps the key to the colonized child's survival can be found in Albert Memmi's assertion that "the colonized's liberation must be carried out through a recovery of self and of autonomous dignity."

Like so many children of immigrant parents, I often translated for my mother. I can remember very clearly being in Rose's (a Woolworth-type store in Columbia, South Carolina) and translating between my mother and saleslady. I say between because that is where I remember being placed, or perhaps placing myself. As a child I was not only linguistic go-between but also physical separator between the hostile (after all, not understanding my mother can only be a hostile act) and the nurturing (my mother who in all other ways is competent, creative, in control). The Conquest-era drawing from the Florentine Codex of Malintzín/La Malinche comes to mind—she/me standing between the conquerors/salesclerks and the Mayans/my mother. A girl child sacrificed to the act of translating, sleeping with the enemy, learning the enemy's language in the enemy's schools. In my case, this battle/conflict imagery/metaphor is especially appropriate; my father the proud U.S. Army officer, my mother his unhappy captive in the Army bases of the United States. Refusing to speak English, refusing to go to the wives' luncheons, refusing to be content separated from her homeland. Her laughter and spirit darkened, shut away. My father says that when we went to visit Charleston (I guess this was sometime in 1963) my mother cried when she saw the sea. She had not seen the sea in all the time we had lived in the U.S. I don't remember her crying. I do remember seeing Fort Sumter off in the distance.

Latina writers often explore the nuances of language and its importance in family life and identity formation. Hear Gloria Anzaldúa on language: "So, if you want to really hurt me, talk badly about my language. Ethnic identity is twin skin to linguistic identity—I am my language. Until I can take pride in my language, I cannot take pride in myself." Cherríe Moraga equates language and return to the mother/woman/*mestiza* as source: "Returning to *la mujer* scares me, re-learning Spanish scares me. . . . In returning to the love of my race, I must return to the fact that not only has the mother been taken from me, but her tongue, her mothertongue. I want the language, feel my tongue rise to the occasion of feeling at home, in common. I know this language in my bones . . . and then it escapes me. . . . 'You don't belong. *¡Quítate!*'" Rosario Morales recalls: "I cried when I heard my voice on tape for the first time. My voice showed no signs of El Barrio, of the South Bronx. I had erased them, helped my teachers erase the signs that I had been a little girl from the tenements who couldn't speak a word of English when she went to kindergarten, not even to say, 'I need to pipi, I'll wet my pants,' to say 'I'm scared, I want to go home.'"

In a poem by Pat Mora, a Mexican mother—a woman perhaps with much in common with my own mother—struggles to learn English in order to understand her children:

> . . . I'm forty,
> embarrassed at mispronouncing words,
> embarrassed at the laughter of my children,
> the grocer, the mailman. Sometimes I take
> my English book and lock myself in the bathroom,
> say the thick words softly,
> for if I stop trying, I will be deaf
> when my children need my help.

In the towns where my father was stationed, there were no Puerto Rican neighborhoods. Our Puerto Rican lives were lived in our home and our backyard, shared with the one or two Puerto Rican families whose time there overlapped with ours. The memory of my mother's *tristeza,* what Judith Ortiz Cofer describes as "the sadness that only place induces and only place cures," hurts even now. Yes, Spanish was my mother's tongue, but my memory of the sound of her voice—reciting poetry, singing old Puerto Rican songs, laughing, scolding—is interrupted by her heart-wrenching silences. She, hostage in U.S. Army bases, made sure that Puerto Rico was alive in her home, that Spanish was alive. Her daily life was an act of subversion.

My mother's story would be incomplete, however, without its denouement. She had graduated in 1945, at seventeen, with a degree in Biology from the University of Puerto Rico. At forty-seven she went back to school, this time enrolling in Spanish literature courses. This was after my father had been reassigned to the island. After finishing a B.A. in Spanish, she earned an M.A. in linguistics, then taught Spanish at Interamerican University. Until then only my mother's private voice had seemed strong; her spirited renditions of Spanish poetry recited from memory filled the house. She had not stood in front of audiences and courtrooms and classrooms like her children were to do. But, back in Puerto Rico my mother, who had spent so many of her years in the United States publicly silent—her psyche bruised by the imposed America of her surroundings—began to talk in the language of transformational grammar and sociolinguistics. She became active in the Puerto Rican Independence Party. Her public voice emerged.

Although I left the island twenty-two years ago, it is always in my consciousness. I often think of the line in Puerto Rican poet Luz María Umpierre's "The Mar/Garita Poem" that says *"hay una isla en Edison, New Jersey"* [there is an island in Edison, New Jersey]. There is, in fact, an island/*hay una isla* in this room in this apartment on this street in Manhattan where I am writing this sentence. Just as I am/there is an island in the academic institution in which I work. The Puerto Rican body/psyche is a geographical space of its own, an island in the ocean of American "ethnicity"—unassimilated, multiaccented, defying the racial paradigms of this country. Being Puerto Rican is an enactment of a virtual reality, the incarnation of our *tierra natal* in the island of our bodies. In a world that is theorizing postcolonial national identities, we are still in an anachronistic colonial relationship with the United States, and that relationship invades both our lifelike dreams at night and our dreamlike daily lives.

As absurd as it may sound, the Caribbean is a problematic, contradictory space in which to anchor Puerto Rican-ness. With our long-standing relationship as its most willing and faithful consumers, Puerto Rico has increasingly become an extension of the United States. We live with strip-malls anchored by Dunkin' Donuts and Burger King franchises, Christmas displays of Santa and snowmen. Yet I daily define myself as a Caribbean person. My Caribbean students and colleagues—from Trinidad and Tobago, Jamaica, Barbados, Dominican Republic, Guadeloupe, Haiti, Cuba—and I sit in my windowless office in a renovated factory recalling colors, sky, light, ocean, the taste of salt in the air.

Inevitably, our nostalgia turns to pain, to the anger of Jamaica Kincaid when she says of her native Antigua:

> Sometimes the beauty of it seems unreal. . . . It is as if, then, the beauty—the beauty of the sea, the land, the air, the trees, the market, the people, the sounds they make—were a prison, and as if everything and everybody inside it were locked in and everything and everybody that is not inside it were locked out. . . .

and we awaken from our daydream remembering why we are no longer there.

Puerto Rico in my dreams is always a city landscape: my grandmother's house in the Condado and the lemon and avocado trees in her backyard, the narrow streets of Old San Juan at night, the nondescript Puerta de Tierra section that separates Old San Juan from the rest of the city, the college I attended in Santurce. But in recent dreams a new image has emerged: a panoramic highway, paid for by federal moneys set aside by the statehood party specifically for this project, rings the island. To build this highway, however, the shoreline has been sacrificed. Beaches have been allowed to erode, towns near the shore have been deliberately flooded, arable land lost. And at night there is no access to the highway or the ocean beyond. Puerto Rico has been converted into an island prison, a self-destructive shrinking body.

Despite a childhood spent on American Army bases, it was my adult choice to live in New York that recontextualized for me the reality of being Puerto Rican. For several years after settling in New York, I continued to identify myself as being "from the island," a survivalist nationalism binding me to the greater possibilities of identifying with those who had, until my own migration, been the "other Puerto Ricans," *los de allá.* Much of my personal struggle with language, exile, and the notion of betrayal of my *madre/patria* played itself out in a narrowly conceived space between pure (i.e., heroic) nationalism and total (i.e., traitorous) assimilation. But, almost unnoticed by me, the conversion happened; they, and I, became *de aquí.* I have become *una puertorriqueña de nueva york.*

Today I share my life with a Dutch-American woman who also owns two languages and cultures. Daily the sounds of Spanish and Dutch and English fill the house in rapid succession. One son calls from the Hague, my father from San Juan; my sisters drop in for dinner, another son and his wife come visiting for the weekend. My brother and his American wife have us all over for Thanksgiving. Our home is Dutch-cozy, *gezellig;* we drink only Puerto Rican *café con leche.* It has become a tradition that we sing "Happy Birthday" in three languages, the candles melting on the cake as we make our way through the last *"hiep-hiep-hoera!"* But the English in which we speak truths and comfort is a language all our own. In our home, it is not the colonizer's language. It recognizes both Puerto Rican and Dutch feelings; its vocabulary includes both our wants and needs. We question its lapses and limitations; we laugh and love in the multiple dimensions of our hybrid, intimately constructed English. Together we confirm the truth of Adrienne Rich's statement: "The relationship to more than one culture, nonassimilating in spirit and therefore living amid contradictions, is a constant act of self-creation." Together we create family and identity, nourished by the deep-seated understanding that there is no room in our lives for the colonizing project of erasing difference or demanding conformity.

Luisa Valenzuela

■

Writing with the Body

Hailed "the heiress of Latin American literature" by Carlos Fuentes, Luisa Valenzuela is a widely translated novelist, journalist, and author of short fiction. Born into a literary family in Buenos Aires, she published her first short story in the journal *Ficción* at age nineteen. *Clara,* her debut novel, appeared just two years later in 1959. Now the author of nearly a dozen publications, she is world renowned for her work's stunning originality and nimble intermingling of personal history with national destinies. A modern master of "ironic, political commentary laced with sex and humor," Valenzuela is the frequent subject of literary scholarship. Her more recent novels include *Bedside Manners, Black Novel with Argentines,* and the critically acclaimed *Lizard's Tail.* In reviewing this startling commentary on the business of politics and terror in Argentina, Susan Sontag asserts that "there is nothing like [*The Lizard's Tail*] in contemporary Latin American literature." Now back in Argentina, Valenzuela has lived, taught, and written in France, Mexico, and the United States.

In the following selection, Valenzuela meditates on the nature of writing under a dictatorship and the distinct but inseparable project of becoming a writer anyway. In a world where words often exact a price too dear (but silence is deadly), Valenzuela realizes that writing is not a passive destiny but a chosen path and, ultimately, "an exercise in liberty." Seeking to make sense of her choice to write no matter the perils, she concludes: "Writing with the body. . . . implies being fully committed"—even in the face of repression, doubt, and fear.

■

As I leave the ambassador's residence in Buenos Aires early one morning in 1977, at the height of my country's military dictatorship, and walk through the dark, tree-lined streets, I think I am being followed. I have been hearing political testimony from people who sought asylum in the Mexican embassy. Enemies of the de facto government. I think that I can be abducted at any moment. Yet I feel immensely vital, filled with an inexplicable strength that may come from my having reached some kind of understanding. I walk back home through those streets that appear to be empty, and take all the precautions I can to make sure that I'm not being followed, that I'm not being aimed at from some doorway, and I feel alive. I would say happy.

Now I know why.

The answer is simple, now, so many years later. I felt—at this moment, I feel—happy because I was—am—writing with the body. Writing that lingers in the memory of my pores. Writing with the body? Yes. I am aware of having done this throughout my life, at intervals, although it may be almost impossible for me to describe. I'm afraid that it's a matter of a secret action or a mode of being that may be ineffable.

But I don't believe in the ineffable. The struggle of every person who writes, of every true writer, is primarily against the demon of that which resists being put into words. It is a struggle that spreads like an oil stain. Often, to surrender to the difficulty is to triumph, because the best text can sometimes be the one that allows words to have their own liberty.

While writing with the body one also works with words, sometimes completely formed in one's mind, sometimes barely suggested. Writing with the body has nothing to do with "body language." It implies being fully committed to an act which is, in essence, a literary act.

At the Mexican embassy that night in 1977, I had just spoken at length with an ex-president who was a political refugee, as well as with a terrorist who had also sought asylum. Both men were sitting at the same table; we were all somewhat drunk and, because of that, more sincere. Then I walked down the streets and as I was walking, I was writing with the body. And not just because of a letter that I was mentally addressing to my friend, Julio Cortázar. I was telling him in the letter—because I knew that I was risking my life and was afraid—that I don't want to play "duck": when I get into the water, I choose to get wet.

I was writing with the body, and fear had much to do with this.

Fear.

I was the kind of child who always poked around wherever there was fear: to see what kind of a creature fear was. I played at being a snake, a snail, or a hippopotamus in a warm African river. Among the animals I avoided was the ostrich. I wanted nothing to do with hiding my head in the sand. I don't know what crazy, morbid impulse made me run through the dark long hallways to the foyer at the entrance of my house, in the middle of the night, when the clock—controlled by witches—struck the hour. Nor do I know what made me go to the terrace where there was supposed to be a two-headed eagle, or behind the house where all kinds of dangers were lurking. I would have preferred hiding my head under the covers. But then who would reassure me? How could my eyes face daylight if they couldn't face shadows in the night? This is why I would go to look, and maybe because I looked came the need, sometime much later, to tell what I had seen.

Why?

Because of surprise

Because of adventure

Because of a question, and a gut rejection of any answers.

You tend to ask yourself why write with your entire body when you have that simple upper extremity which, thanks to the evolution of the species, has an opposable thumb especially made for holding a pen.

You also ask yourself—and this is really overwhelming—why write at all? In my case, I belong, body and soul and mind, to the so-called Third World where certain needs exist that are not at all literary.

Then other responses (or perhaps they are excuses) come to mind. The need to preserve collective memory is undoubtedly one of them.

There is yet another good excuse: writing as one's destined vocation. But I don't know if literature was my destiny. I wanted to be a physicist, or a mathematician, and, before that, an archaeologist or anthropologist, and for a long time I wanted to be a painter. Because I was raised in a house full of writers and that wasn't for me. No, ma'am. No thanks.

Fernando Alegría now describes that moment and place as the Buenos Aires Bloomsbury and this description isn't as crazy as it may appear. In our old house in the Belgrano section of town, the habitués were named Borges, Sábato, Mallea. My mother, the writer Luisa Mercedes Levinson, was the most sociable person in the world when she wasn't in bed, writing.

When I was a child, I would look from the door of her room and she would be in her bed surrounded by papers, all day until sunset when the others arrived. I would watch her with admiration and with the conviction that that life wasn't for me. I wanted a different future.

Disguises I chose Carnivals:

Aviatrix

Woman Explorer

Robin Hood

Those were the masks that belonged to the official Carnival. But other masks at other times also took the shape of exploration and adventure. I would climb onto the roofs of the neighboring houses to try and reach the end of the block, something which was impossible to do because of the gardens in between. On those days when I felt really daring, I would climb up to a stone angel that clung to a column and that needed my presence, because otherwise no one would ever see it. I would also sneak into empty lots, or explore an abandoned house around the block. I was always looking for treasures that changed according to my ambitions: colorful figurines, stamps, coins. There was an old guard at the abandoned house who would let us in and was our friend. Until one afternoon, after exploring the basement looking for secret passages—at that time we pretended that the house belonged to German spies or was it a smuggler's hideout?—the old guard greeted us with his fly open and all those strange things hanging out. I ran away with my best friend in tow. I never went back, but years, thousands of years later, I wondered if that was the treasure for which we searched.

Now I know: with that small adventure around the block and with those big stories I made up, I began the slow learning process of writing with the body.

Because

pores or ink, it is the same thing

the same stakes.

Clarice Lispector knew it and in her books focused on that love-hate, that happiness-misfortune we call literature. Her novels appear to be about love and the search for knowledge but they are also different ways of speaking about writing.

One's happiness is greatest when the story flows like a stream of clear water, even if the worst abominations are being narrated. It is only during the reading of those passages that the fear of what has flowed from one's own pen takes over.

There is another misfortune in writing and it is perhaps the most painful. It is inscribed during times of silence, when nothing is written with the body or mind or hand. Periods of drought which seem to be of nonexistence.

This is why I say sometimes that writing is a full-time curse.

I also say that, in its best moments, writing a novel is a euphoric feeling, like being in love.

And to think that my mother, the writer, is to blame for all of this. Not because of the example she set, nor because of my emulation of her, which I acknowledge. She is to blame because when I was in the sixth grade in elementary school, my teacher asked her to help me with my compositions. "Your daughter is so bright in science," my teacher told her, "it's a shame that her grade should go down because she can't write." So my mother, overzealous in trying to help me, wrote a composition as she thought a tender eleven-year-old would.

I didn't think it was a very dignified text. From that moment on, I decided to assume the responsibility of my own writings. And that's how things are.

Because writing is the path that leads to the unknown. The way back is made of reflection, trying to come to terms with yourself and with that which has been produced. I strongly believe in the fluctuation from intuition to understanding. Placing ourselves right there

at the border
between two currents
at the center of the whirlpool,
the eye of the tornado?

"You are too intelligent to be beautiful" is what many of us have been told at some time by a man we've loved. Or, supposing literature is your profession: "You are too intelligent to be a good writer." Contrasting, of course, that ugly masculine thing which is intelligence with female intuition. You wouldn't tell that to Susan Sontag is what someone with clearer ideas would reply. But those marks were made on young and tender skin, and from that moment on, one will always have a feeling of inadequacy.

Incapable, inactive, unproductive. I think all of us, from the time we're very young, feel at some time what could be called a nostalgia for imprisonment: the crazy, romantic fantasy that a prisoner has all the time to herself, to write. Only later do we realize that writing is an exercise of liberty.

From exigencies and from temptations, the stuff of literature is made. And from reflection, also. From everything. There is no unworthy material, although a great deal must be discarded.

When I was seventeen years old, I started working in journalism. For many years it was the perfect combination, one that allowed me to be part of all the disciplines, to go everywhere, and, at the same time, to write. A gift of ubiquity wrapped in words. I had the tremendous luck, almost a miracle, of having a boss who was a true teacher. Ambrosio Vencino was not a journalist; he was a displaced man of letters. To him I owe my obsessive precision with language.

I owe my travels to myself, to my need to touch the world with my own hands. I never paid attention to the premise that you don't have to leave your own bedroom to know the world. I traveled, I continue traveling, and I sometimes think that in all those displacements, parts of my self are being left behind.

Rodolfo Walsh, the Argentine writer and activist, once told me when I was complaining about how much I went from one place to the next and how little I wrote: "Your writing is also made from your travels."

Many years later, my writing was also made from another of Rodolfo Walsh's lesions to which I didn't pay much attention at the time. One day he showed me the difficult physical exercises that Cuban guerrillas practiced then in the Sierra Maestra. That physical guerrilla wisdom seemed to stand me in good stead in 1975 and 1976, when I sat in the cafes of Buenos Aires, devastated by state terrorism, and wrote stories that were, in a way, guerrilla exercises.

I put my body where my words are.

The physical loss hasn't been as great for me as it has been for others. I haven't been tortured, beaten, or persecuted. Knock on wood. I've been spared, perhaps because my statements aren't frontal; they are visions from the corner of my eye, oblique. I think we must continue writing about the horrors so that memory isn't lost and history won't repeat itself.

As a teenager, I was a voracious reader and I bragged about it but there were two books that I read in secret: *Freud* by Emil Ludwig and *The Devil in the Flesh (Le Diable au Corps)* by Raymond Radiguet. With these two books I may not have gone very far in terms of pornographic material but it's clear that my libido was already acting up.

That writing with the body known as the act of love happened later, as it should have, and turned out quite well, with great style, but with more of an inclination toward the short story than the novel.

I love the short story for being round, suggestive, insinuating, microcosmic. The story has both the inconvenience and the fascination of new beginnings.

The novel, on the other hand, requires more concentration, more time, a state of grace. I love it because of the joy in opening new paths as words progress.

Paths to the unknown, the only interesting ones.

What I already know bores me, makes me repetitive. This is why whenever I have had a good plot that was clearly thought out, I was forced to give it up or at least to compress it, trying to squeeze out the juice that wasn't visible at first sight.

If I had to write my creed, I would first mention humor:

I believe in having a sense of humor at all costs

I believe in sharp, black humor

I believe in the absurd

in the grotesque

in everything which allows us to move beyond our limited thinking, beyond self-censorship and the censorship by others, which tends to be much more lethal. Taking a step to one side to observe the action as it is happening. A necessary step so that the vision of political reality is not contaminated by dogmas or messages.

I have nothing to say.

With luck, something will be said through me, despite myself, and I might not even realize it.

It is said that women's literature is made of questions.

I say that women's literature consequently is much more realistic.

Questions, uncertainties, searches, contradictions.

Everything is fused, and sometimes confused, and implicates us. The true act of writing with the body implies being fully involved. I am my own bet; I play myself, as though lying on the roulette table, calling out "All or nothing!"

What is interesting about the literary wager is that we do wager everything, but we don't know against what.

They say that women's literature is made of fragments.

I repeat that it is a matter of realism.

It is made of rips, shreds of your own skin which adhere to the paper but are not always read or even legible. Shreds that can be of laughter, of sheer delight.

Sometimes while writing, I have to get up to dance, to celebrate the flow of energy transforming itself into words. Sometimes the energy becomes words that are not printed, not even with the delicate line of a fountain pen, which is the most voluptuous in the act of writing. You must always celebrate when—whether in a cafe or subway—a happy combination of words, a fortuitous allusion, elicits associations that unwind the mental thread of writing without a mark. The mark comes next. And I will do my best to retain the freshness of that first moment of awe and transformation.

Translated from the Spanish by Cynthia Ventura and Janet Sternburg

Margaret Atwood

■

On Writing Poetry

Margaret Atwood is the best-selling author of over thirty works of fiction, poetry, criticism, and more. Widely read the world over, her work has been translated into dozens of languages. Born in 1939 in Ottawa, she grew up in northern Ontario, Quebec, and Toronto, where she now lives. Her second and best-known novel, *The Handmaid's Tale* (1983), remains a timeless science fiction and feminist cult classic, and was adapted for the screen in 1990. Declared by E. L. Doctorow a companion to "Orwell's *1984*, its verso in fact," this chilling dystopic commentary on U.S. sexual politics was shortlisted for the Booker Prize, as were *Cat's Eye* and *Alias Grace*. In 2000 Atwood won the prestigious award for her critically acclaimed *The Blind Assassin,* which *Newsday* pronounced "the first great novel of the new millennium." *Oryx and Crake,* her eleventh novel, earned Atwood her fifth nod from the Booker Prize in 2003. In addition to several honorary degrees, she is also the recipient of the Giller Prize and the Premio Mondello. The former president of PEN Canada, an international advocacy group dedicated to writers suffering persecution, Atwood is also a leading anti-censorship and human rights activist.

Best known for her fiction, Atwood is also distinguished for her poetry—her first love, as she reveals in the following selection. "On Writing Poetry" (1995) was originally delivered as a lecture in Hay on Wye, Wales. With her famous wit and pithy observation, she delights live and reading audiences alike with "the official version" of her coming into her own as a poet. Bulging cheek notwithstanding, here she surveys the long, jagged road from there to here, and marvels at her own arrival: "When I was sixteen, it was simple. Poetry existed; therefore it could be written; and nobody had told me—yet—the many, many reasons why it could not be written by me."

■

I'm supposed to be talking in a vaguely autobiographical way about the connection between life and poetry, or at least between my life and my poetry. I recently read an account of a study which intends to show

how writers of a certain age—my age, roughly—attempt to "seize control" of the stories of their own lives by deviously concocting their own biographies. However, it's a feature of our age that if you write a work of fiction, everyone assumes that the people and events in it are disguised biography—but if you write your biography, it's equally assumed you're lying your head off.

This last may be true, at any rate of poets: Plato said that poets should be excluded from the ideal republic because they are such liars. I am a poet, and I affirm that this is true. About no subject are poets tempted to lie so much as about their own lives; I know one of them who has floated at least five versions of his autobiography, none of them true. I of course—being also a novelist—am a much more truthful person than that. But since poets lie, how can you believe me?

Here then is the official version of my life as a poet:

I was once a snub-nosed blonde. My name was Betty. I had a perky personality and was a cheerleader for the college football team. My favourite colour was pink. Then I became a poet. My hair darkened overnight, my nose lengthened, I gave up football for the cello, my real name disappeared and was replaced by one that had a chance of being taken seriously by the literati, and my clothes changed colour in the closet, all by themselves, from pink to black. I stopped humming the songs from *Oklahoma* and began quoting Kierkegaard. And not only that—all of my high-heeled shoes lost their heels, and were magically transformed into sandals. Needless to say, my many boyfriends took one look at this and ran screaming from the scene as if their toenails were on fire. New ones replaced them; they all had beards.

Believe it or not, there is an element of truth in this story. It's the bit about the name, which was not Betty but something equally non-poetic, and with the same number of letters. It's also the bit about the boyfriends. But meanwhile, here is the real truth:

I became a poet at the age of sixteen. I did not intend to do it. It was not my fault.

Allow me to set the scene for you. The year was 1956. Elvis Presley had just appeared on the Ed Sullivan Show, from the waist up. At school dances, which were held in the gymnasium and smelled like armpits, the dance with the most charisma was rock'n'roll. The approved shoes were saddle shoes and white bucks, the evening gowns were strapless, if you could manage it; they had crinolined skirts that made you look like half a cabbage with a little radish head. Girls were forbidden to wear jeans to school, except on football days, when they sat on the hill to watch, and it was feared that the boys would be able to see up their dresses unless they wore pants. TV dinners had just been invented.

None of this—you might think, and rightly—was conducive to the production of poetry. If someone had told me a year previously that I would suddenly turn into a poet, I would have giggled. Yet this is what did happen.

I was in my fourth year of high school. The high school was in Toronto, which in the year 1956 was still known as Toronto the Good because of its puritanical liquor laws. It had a population of six hundred and fifty thousand, five hundred and nine people at the time, and was a synonym for bland propriety. The high school I attended was also a synonym for bland propriety, and although it has produced a steady stream of chartered accountants and one cabinet minister, no other poets have ever emerged from it, before or since.

The day I became a poet was a sunny day of no particular ominousness. I was walking across the football field, not because I was sports-minded or had plans to smoke a cigarette behind the field house—the only other reason for going there—but because this was my normal way home from school. I was scuttling along in my usual furtive way, suspecting no ill, when a large invisible thumb descended from the sky and pressed down on the top of my head. A poem formed. It was quite a gloomy poem: the poems of the young usually are. It was a gift, this poem—a gift from an anonymous donor, and, as such, both exciting and sinister at the same time.

I suspect this is the way all poets begin writing poetry, only they don't want to admit it, so they make up more rational explanations. But this is the true explanation, and I defy anyone to disprove it.

The poem that I composed on that eventful day, although entirely without merit or even promise, did have some features. It rhymed and scanned, because we had been taught rhyming and scansion at school. It resembled the poetry of Lord Byron and Edgar Allan Poe, with a little Shelley and Keats thrown in. The fact is that at the time I became a poet, I had read very few poems written after the year 1900. I knew nothing of modernism or free verse. These were not the only things I knew nothing of. I had no idea, for instance, that I was about to step into a whole set of preconceptions and social roles which had to do with what poets were like, how they should behave, and what they ought to wear; moreover, I did not know that the rules about these things were different if you were female. I did not know that "poetess" was an insult, and that I myself would some day be called one. I did not know that to be told I had transcended my gender would be considered a compliment. I didn't know—yet—that black was compulsory. All of that was in the future. When I was sixteen, it was simple. Poetry existed; therefore it could be written; and nobody had told me—yet—the many, many reasons why it could not be written by me.

At first glance, there was little in my background to account for the descent of the large thumb of poetry onto the top of my head. But let me try to account for my own poetic genesis.

I was born on November 18, 1939, in the Ottawa General Hospital, two and a half months after the beginning of the Second World War. Being born at the beginning of the war gave me a substratum of anxiety and dread to draw on, which is very useful to a poet. It also meant that I was malnourished. This is why I am short. If it hadn't been for food rationing, I would have been six feet tall.

I saw my first balloon in 1946, one that had been saved from before the war. It was inflated for me as a treat when I had the mumps on my sixth birthday, and it broke immediately. This was a major influence on my later work.

As for my birth month, a detail of much interest to poets, obsessed as they are with symbolic systems of all kinds: I was not pleased, during my childhood, to have been born in November, as there wasn't much inspiration for birthday party motifs. February children got hearts, May ones flowers, but what was there for me? A cake surrounded by withered leaves? November was a drab, dark and wet month, lacking even snow; its only noteworthy festival was Remembrance Day. But in adult life I discovered that November was, astrologically speaking, the month of sex, death and regeneration, and that November First was the Day of the Dead. It still wouldn't have been much good for birthday parties, but it was just fine for poetry, which tends to revolve a good deal around sex and death, with regeneration optional.

Six months after I was born, I was taken by packsack to a remote cabin in north-western Quebec, where my father was doing research as a forest entomologist. I should add here that my parents were unusual for their time. Both of them liked being as far away from civilization as possible, my mother because she hated housework and tea parties, my father because he liked chopping wood. They also weren't much interested in what the sociologists would call rigid sex-role stereotyping. This was a help to me in later life, and helped me to get a job at summer camp teaching small boys to start fires.

My childhood was divided between the forest, in the warmer parts of the year, and various cities, in the colder parts. I was thus able to develop the rudiments of the double personality so necessary for a poet. I also had lots of time for meditation. In the bush there were no theatres, movies, parades, or very functional radios; there were also not many other people. The result was that I learned to read early—I was lucky enough to have a mother who read out loud, but she couldn't be doing it all the time and you had to amuse yourself with something or other when it rained. I became a reading addict, and have remained so ever since. "You'll ruin your eyes," I was told when caught at my secret vice under the covers with a flashlight. I did so, and would do it again. Like cigarette addicts who will smoke mattress stuffing if all else fails, I will read anything. As a child I read a good many things I shouldn't have, but this also is useful for poetry.

As the critic Northrop Frye has said, we learn poetry through the seat of our pants, by being bounced up and down to nursery rhymes as children. Poetry is essentially oral, and is close to song; rhythm precedes meaning. My first experiences with poetry were Mother Goose, which contains some of the most surrealistic poems in the English language, and whatever singing commercials could be picked up on the radio, such as:

> You'll wonder where the yellow went
> When you brush your teeth with Pepsodent!

I created my first book of poetry at the age of five. To begin with, I made the book itself, cutting the pages out of scribbler paper and sewing them together in what I did not know was the traditional signature fashion. Then I copied into the book all the poems I could remember, and when there were some blank pages left at the end, I added a few of my own to complete it. This book was an entirely satisfying art object for me; so satisfying that I felt I had nothing more to say in that direction, and gave up writing poetry altogether for another eleven years.

My English teacher from 1955, run to ground by some documentary crew trying to explain my life, said that in her class I had showed no particular promise. This was true. Until the descent of the giant thumb, I showed no particular promise. I also showed no particular promise for some time afterwards, but I did not know this. A lot of being a poet consists of willed ignorance. If you woke up from your trance and realised the nature of the life-threatening and dignity-destroying precipice you were walking along, you would switch into actuarial sciences immediately.

If I had not been ignorant in this particular way, I would not have announced to an assortment of my high school female friends, in the cafeteria one brown-bag lunchtime, that I was going to be a writer. I said "writer," not "poet"; I did have some common sense. But my announcement was certainly a conversation-stopper. Sticks of celery were suspended in mid-crunch, peanut-butter sandwiches paused halfway between table and mouth; nobody said a word. One of those present reminded me of this incident recently—I had repressed it— and said she had been simply astounded. "Why?" I said. "Because I wanted to be a writer?" "No," she said. "Because you had the guts to say it out loud."

But I was not conscious of having guts, or even of needing them. We obsessed folks, in our youth, are oblivious to the effects of our obsessions; only later do we develop enough cunning to conceal them, or at least to avoid mentioning them at cocktail parties. The one good thing to be said about announcing yourself as a writer in the colonial Canadian fifties is that nobody told me I couldn't do it because I was a girl. They simply found the entire proposition ridiculous. Writers were dead and English, or else extremely elderly and American; they were not sixteen years old and Canadian. It would have been worse if I'd been a boy, though. Never mind the fact that all the really stirring poems I'd read at that time had been about slaughter, mayhem, sex and death—poetry was thought of as existing in the pastel female realm, along with embroidery and flower arranging. If I'd been male I would probably have had to roll around in the mud, in some boring skirmish over whether or not I was a sissy.

I'll skip over the embarrassingly bad poems I published in the high school year book—had I no shame?—well, actually, no—mentioning only briefly the word of encouragement I received from my wonderful Grade 12 English teacher, Miss Bessie Billings—"I can't understand a word of this, dear, so it must be good." I will not go into the dismay of my parents, who worried—with good reason—over how I would support myself. I will pass over my flirtation with journalism as a way of making a living, an idea I dropped when I discovered that in the fifties—unlike now—female journalists always ended up writing the obituaries and the ladies' page.

But how was I to make a living? There was not a roaring market in poetry, there, then. I thought of running away and being a waitress, which I later tried, but got very tired and thin; there's nothing like clearing away other people's mushed-up dinners to make you lose your appetite. Finally I went into English literature at university, having decided in a cynical manner that I could always teach to support my writing habit. Once I got past the Anglo Saxon it was fun, although I did suffer a simulated cardiac arrest the first time I encountered T. S. Eliot and realised that not all poems rhymed, anymore. "I don't understand a word of this," I thought, "so it must be good."

After a year or two of keeping my head down and trying to pass myself off as a normal person, I made contact with the five other people at my university who were interested in writing; and through them, and some of my teachers, I discovered that there was a whole subterranean Wonderland of Canadian writing that was going on just out of general earshot and sight. It was not large—in 1960 you were doing well to sell 200 copies of a book of poems by a Canadian, and a thousand novels was a best-seller; there were only five literary magazines, which ran on the life blood of their editors; but it was very integrated. Once in—that is, once published in a magazine—it was as if you'd been given a Masonic handshake or a key to the underground railroad. All of a sudden you were part of a conspiracy.

People sometimes ask me about my influences; these were, by and large, the Canadians poets of my own generation and that just before mine. P. K. Page, Margaret Avison, Jay MacPherson, James Reaney, Irving Layton, Leonard Cohen, Al Purdy, D. G. Jones, Eli Mandel, John Newlove, Gwendolyn MacEwen, Michael Ondaatje, Pat Lane, George Bowering, Milton Acorn, A. M. Klein, Alden Nowlan,

Elizabeth Brewster, Anne Wilkinson—these are some of the poets who were writing and publishing then, whom I knew, and whose poetry I read. People writing about Canadian poetry at that time spoke a lot about the necessity of creating a Canadian literature. There was a good deal of excitement, and the feeling that you were in on the ground floor, so to speak.

So poetry was a vital form, and it quickly acquired a public dimension. Above ground the bourgeoisie reined supreme, in their two-piece suits and ties and camel-hair coats and pearl earrings (not all of this worn by the same sex); but at night the Bohemian world came alive, in various nooks and crannies of Toronto, sporting black turtlenecks, drinking coffee at little tables with red-checked tablecloths and candles stuck in chianti bottles, in coffee houses—well—in the one coffee house in town—listening to jazz and folk singing, reading their poems out loud as if they'd never heard it was stupid, and putting swear words into them. For a twenty-year-old this was intoxicating stuff.

By this time I had my black wardrobe more or less together, and had learned not to say, "Well, hi there!" in sprightly tones. I was publishing in little magazines, and shortly thereafter I started to write reviews for them too. I didn't know what I was talking about, but I soon began to find out. Every year for four years, I put together a collection of my poems and submitted it to a publishing house; every year it was—to my dismay then, to my relief now—rejected. Why was I so eager to be published right away? Like all twenty-one-year-old poets, I thought I would be dead by thirty, and Sylvia Plath had not set a helpful example. For a while there, you were made to feel that, if a poet and female, you could not really be serious about it unless you'd made at least one suicide attempt. So I felt I was running out of time.

My poems were still not very good, but by now they showed—how shall I put it?—a sort of twisted and febrile glimmer. In my graduating year, a group of them won the main poetry prize at the University. Madness took hold of me, and with the aid of a friend, and another friend's flatbed press, we printed them. A lot of poets published their own work then; unlike novels, poetry was short, and therefore cheap to do. We had to print each poem separately, and then disassemble it, as there were not enough a's for the whole book; the cover was done with a lino-block. We printed 250 copies, and sold them through bookstores, for 50 cents each. They now go in the rare book trade for eighteen hundred dollars a pop. Wish I'd kept some.

Three years or so later—after two years at graduate school at the dreaded Harvard University, two broken engagements, a year of living in a tiny rooming-house room and working at a market research company which was more fun than a barrel of drugged monkeys and a tin of orange-flavoured rice pudding—and after the massive rejection of my first novel, and of several other poetry collections as well—and not to mention my first confusing trip to Europe, I ended up in British Columbia, teaching grammar to Engineering students at eight-thirty in the morning in a Quonset hut. It was all right, as none of us were awake; I made them write imitations of Kafka, which I thought might help them in their chosen profession.

In comparison with the few years I had just gone through, this was sort of like going to heaven. I lived in an apartment built on top of somebody's house, and had scant furniture; but not only did I have a 180-degree view of Vancouver harbour, but I also had all night to write in. I taught in the daytime, ate canned food, did not wash my dishes until all of them were dirty—the biologist in me became very interested in the different varieties of moulds that could be grown on left-over Kraft dinner—and stayed up until four in the morning. I completed, in that one year, my first officially published book of poems and my first published novel, which I wrote on blank exam booklets, as well as a number of short stories and the beginnings of two other novels, later completed. It was an astonishingly productive year for me. I looked like the Night of the Living Dead. Art has its price.

This first book of poems was called *The Circle Game;* I designed the cover myself, using stick-on dots—we were very cost-effective in those days—and to everyone's surprise, especially mine, it won a prize called The Governor General's Award, which in Canada was the big one to win. Literary prizes are a crapshoot, and I was lucky that year. I was back at Harvard by then, mopping up the uncompleted work for my doctorate—I never did finish it—and living with three roommates, whose names were Judy and Sue and Karen. To collect the prize I had to attend a ceremony in Ottawa, at Government House, which meant dressups—and it was obvious to all of us, as we went through the two items in my wardrobe, that I had nothing to wear. Sue leant me the dress and earrings, Judy the shoes, and while I was away they incinerated my clunky rubber-soled Hush Puppy shoes, having decided that these did not go with my new, poetic image.

This was an act of treachery, but they were right. I was now a recognised poet, and had a thing or two to live up to. It took me a while to get the hair right, but I have finally settled down with a sort of modified Celtic look, which is about the only thing available to me short of baldness. I no longer feel I'll be dead by thirty; now it's sixty. I suppose these deadlines we set for ourselves are really a way of saying we appreciate time, and want to use all of it. I'm still writing, I'm still writing poetry, I still can't explain why, and I'm still running out of time.

Wordsworth was sort of right when he said, "Poets in their youth begin in gladness / But thereof comes in the end despondency and madness." Except that sometimes poets skip the gladness and go straight to the despondency. Why is that? Part of it is the conditions under which poets work—giving all, receiving little in return from an age that by and large ignores them—and part of it is cultural expectation—"The lunatic, the lover and the poet," says Shakespeare, and notice which comes first. My own theory is that poetry is composed with the melancholy side of the brain, and that if you do nothing but, you may find yourself going slowly down a long dark tunnel with no exit. I have avoided this by being ambidextrous: I write novels too. But when I find myself writing poetry again, it always has the surprise of that first unexpected and anonymous gift.

Barbara Kingsolver

■

Stealing Apples

Proclaimed an "extravagantly gifted narrative voice" by the *New York Times,* Barbara Kingsolver is a best-selling novelist, essayist, and poet. The author of five critically successful novels and several nonfiction books, she was recognized by the *San Francisco Chronicle* as "a writer we will keep reading for as long as she continues to grace us with her bounty." Born in 1955, she grew up in eastern Kentucky and started writing as a young child. Faced with the narrow prospects offered by rural Kentucky in the early 1970s, particularly for women, she struck out on her own at age eighteen. Nevertheless, Kingsolver's deep Kentucky roots would figure prominently in her later work as a creative writer. Initially shelving her love of writing, she studied science at DePauw University and the University of Arizona in Tucson, where she took one creative writing course. In the 1980s she began a successful career as a science writer and award-winning journalist. But the lifelong call to storytelling continued to tug at Kingsolver, who finally answered in the latter part of the decade. According to one source, she wrote most of her remarkable first novel in a closet during the sleepless nights of her first pregnancy. The story of a young woman from Kentucky who moves out West, *The Bean Trees* (1988) was a *New York Times* Notable Book and an American Library Association selection. Several stunning publications have followed, including the poetry collection *Another America: Otra America* and *The Poisonwood Bible,* which was nominated for the Pulitzer Prize and the PEN/Faulkner Award. As a writer she has also paid the sometimes painful costs of her craft, most notably with the harsh public condemnation of her outspoken essays on the September 11, 2001, attacks. Kingsolver is a recipient of the National Humanities Medal, the "highest honor for service through the arts" awarded in the United States.

In 2002 Kingsolver again earned wide critical acclaim with *Small Wonder,* a collection of essays on nature, post-9/11 politics, and life. In "Stealing Apples," this world-famous novelist turns her attention to the mysteries of writing poetry—and its everyday importance. With quiet power, here Kingsolver reflects as writer, mother, and human rights activist on writing as resistance: "My way of finding a place in this world is to write one."

I have never yet been able to say out loud that I am a *poet*.

It took me many years and several published novels to begin calling myself a *novelist*, but finally now I can do that, I own up to it, and will say so in capital letters on any document requiring me to identify myself with an honest living. "Novelist," I'll write gleefully, chortling to think that the business of making up stories can be called an honest living, but there you are. It's how I keep shoes on my kids and a roof above us. I sit down at my desk every day and make novels happen: I design them, construct them, revise them, I tinker and bang away with the confidence of an experienced mechanic, knowing that my patience and effort will get this troubled engine overhauled, and this baby will hum.

Poetry is a different beast. I rarely think of poetry as something I make happen; it is more accurate to say that it happens to *me*. Like a summer storm, a house afire, or the coincidence of both on the same day. Like a car wreck, only with more illuminating results. I've overheard poems, virtually complete, in elevators or restaurants where I was minding my own business. (A writer's occupational hazard: I think of eavesdropping as minding my business.) When a poem does arrive, I gasp as if an apple had fallen into my hand, and give thanks for the luck involved. Poems are everywhere, but easy to miss. I know I might very well stand under that tree all day, whistling, looking off to the side, waiting for a red delicious poem to fall so I could own it forever. But like as not, it wouldn't. Instead it will fall right while I'm in the middle of changing the baby, or breaking up a rodeo event involving my children and the dog, or wiping my teary eyes while I'm chopping onions and listening to the news; *then* that apple will land with a thud and roll under the bed with the dust bunnies and lie there forgotten and lost for all time. There are dusty, lost poems all over my house, I assure you. In yours, too, I'd be willing to bet. Years ago I got some inkling of this when I attended a reading by one of my favorite poets, Lucille Clifton. A student asked her about the brevity of her poems (thinking, I suspect, that the answer would involve terms such as "literary retrenchment" and "parsimony"). Ms. Clifton replied simply that she had six children and could hold only about twenty lines in memory until the end of the day. I felt such relief, to know that this great poet was bound by ordinary life, like me.

I've learned since then that most great poets are more like me, and more like you, than not. They raise children and chop onions, they suffer and rejoice, they feel blessed by any poem they can still remember at the end of the day. They may be more confident about tinkering with the engine, but they'll generally allow that there's magic involved, and that the main thing is to pay attention. I have several friends who are poets of great renown, to whom I've confessed that creating a poem is a process I can't really understand or control. Every one of them, on hearing this, looked off to the side and whispered, "Me either!"

We're reluctant to claim ownership of this mystery. In addition, we live in a culture that doesn't put much stock in it. Elsewhere in the world—say in Poland or Nicaragua—people elect their poets to public office, or at the very least pay them a stipend to produce poetry, regularly and well, for the public good. Here we have no such class of person. Here a poet may be prolific and magnificently skilled, but even so, it's not the *poetry* that's going to keep shoes on the kids and a roof overhead. I don't know of a single American poet who ever made a living solely by writing poetry. That's sad, but it's true. Identifying your livelihood as "Poet" on an official form is the kind of daring gesture that will make your bank's mortgage officer laugh very hard all the way into the manager's office and back. So poets, of necessity, tend to demur. At the most we might confess, "I write poetry sometimes."

And so we do. Whether anyone pays us or respects us or calls us a poet or not, just about any person alive will feel a tickle behind the left ear when we catch ourselves saying, "It was a little big and pretty ugly, but it's coming along shortly. . . ." We stop in our tracks when a child pointing to the sunset cries that the day is bleeding and is going to die. Poetry approaches, pauses, then skirts around us like a cat. I sense its presence in my house when I am chopping onions and crying but not really *crying* while I listen to the lilting radio newsman promise, "Up *next:* The city's oldest homeless shelter shut down by neighborhood protest, *and,* Thousands offer to adopt baby Jasmine abandoned in Disneyland!" There is some secret grief here I need to declare, and my fingers itch for a pencil. But then the advertisement blares that I should expect the unexpected, while my elder child announces that a shelter can't be homeless, and onions make her eyes run away with her nose, and my toddler marches in a circle shouting "Apple-Dapple! Come-Thumb-Drum!" and poems roll under the furniture, left and right. I've lost so many I can't count them. I do understand that they fall when I'm least able to pay attention because poems fall not from a tree, really, but from the richly pollinated boughs of an ordinary life, buzzing, as lives do, with clamor and glory. They are easy to miss but everywhere: poetry just *is,* whether we revere it or try to put it in prison. It is elementary grace, communicated from one soul to another. It reassures us of what we know and socks us in the gut with what we don't, it sings us awake, it's irresistible, it's congenial.

Over the years I've forgotten enough poems to fill several books and remembered enough to fill just one. By the grace of a small, devoted press and a small, devoted contingent of North Americans who read poetry, it remains in print. I began writing poems when I was very young; the most noticeable virtue of my early works was that they rhymed. Then, in high school, I abandoned rhyme scheme in favor of free verse and produced rafts of poems whose most noticeable characteristics were that they were earnest and frequently whiny. I returned again to rhyme scheme and more rigorous structure when I was in college, after seeking my first writing advice from an English professor who advised, "Write sonnets. It will teach you discipline." I dutifully wrote a hundred dreadful sonnets and just one that seemed successful, insofar as its subject suited the extremely confining sonnet form.

Although I had been working at poems and stories all my life, I didn't really begin to understand what it meant to be a writer until my adulthood commenced in Tucson, Arizona, following my arrival here at the very end of the 1970s. I had come to the Southwest expecting cactus, wide-open spaces, and adventure. I found instead, another whole America. This other America didn't appear on picture postcards, nor did it resemble anything I had previously supposed to be American culture. Arizona was cactus, all right, and purple mountain majesties, but this desert that burned with raw beauty had a great fence built across it, attempting to divide north from south. I'd stumbled upon a borderland where people perished of heat by day and of cold hostility by night.

This is where poetry and adulthood commenced for me, as I understand both these things, because of remarkable events that fell into my quite ordinary way. Oh, I suffered the extremes of love and loss, poverty and menial jobs and exhilarating recuperations, obsessive explorations of a new landscape—all common preoccupations for a young adult in the America I knew. But I also met people, some of them very uncommon. In particular, some of them were organizing the Sanctuary movement, an undertaking I could not previously have imagined in the America I knew. This was an underground railroad run by a few North Americans who placed conscience above law. Their risk was to provide safety for Latin American refugees—many hundreds of them—who faced death in their own countries but could not, though innocent of any crime or ill will, gain legal entry into ours.

I learned, slowly, with horror, that the persecution these refugees were fleeing was partly my responsibility. The dictators of El Salvador, Guatemala, and Chile received hearty support from my government; their brutish armies were supplied and trained by my government. Some of the police who tortured protestors in those countries had been trained in that skill at a camp in Fort Benning, Georgia. My taxes had helped pay for that, and also the barbed wire and bullets that prevented war-weary families from finding refuge here. I wasn't prepared for the knowledge of what one nation might do to another. But that knowledge arrived regardless. I saw that every American proverb had two sides, could be told in two languages, and that injustice did not disappear when I looked away, but instead seeped in at the back of my neck to poison my heart's desires. I saw that unspeakable things could be survived, and that sometimes there was even joy on the other side. I learned all this, one story at a time, from people who had lived enough to know it. Some of them became my friends. Others vanished again, into places I can't know. This great apple that had fallen into my lap became my first novel, *The Bean Trees*. I doubted whether my compatriot readers would really want to hear all that much about what one country would do to another, particularly when one of the countries was ours. I have been wrong about that: once, twice, always.

I believe there are wars in every part of every continent, and a world of clamor and glory in every life. Mine is right here, where I raise my voice and my children, and where we must find our peace, if there is any to be had. Heartbreak and love and poetry abound. We live in a place where north meets south and many people are running for their lives, while many others rest easy with the embarrassments of privilege. Others still are trying to find a place in between, a place of honest living where they can abide themselves and one another without howling in the darkness. My way of finding a place in this world is to write one. This work is less about making a living, really, than about finding a way to be alive. "Poet" is too much of a title for something so incorrigible, and so I may never call myself by that name. But when I want to howl and cry and laugh all at once, I'll raise up a poem against the darkness, or an essay, or a tale. That is my testament to the two boldly different faces of America and the places I've found, or made or dreamed, in between.

One afternoon, as my one-year-old stood on a chair reciting the poems she seems to have brought with her onto this planet, I heard on the news that our state board of education was dropping the poetry requirement from our schools. The secretary of education explained that it took too much time to teach children poetry, when they were harder pressed than ever to master the essentials of the curriculum. He said we had to take a good, hard look at what was essential, and what was superfluous.

"Superfluous," I said to the radio.

"Math path boo!" said my child, undaunted by her new outlaw status.

This one was not going to get away. I threw down my dishtowel, swept the baby off her podium, and carried her under my arm as we stalked off to find a pencil. In my opinion, when you find yourself laughing and crying both at once, that is the time to write a poem. Maybe that's the only honest living there is.

Judith Ortiz Cofer

∎

The Woman Who Slept with One Eye Open

The critically acclaimed author of fiction, poetry, essays, and memoir, Judith Ortiz Cofer was born in Hormigueros, Puerto Rico. Nominated for the Pulitzer Prize for her first novel, *The Line of the Sun* (1989), she was named in the *New York Times* "a novelist of historical compass and sensitivity." Now acknowledged as a major "Latina writer," Ortiz Cofer has taken the critical establishment to task for its often reductive treatment of works by marginalized artists. In an interview with Edna Acosta-Belén, she also observes this dangerous tendency in the publishing industry, citing early encounters with mainstream houses that were unwilling to publish her "exotic" novels (about growing up Puerto Rican) in an untried market. Still, her determination to create her own voice was unwavering, and like many other literary pioneers, her work was first welcomed by independent presses. In 1993, *Latin Deli: Prose and Poetry* won the Anisfeld-Wolf Book Award; two years later, the American Library Association named *An Island Like You: Stories of the Barrio* a Best Book of the Year. Ortiz Cofer is also coeditor of *Sleeping with One Eye Open: Women Writers and the Art of Survival* (1998). Widely studied and anthologized, her work has appeared in *Best American Essays 1991, The Norton Introduction to Poetry, The Pushcart Prize, O. Henry Prize Stories,* and scores of other collections. Now the Franklin Professor of English at the University of Georgia, she is the recipient of several distinguished fellowships and residencies. Her most recent novel, *The Meaning of Conseulo,* apppeared in 2003.

In "The Woman Who Slept with One Eye Open," Ortiz Cofer (re)introduces readers to the vibrant storytelling tradition of Puerto Rican women, a tradition that brought comfort and inspiration to "a child caught in that lonely place between two cultures and two languages." Here she articulates the enduring influence of the legendary María Sabida—and her alter ego, *la sufrida*—on the writer and woman she would choose to become. She also retells brave new *cuentos* learned from a community of working-class Latinas struggling to find a room of their own, even "in a cramped apartment where the only table had to be used to store groceries, change babies, and iron." Like them, like María Sabida, Judith Ortiz Cofer is a writer who will either find a way or make one.

As a child caught in that lonely place between two cultures and two languages, I wrapped myself in the magical veil of folktales and fairy tales. The earliest stories I heard were those told by the women of my family in Puerto Rico, some of the tales being versions of Spanish, European, and even ancient Greek and Roman myths that had been translated by time and by each generation's needs into the *cuentos* that I heard. They taught me the power of the word. These *cuentos* have been surfacing in my poems and my prose since I decided to translate them for myself and to use them as my palette, the primary colors from which all creation begins.

The stories that have become the germinal point for not only my work as a creative artist but also my development as a free woman are those of two women. One is María Sabida, "the smartest woman on the whole island," who conquered the heart of a villain and "slept with one eye open." And the other is María Sabida's opposite, María La Loca, the woman who was left at the altar, the tragic woman who went crazy as a result of a broken heart. Once a beautiful girl, María La Loca ends up, in my grandmother's *cuento,* a pitiful woman who retreats into insanity because she is shamed by a man, cheated out of the one option she allowed herself to claim: marriage.

The crude and violent tale of María Sabida, which I have found in collections of folktales recorded from the oral tellings of old people at the turn of the century, revealed to me the amazing concept that a woman can have "macho"—that quality that men in certain countries, including my native island, have claimed as a male prerogative. The term "macho," when divested of gender, to me simply means the arrogance to assume that you belong where you choose to stand, that you are inferior to no one, and that you will defend your domain at whatever cost. In most cases, I do not recommend this mode as the best way to make room for yourself in a crowded world. But I grew up in a place and time where modesty and submissiveness were the qualities a girl was supposed to internalize. So the woman who slept with one eye open intrigued me as a possible model in my formative years as a creative artist. Of course, it would be a long time before I articulated what I knew then instinctively: María Sabida's "macho" was what I myself would need to claim for my art. It is almost bravado to say "I am a writer" in a society where that condition usually means "I am unemployed," "I live on the fringes of civilization," "I am declaring myself better/different," and so forth. I know writers who will put anything else under "occupation" on a passport or job application rather than call up a red flag of distrust that the word "writer" has come to have for many people.

When I feel that I need a dose of "macho," I follow a woman's voice back to María Sabida. I have come to believe that she was the smartest woman on the island because she learned how to use the power of words to conquer her fears; she knew that this was what gave men their aura of power. They knew how to convince themselves and others that they were brave. Of course, she still had to sleep with one eye open because when you steal secrets, you are never again safe in your bed. María Sabida's message may be entirely different to me from what it was to the generations of women who heard and told the old tale. As a writer I chose to make my alter ego, my *comadre*. In Catholic cultures two women otherwise unrelated can enter into a sacred bond, usually for the sake of a child, called the *comadrazgo*. One woman swears to stand in for the other as a surrogate mother if the need arises. It is a sacrament that joins them, more sacred than friendship, more binding than blood. And if these women violate the trust of their holy alliance, they will have committed a mortal sin. Their souls are endangered. I feel similarly about my commitment to the mythical María Sabida. My *comadre* taught me how to defend my art, how to conquer the villain by my wits. If I should ever weaken my resolve, I will become María La Loca, who failed herself, who allowed herself to be left at the altar.

Comadres y compadres, let me tell you the *cuento* of María Sabida, the smartest woman on the whole island.

Once upon a time, there was a widower merchant who had no other children, only a daughter. He often had to leave her alone while he traveled on business to foreign lands. She was called María Sabida because she was smart and daring and knew how to take care of herself. One day, the merchant told her that he would be away on a trip for a long time and left María Sabida in the company of her women friends.

One moonless night when she and her *compañeras* were sitting on the veranda of her father's house talking, María Sabida saw a bright light in the distance. Because the house was far away from the pueblo, she was very curious about what the light could be. She told her friends that they would investigate the source of light very next morning.

As planned, early the next day, María Sabida and her friends set out through the woods in the direction where they had seen the light. They arrived at a house that seemed to be unoccupied. They went in and peered into each room. It looked like a man's place. But they smelled cooking. So they followed their noses to the kitchen, where an old man was stirring a huge cauldron. He welcomed them and asked them to stay and eat. María Sabida looked in the pot and saw that it was filled with the arms and legs of little children. Then she knew that this was the house of a gang of killers, kidnappers, and thieves that had been terrorizing the countryside for years. Sickened by the sight, María Sabida picked up the pot and poured its contents out of the window. The old man screamed at her: "You will pay for this, woman! When my master comes home, he will kill you and your *compañeras!*" Then at gunpoint he led them upstairs where he locked them up.

When the leader of the thieves arrived with his gang, María Sabida heard him conspiring with his men to trick the women. Bearing a tray of *higos de sueño,* sleep-inducing figs, the *jefe* came up to the bedroom where the women were being kept. In a charming voice he persuaded the women to eat the fruit. María Sabida watched her friends fall deeply asleep one by one. She helped the *jefe* settle them in beds as she planned. Then she pretended to eat a fig and lay down yawning. To test how well the potion in the fruit had worked, the *jefe* of the thieves lit a candle and dripped a few drops of hot wax on the women's faces. María Sabida bore the pain without making a sound.

Certain now that the women were deeply asleep, the *jefe* went to the second-floor veranda and whistled for his comrades to come into the house. María Sabida leaped from the bed as he was leaning over the rail, and she pushed him off. While his men were tending to their injured leader, María Sabida awakened the women and they followed her to safety.

When María Sabida's father returned from his journey days later, she told him that she had decided to marry the leader of the thieves. The father sent a letter to the man asking him if he would marry his daughter. The *jefe* responded immediately that he had been unable to forget the smart and brave María Sabida. Yes, he would marry her. The wedding took place with a great fiesta. Everyone in the pueblo hoped that María Sabida would reform this criminal and that they could stop fearing his gang. But as soon as the couple had arrived at the thieves' house, the new husband told his bride that now she would pay for having humiliated him in front of his men. He told her to go to

the bedroom and wait for him. María Sabida knew that he was going to murder her. She had an idea. She asked her husband if he would let her take some
honey to eat before she went to bed. He agreed. And while he drank his rum
and celebrated her death with his gang, María Sabida worked in the kitchen
making a life-size honey doll out of burlap sacks. She filled the doll with
honey, cutting off some of her own hair to affix to its head. She even tied a
string to its neck so that she could make the doll move from where she planned
to hide under the marriage bed. She took the honey doll upstairs and placed it
on the bed. Then she slid underneath the bed where she could see the door.

It was not long before the husband came in drunk and ready for blood. He
struck the honey doll, thinking that it was María Sabida. He insulted her and
asked if she thought she was smart now. Then he plunged a dagger into the
doll's heart. A stream of honey hit him on the face. Tasting the sweetness on
his mouth and tongue, the assassin exclaimed: "María Sabida, how sweet you
are in death, how bitter in life. If I had known your blood contained such
sweetness, I would not have killed you!"

María Sabida then came out from under the bed. In awe that María Sabida
had outsmarted him again, the leader of the thieves begged her to forgive him.
María Sabida embraced her husband. They lived happily together, so they say.
But on that night of her wedding, and every other night, María Sabida slept
with one eye open.

I have translated the tale of María Sabida several times for different purposes, and each time the story yields new meanings. Time and again the
words I use to roughly equate the powerful Spanish change meanings
subtly as if the story were a Ouija board, drawing letters out of my
mind to form new patterns. This is not hocus-pocus. It is the untapped
power of creativity. When a writer abandons herself to its call, amazing
things happen. On the surface the *cuento* of María Sabida may be inter-
preted as a parable of how a good woman conquers and tames a bad
man. In the Spanish cultures, with their Holy Mother Mary mystique,
the role of the woman as spiritual center and guide in a marriage is a
central one. Men were born to sin; women, to redeem. But as a writer,
I choose to interpret the tale of the woman who outmaneuvers the
killer, who marries him so that she does not have to fear him, as a
metaphor for the woman creator. The assassin is the destroyer of ambi-
tion, drive, and talent—the killer of dreams. It does not have to be a
man. It is anything or anyone who keeps the artist from her work. The

smartest woman on the island knows that she must trap the assassin so that he/she/it does not deprive her of her creative power. To marry the killer means to me that the artist has wedded the negative forces in her life that would keep her from fulfilling her mission and, furthermore, that she has made the negative forces work for her instead of against her.

Her sweetness is the vision of beauty that the artist carries within her, that few see unless she sacrifices herself. Does she have to be destroyed, or destroy herself so that the world can taste her sweet blood? Woolf, Plath, and Sexton may have thought so. I would rather believe that the sweetness may be shared without total annihilation, but not without pain or sacrifice: that is part of the formula for the honey-filled burlap sack that will save your life. The transaction that took place between María Sabida and her assassin-husband was a trade-off on macho. She took on his macho. He understood that. So they embraced. The artist and the world struck a compromise, albeit an uneasy one on her part. She had to sleep with one eye open and watch what was offered her to eat. Remember the sleep-inducing figs.

Some women eat sleep-inducing figs early in their lives. At first they are unwitting victims of this feminine appetizer. Later they reach for the plate. It is easier to sleep while life happens around you. Better to dream while others *do*. The writer recognizes the poisoned fruit. She may pretend to sleep and bear the pain of hot wax as she prepares herself for battle. But she knows what is happening around her at all times. And when she is ready, she will act. Occasionally my *comadre* will try to save other women who have eaten the *higos de sueño*. She will try to rouse them, to wake them up. And sometimes, the sleepers will rise and follow her to freedom. But very often, they choose to remain unconscious. They rise briefly, look around them. They see that the world goes on without them. They eat another fig and go back to sleep.

There is another kind of woman that my *comadre* cannot save: María La Loca, the woman who was left at the altar. I first heard my grandmother tell this *cuento* when I was a child in Puerto Rico. Later I wrote this poem:

The Woman Who Was Left at the Altar

She calls her shadow Juan,
looking back often as she walks.

She has grown fat, breasts huge
as reservoirs. She once opened her blouse
in church to show the silent town
what a plentiful mother she could be.
Since her old mother died, buried in black,
she lives alone. Out of the lace
she made curtains for her room,
doilies out of the veil. They are now
yellow as malaria.
She hangs live chickens from her waist to sell,
walks to the silent town swinging her skirts of flesh.
She doesn't speak to anyone. Dogs follow
the scent of blood to be shed. In their hungry,
yellow eyes she sees his face.
She takes him to the knife time after time.

Again this is a tale that is on the surface about the harsh lessons of love. But even my Mamá knew that it had a subtext. It was about failing oneself and blaming it on another. In my book *Silent Dancing*, I wrote around my Mamá's *cuento,* showing how she taught me about the power of storytelling through the tale of María La Loca. Mamá told it as a parable to teach her daughters how love can defeat you, if you are weak enough to let it.

There is a woman who comes to my *comadre* and complains that she knows that she has talent, that she has poetry in her, but that her life is too hard, too busy; her husband, her children are too demanding. She is a moral, responsible person and cannot in good conscience allow herself the luxury of practicing art. My *comadre* takes the time to tell this woman that she can choose to "learn to sleep with one eye open," to conjure up some female macho and claim the right to be an artist. But the woman is always prepared with an arsenal of reasons, all bigger than her needs, as to why she will die an unfulfilled woman, yearning to express herself in lyrical lines. She will, if pressed, imply that my *comadre* cannot possibly be a nurturing mother or caring partner, if she can find the time to write. In my culture, this type of woman who has perfected one art—that of self-abnegation, sometimes even martyrdom—is called *la sufrida*, the suffering one. There is much more admiration and respect for *la sufrida* in our society than there is for the artist.

The artist, too, suffers—but selfishly. She suffers mainly because the need to create torments her. If she is not fortunate enough to be truly selfish (or doesn't have enough macho in her to do as men have always done and claim the right, the time, and the space she needs), then she is doomed to do a balancing act, to walk the proverbial line that is drawn taut between the demands of her life—which may include choices that were made *before* she discovered her calling, such as marriage and children—and her art. The true artist will use her creativity to find a way, to carve the time, to claim a kitchen table, a library carrel, if a room of her own is not possible. She will use subterfuge if necessary, write poems in her recipe book, give up sleeping time or social time, and write.

Once I was asked to teach an evening writing class for a group of working-class Latinas who had taken the initiative to ask a community arts organization for a workshop they could attend. These women toiled at mind-numbing jobs eight or more hours each day, and most of them had several small children and a tired husband at home waiting for them to cook at the end of the workday. Yet somehow the women had found one another as artists. Perhaps on a lunch break one of them had dared to mention that she wrote poems or kept a journal. In any case, I met a determined group of tired women that first night, many nervously watching the clock because they had had to make complex arrangements to leave their homes on a weeknight. Perceiving that the needs of this class would be different from those of my usual writing students, I asked these women to write down their most pressing artistic problem. I read the slips of paper during the break and confirmed my intuition about them. Almost unanimously they had said that their main problem was no time and no place to write. When we came together again, I told them about my method of writing, how I had developed it because, by the time I knew I had to write, I was a young mother and wife and was teaching full-time. At the end of the day, after giving my child all of the attention I *wanted* to give her, grading papers, and doing the normal tasks involved with family life, I was done for. I could not summon a thought into my head, much less try to create. After trying various ways of finding time for myself, short of leaving everyone I loved behind for the sake of Art, I decided on the sacrifice I had to make—and there is always one: I had to give up some of my precious sleep time. In order to give myself what I needed, I had to stop eating the delicious sleep-inducing figs that also make you good at finding excuses for not becoming what you need to be. I started going to bed when my daughter did and rising at 5:00 A.M. And in the two hours before the household came alive and the demands on me began, I wrote and I wrote and I wrote. Actually, I usually had just enough time, after drinking coffee and bringing order to the chaos in my head, to write a few lines of a poem, or one or two pages on my novel—which took me, at that pace, three and one-half years to complete. But I was working, at a rate that many unencumbered writers would probably find laughably slow. But I wrote, and I write. And I am not left at the altar. Each line that I lay on a page points me toward my *comadre* María Sabida and takes me farther away from falling into the role of *la sufrida*.

The first assignment I gave that group of women was this: to go home and create a place to write for themselves. It had to be a place that could be cordoned off somehow, a place where books and notes could be left without fear of someone disturbing them and ruining a thought left unfinished, and, also important, a place where no one would feel free to read a work in progress—to ridicule and perhaps inhibit the writer. Their second assignment: to come up with a plan to make time to write every day.

As I expected, this latter injunction caused an uproar. They each claimed that their situation was impossible: no room, no privacy, no time, no time, no time. But I remained firm. They were going to write their version of Virginia Woolf's "A Room of One's Own" to fit their individual lives.

Two evenings later I met them again. I recall the faces of those weary women on that night. They were tired but not beaten, as they were used to challenges and to dealing with nearly impossible odds. I had dared them to use the strength of character that allowed them to survive in a harsh world of barrio and factory and their endless *lucha*. The struggle for survival was familiar to them. One by one they read their *cuentos* of how they had made a writing corner for themselves, the most fortunate among them having a guest room that her mother-in-law often occupied. She turned it into her study and bought a lock; permission for other uses would have to be requested. Others had appropriated a corner here and there, set up a table and a chair, and screened off a space for themselves. The *No Trespassing* rules had been discussed with family members; even mild threats had been issued to nosy teenage children: You mess with my papers, I'll make free with your things. It was a celebration, minor declarations of independence by women used to yielding their private territory to others.

That night I saw that the act of claiming a bit of space and time for themselves was the beginning of something important for some of these women. Of course, not all of them would succeed against the thief of time. Some would find it easier to revert to the less fatiguing norm of the usual daily struggle. It takes a fierce devotion to defend your artistic space, and eternal vigilance over it, because the needs of others will grow like vines in your little plot and claim it back for the jungle. Finally, we came to the last writer in the circle. This was a young woman who always looked harried and disheveled in her old jeans and man's shirt. She had two sons, little hellions, both under six years of age, and an absent husband. The story she had brought to class the first night had made us cry and laugh. She had the gift, no doubt about it, but had been almost angry about the writing space and time assignment. She lived in a cramped apartment where the only table had to be used to store groceries, change babies, and iron. The story she had read to us had been written during a hospital stay. What was she to do, cut her wrists so that she could find time to write? We waited in respectful silence for her to begin reading. She surprised us by standing up and announcing that she had brought her writing place with her that night. Out of the back pocket of her jeans she pulled a handmade notebook. It had a sturdy cardboard covering, and within it was paper cut to fit and stitched together. There was also a small pencil that fit just right in the groove. She flipped the notebook open and began to read her essay. She had nearly given up trying to find a place to write. Everywhere she laid down her papers the kids had gotten to them. It became a game for them. At first she had been angry, but then she had decided to use her imagination to devise a way to write that was child-proof. So she had come up with the idea of a portable room of her own. Because she could not leave her children and lock herself up in a room to write, she constructed a notebook that fit her jeans' pocket precisely. It had a hard back so that she could write on it while she went around the house or took the kids to the park, or even while grocery shopping. No one thought anything of it because it just looked like a housewife making a laundry list. She had even written this essay on her son's head while he leaned on her knees watching television.

Again there was laughter and tears. We had all learned a lesson that night about the will to create. I often think about this woman carrying her writing room with her wherever she went, and I have told her story often to other women who claim that the world keeps them from giving themselves to art. And I have put this young woman, who knew the meaning of *being* an artist, in my little pantheon of women who sleep with one eye open, the clapboard temple where I visit my story-telling *comadre*, María Sabida, to seek her counsel.

There are no altars in this holy place, nor women who were left at one.

IV.

In Tribute

■

There is more to be said
—Edna St. Vincent Millay

June Jordan

■

The Difficult Miracle of Black Poetry in America or Something Like a Sonnet for Phillis Wheatley

A major American writer, June Jordan (1936–2002) was an award-winning poet, essayist, and journalist. She is the author or editor of over thirty publications. In 2002 she succumbed to a decade-long fight with breast cancer, a loss still mourned by the literary and activist worlds. Reflecting on Jordan's extraordinary contribution to American letters and global social justice movements, Toni Morrison sums it best: "Forty years of tireless activism coupled with and fueled by flawless art." Recently *Ms.* magazine named her "one of America's fiercest literary figures and social activists" and "the hope of a generation." The daughter of Jamaican immigrants, Jordan was born in Harlem and raised in the Bedford-Stuyvesant section of Brooklyn. Growing up in a difficult and often violent household, she began writing poetry at age seven. In the 1960s she became a passionately engaged political activist, and it was against the backdrop of the civil rights and U.S. feminist movements that her public voice emerged. Among her most celebrated works are the breakthrough essay collection *Civil Wars* and *Kissing God Goodbye: Poems 1991–1997.* Best known for her poetry and radical political commentary, she is also the author of several plays and children's books. She founded the arts empowerment organization Poetry for the People at the University of California, Berkeley, where she was also a distinguished professor of African American studies. In 1998 she received a lifetime achievement award from the National Black Writers' Conference.

With this prize-winning essay, Jordan remembers the brilliant legacy of Phillis Wheatley (1755?–1784), "the first decidedly American poet on this continent, Black or white, male or female." More than a tribute to this "astonishing" literary pioneer, "The Difficult Miracle" dares us to imagine American poetry without her. With poetic urgency and uncommon insight, Jordan evokes a history that is at once proud and decidedly "not natural," a long river of subjugation and song from which, ultimately, the poets of tomorrow will spring: "This is the difficult miracle of Black poetry in America: that we persist, published or not, and loved or unloved: we persist."

■

It was not natural. And she was the first. Come from a country of many tongues tortured by rupture, by theft, by travel like mismatched clothing packed down into the cargo hold of evil ships sailing, irreversible, into slavery. Come to a country to be docile and dumb, to be big and breeding easily, to be turkey/horse/cow, to be cook/carpenter/plow, to be 5'6" 140 lbs., in good condition and answering to the name of Tom or Mary: to be bed bait, to be legally spread legs for rape by the master/the master's son, the master's overseer/the master's visiting nephew: to be nothing human nothing family nothing from nowhere nothing that screams nothing that weeps nothing that dreams nothing that keeps anything/anyone deep in your heart: to live forcibly illiterate, forcibly itinerant: to live eyes lowered head bowed: to be worked without rest, to be worked without pay, to be worked without thanks, to be worked day up to nightfall: to be three-fifths of a human being at best: to be this valuable/this hated thing among strangers who purchased your life and then cursed it unceasingly: to be a slave: to be a slave. Come to this country a slave and how should you sing? After the flogging the lynch rope the general terror and weariness what should you know of a lyrical life? How could you, belonging to no one, but property to those despising the smiles of your soul, how could you dare to create yourself: a poet?

A poet can read. A poet can write.

A poet is African in Africa, or Irish in Ireland, or French on the left bank in Paris, or white in Wisconsin. A poet writes in her own language. A poet writes of her own people, her own history, her own vision, her own room, her own house where she sits at her own table quietly placing one word after another word until she builds a line and a movement and an image and a meaning that somersaults all of these into the singing, the absolutely individual voice of the poet: at liberty. A poet is somebody free. A poet is someone at home.

How should there be Black poets in America?

It was not natural. And she was the first. It was 1761—so far back before the revolution that produced these United States, so far back before the concept of freedom disturbed the insolent crimes of this continent—

in 1761, when seven-year-old Phillis stood, as she must, when she stood nearly naked, as small as a seven-year-old by herself, standing on land at last, at last after the long, annihilating horrors of the Middle Passage. Phillis, standing on the auctioneer's rude platform: Phillis For Sale.

Was it a nice day?

Does it matter? Should she muse on the sky or remember the sea? Until then Phillis had been somebody's child. Now she was about to become somebody's slave.

Suzannah and John Wheatley finished their breakfast and ordered the carriage brought 'round. They would ride to the auction. This would be an important outing. They planned to buy yet another human being to help with the happiness of their comfortable life in Boston. You don't buy a human being, you don't purchase a slave, without thinking ahead. So they had planned this excursion. They were dressed for the occasion, and excited, probably. And experienced, certainly. The Wheatleys already owned several slaves. They had done this before; the transaction would not startle or confound or embarrass or appall either one of them.

Was it a nice day?

When the Wheatleys arrived at the auction they greeted their neighbors, they enjoyed this business of mingling with other townsfolk politely shifting about the platform, politely adjusting positions for gain of a better view of the bodies for sale. The Wheatleys were good people. They were kind people. They were openminded and thoughtful. They looked at the bodies for sale. They looked and they looked. This one could be useful for that. That one might be useful for this. But then they looked at that child, that Black child standing nearly naked, by herself. Seven or eight years old, at the most, and frail. Now that was a different proposal! Not a strong body, not a grown set of shoulders, not a promising wide set of hips, but a little body, a delicate body, a young, surely terrified face! John Wheatley agreed to the whim of his wife, Suzannah. He put in his bid. He put down his cash. He called out the numbers. He competed successfully. He had a good time. He got what he wanted. He purchased yet another slave. He bought that Black girls standing on the platform, nearly naked. He gave this new slave to his wife and Suzannah Wheatley was delighted. She and her husband went home. They rode there by carriage. They took that new slave with them. An old slave commanded the horses that pulled the carriage that carried the Wheatleys home, along with the new slave, that little girl they named Phillis.

Why did they give her that name?

Was it a nice day?

Does it matter?

It was not natural. And she was the first: Phillis Miracle: Phillis Miracle Wheatley: the first Black human being to be published in America. She was the second female to be published in America.

And the miracle begins in Africa. It was there that a bitterly anonymous man and a woman conjoined to create this genius, this lost child of such prodigious aptitude and such beguiling attributes that she very soon interposed the reality of her particular, dear life between the Wheatley's notions about slaves and the predictable outcome of such usual blasphemies against Black human beings.

Seven-year-old Phillis changed the slaveholding Wheatleys. She altered their minds. She entered their hearts. She made them see her and then they truly saw her, Phillis, darkly amazing them with the sweetness of her spirit and the alacrity of her forbidden, strange intelligence, they, in their own way, loved her as a prodigy, as a girl mysterious but godly.

Sixteen months after her entry into the Wheatley household Phillis was talking the language of her owners. Phillis was fluently reading the Scriptures. At eight and a half years of age, this Black child, or "Africa's Muse," as she would later describe herself, was fully literate in the language of this slaveholding land. She was competent and eagerly asking for more: more books, more and more information. And Suzannah Wheatley loved this child of her whimsical good luck. It pleased her to teach and to train and to tutor this Black girl, this Black darling of God. And so Phillis delved into kitchen studies commensurate, finally, to a classical education available to young white men at Harvard.

She was nine years old.

What did she read? What did she memorize? What did the Wheatleys give to this African child? Of course, it was white, all of it: white. It was English, most of it, from England. It was written, all of it, by white men taking their pleasure, their walks, their pipes, their pens and their paper, rather seriously, while somebody else cleaned the house, washed the clothes, cooked the food, watched the children: probably not slaves, but possibly a servant, or, commonly, a wife. It was written, this white man's literature of England, while somebody else did the other things that have to be done. And that was the literature absorbed by the slave, Phillis Wheatley. That was the writing, the thoughts, the nostalgia, the lust, the conceits, the ambitions, the mannerisms, the games, the illusions, the discoveries, the filth and the flowers that filled up the mind of the African child.

At fourteen, Phillis published her first poem, "To the University of Cambridge": not a brief limerick or desultory teenager's verse, but thirty-two lines of blank verse telling those fellows what for and whereas, according to their own strict Christian codes of behavior. It is in that poem that Phillis describes the miracle of her own Black poetry in America:

> While an intrinsic ardor bids me write
> the muse doth promise to assist my pen

She says that her poetry results from "an intrinsic ardor," not to dismiss the extraordinary kindness of the Wheatleys, and not to diminish the wealth of white men's literature with which she found herself quite saturated, but it was none of these extrinsic factors that compelled the labors of her poetry. It was she who created herself a poet, notwithstanding and in despite of everything around her.

Two years later, Phillis Wheatley, at the age of sixteen, had composed three additional, noteworthy poems. This is one of them, "On Being Brought from Africa to America":

> Twas mercy brought me from my Pagan land,
> Taught my benighted soul to understand
> That there's a God, that there's a Savior too:
> Once I redemption neither sought nor knew
> Some view our sable race with scornful eye,
> "Their color is a diabolic die."
> Remember, *Christians,* Negroes, black as Cain,
> May be refin'd, and join the angelic train.

Where did Phillis get these ideas?

It's simple enough to track the nonsense about herself "benighted": *benighted* means surrounded and preyed upon by darkness. That clearly reverses what had happened to that African child, surrounded by and captured by the greed of white men. Nor should we find puzzling her depiction of Africa as "Pagan" versus somewhere "refined." Even her bizarre interpretation of slavery's theft of Black life as a merciful rescue should not bewilder anyone. These are regular kinds of iniquitous nonsense found in white literature, the literature that Phillis Wheatley assimilated, with no choice in the matter.

But here, in this surprising poem, this first Black poet presents us with something wholly her own, something entirely new. It is her matter-of-fact assertion that, "Once I redemption neither sought nor knew," as in: once I existed beyond and without these terms under consideration. *Once I existed on other than your terms.* And, she says, *but* since we are talking your talk about good and evil/redemption and damnation, let me tell you something you had better understand. I am Black as Cain *and* I may very well be an angel of the Lord. Take care not to offend the Lord!

Where did that thought come to Phillis Wheatley?

Was it a nice day?

Does it matter?

Following her "intrinsic ardor," and attuned to the core of her own person, this girl, the first Black poet in America, had dared to redefine herself from house slave to, possibly, an angel of the Almighty.

She was making herself at home.

And depending on whether you estimated that nearly naked Black girl on the auction block to be seven or eight years old, in 1761, by the time she was eighteen or nineteen, she had published her first book of poetry, *Poems on Various Subjects Religious and Moral.* It was published in London, in 1773, and the American edition appeared, years later, in 1786. Here are some examples from the poems of Phillis Wheatley:

From "On the Death of Rev. Dr. Sewell":

> Come let us all behold with wishful eyes
> The saint ascending to his native skies.

From "On the Death of the Rev. Mr. George Whitefield":

> Take him, ye Africans, he longs for you,
> *Impartial Savior* is his title due,
> Washed in the fountain of redeeming blood,
> You shall be sons and kings, and priest to God.

Here is an especially graceful and musical couplet, penned by the first Black poet in America:

> But, see the softly stealing tears apace,
> Pursue each other down the mourner's face;

This is an especially awful, virtually absurd set of lines by Ms. Wheatley:

> "Go Thebons! great nations will obey
> And pious tribute to her altars pay:
> With rights divine, the goddess be implor'd,
> Nor be her sacred offspring nor ador'd."
> Thus Manto spoke. The Thebon maids obey,
> And pious tribute to the goddess pay.

Awful, yes. Virtually absurd; well, yes, except, consider what it took for that young African to undertake such personal abstraction and mythologies a million million miles remote from her own ancestry, and her own darkly formulating face! Consider what might meet her laborings, as poet, should she, instead, invent a vernacular precise to Senegal, precise to slavery, and, therefore, accurate to the secret wishings of her lost and secret heart?

If she, this genius teenager, should, instead of writing verse to comfort a white man upon the death of his wife, or a white woman upon the death of her husband, or verse commemorating weirdly fabled white characters bereft of children diabolically dispersed; if she, instead, composed a poetry to speak her pain, to say her grief, to find her parents, or to stir her people into insurrection, what would we now know about God's darling girl, that Phillis?

Who would publish that poetry, then?

But Phillis Miracle, she managed, nonetheless, to write, sometimes, towards the personal truth of her experience.

For example, we find in a monumental poem entitled "Thoughts on the Works of Providence," these five provocative lines, confirming every suspicion that most of the published Phillis Wheatley represents a meager portion of her concerns and inclinations:

> As reason's pow'rs by day our God disclose,

So we may trace him in the night's repose.
Say what is sleep? and dreams how passing strange!
When action ceases, and ideas range
Licentious and unbounded o'er the plains.

And, concluding this long work, there are these lines:

Infinite *love* whene'er we turn our eyes
Appears: this ev'ry creature's wants supplies,
This most is heard in Nature's constant voice,
This makes the morn, and this the eve rejoice,
This bids the fost'ring rains and dews descend
To nourish all, to serve one gen'ral end,
The good of man: Yet man ungrateful pays
But little homage, and but little praise.

Now and again and again these surviving works of genius Phillis
Wheatley veer incisive and unmistakable, completely away from the
verse of good girl Phillis ever compassionate upon the death of someone else's beloved, pious Phillis modestly enraptured by the glorious
trials of virtue on the road to Christ, arcane Phillis intent upon an
"Ode to Neptune," or patriotic Phillis penning an encomium to
General George Washington ("Thee, first in peace and honor"). Then
do we find that "Ethiop," as she once called herself, that "Africa's
muse," knowledgeable, but succinct, on "dreams how passing strange!
/ When action ceases, and ideas range / Licentious and unbounded
o'er the plains."
Phillis Licentious Wheatley?
Phillis Miracle Wheatley in contemplation of love and want of love?
Was it a nice day?
It was not natural. And she was the first.
Repeatedly singing for liberty, singing against the tyrannical, repeatedly avid in her trusting support of the American Revolution (how
could men want freedom enough to die for it but then want slavery
enough to die for that?) repeatedly lifting witness to the righteous and
the kindly factors of her days, this was no ordinary teenaged poet, male
or female, Black or white. Indeed, the insistently concrete content of
her tribute to the revolutionaries who would forge America, an inde-

pendent nation state, indeed the specific daily substance of her poetry establishes Phillis Wheatley as the first decidedly American poet on this continent, Black or white, male or female.

Nor did she only love the ones who purchased her, a slave, those ones who loved her, yes, but with astonishment. Her lifelong friend was a young Black woman, Obour Tanner, who lived in Newport, Rhode Island, and one of her few poems dedicated to a living person, neither morbid nor ethereal, was written to the young Black visual artist Scipio Moorhead, himself a slave. It is he who crafted the portrait of Phillis that serves as her frontispiece profile in her book of poems. Here are the opening lines from her poem, "To S.M., A Young African Painter, on Seeing His Works."

> To show the lab'ring bosom's deep intent,
> And thought in living characters to paint.
> When first thy pencil did those beauties give,
> And breathing figures learnt from thee to live,
> How did those prospects give my soul delight,
> A new creation rushing on my sight?
> Still, wondrous youth! each noble path pusue,
> On deathless glories fix thine ardent view:
> Still may the painter's and the poet's fire
> To aid thy pencil, and thy verse conspire!
> And many the charms of each seraphic theme
> Conduct thy footsteps to immortal fame!

Remember that the poet so generously addressing the "wondrous youth" is certainly no older than eighteen, herself! And this, years before the American Revolution, and how many many years before the 1960s! This is the first Black poet of America addressing her Brother Artist not as so-and-so's Boy, but as "Scipio Moorhead, A Young African Painter."

Where did Phillis Miracle acquire this consciousness?

Was it a nice day?

It was not natural. And she was the first.

But did she—we may persevere, critical from the ease of the 1980s—did she love, did she need, freedom?

In the poem (typically titled at such length and in such deferential rectitude as to discourage most readers from scanning what follows), in the poem titled "To the Right Honorable William, Earl of Dartmouth, His Majesty's Principal Secretary of State for North America, etc.," Phillis Miracle has written these irresistible, authentic, felt lines:

> No more America in mournful strain
> Of wrongs, and grievances unredress's complain,
> No longer shalt Thou dread the iron chain,
> Which wanton tyranny with lawless head
> Had made, and with it meant t' enslave the land.
> Should you, my Lord, while you peruse my song,
> Wonder from whence my love of Freedom sprung,
> Whence flow these wishes for the common good,
> By feeling hearts alone best understood,
> I, young in life, by seeming cruel of fate
> Was snatch'd from Afric's fancy'd happy seat.
> What pangs excruciating must molest
> What sorrows labour in my parent's breast?
> Steel'd was that soul and by no misery mov'd
> That from a father seized his babe belov'd
> Such, such as my case. And can I then but pray
> Others may never feel tyrannic sway?

So did the darling girl of God compose her thoughts, prior to 1776. And then.

And then her poetry, these poems, were published in London.

And then, during her twenty-first year, Suzannah Wheatley, the white woman slaveholder who had been changed into the white mother, the white mentor, the white protector of Phillis, died.

Without that white indulgence, that white love, without that white sponsorship, what happened to the young African daughter, the young African poet?

No one knows for sure.

With the death of Mrs. Wheatley, Phillis came of age, a Black slave in America.

Where did she live?

How did she eat?

No one knows for sure.

But four years later she met and married a Black man, John Peters. Mr. Peters apparently thought well of himself, and of his people. He comported himself with dignity, studied law, argued for the liberation of Black people, and earned the everyday dislike of white folks. His wife bore him three children; all of them died.

His wife continued to be Phillis Miracle.

His wife continued to obey the "intrinsic ardor" of her calling and she never ceased the practice of her poetry. She hoped, in fact, to publish a second volume of her verse.

This would be the poetry of Phillis, the lover of John, Phillis the woman, Phillis the wife of a Black man pragmatically premature in his defiant self-respect, Phillis giving birth to three children, Phillis the mother, who must bury the three children she delivered into American life.

None of these poems was ever published.

This would have been the poetry of someone who had chosen herself, free, and brave to be free in a land of slavery.

When she was thirty-one years old, in 1784, Phillis Wheatley, the first Black poet in America, she died.

Her husband, John Peters, advertised and begged that the manuscript of her poems that she had given to someone, please be returned. But no one returned them.

And I believe we would not have seen them anyway. I believe no one would have published the poetry of Black Phillis Wheatley, that grown woman who stayed with her chosen Black man. I believe that the death of Suzannah Wheatley, coincident with the African poet's twenty-first birthday, signalled, decisively, the end of her status as a child, as a dependent. From there we would hear from an independent Black woman poet in America.

Can you imagine that, in 1775?

Can you imagine that, today?

America has long been tolerant of Black children, compared to its reception of independent Black men and Black women.

She died in 1784.

Was it a nice day?

It was not natural. And she was the first.

Last week, as the final judge for this year's Loft McKnight Awards in creative writing, awards distributed in Minneapolis, Minnesota, I read through sixteen manuscripts of rather fine poetry.

These are the terms, the lexical terms, that I encountered there:

> Rock, moon, star, roses, chimney, Prague, elms, lilac, railroad
> tracks, lake, lilies, snow geese, crow, mountain, arrow feath-
> ers, ear of corn, marsh, sandstone, rabbit-bush, gulley, pump-
> kins, eagle, tundra, dwarf willow, dipper-bird, brown creek,
> lizards, sycamores, glacier, canteen, skate eggs, birch, spruce,
> pumphandle

Is anything about that listing odd? I don't suppose so. These are the terms, the lexical items accurate to the specific Minnesota daily life of those white poets.

And so I did not reject these poems, I did not despise them saying, "How is this possible? Sixteen different manuscripts of poetry written in 1985 and not one of them uses the terms of my own Black life! Not one of them writes about the police murder of Eleanor Bumpurs or the Bernard Goetz shooting of four Black boys or apartheid in South Africa, or unemployment, or famine in Ethiopia, or rape, or fire escapes, or cruise missiles in the New York harbor, or medicare, or alleyways, or napalm, or $4.00 an hour, and no time off for lunch."

I did not and I would not presume to impose my urgencies upon white poets writing in America. But the miracle of Black poetry in America, the *difficult* miracle of Black poetry in America, is that we have been rejected and we are frequently dismissed as "political" or "topical" or "sloganeer-ing" and "crude" and "insignificant" because, like Phillis Wheatley, we have persisted for freedom. We will write against South Africa and we will seldom pen a poem about wild geese flying over Prague, or grizzlies at the rain barrel under the dwarf willow trees. We will write, published or not, however we may, like Phillis Wheatley, of the terror and the hungering and the quandaries of our African lives on this North American soil. And as long as we study white literature, as long as assimilate the English lan-guage and its implicit English values, as long as we allude and defer to gods we "neither sought nor knew," as long as we, Black poets in America, remain the children of slavery, as long as we do not come of age and attempt, then to speak the truth of our difficult maturity in an alien place, then we will be beloved, and sheltered, and published.

But not otherwise. And yet we persist.

And it was not natural. And she was the first.

This is the difficult miracle of Black poetry in America: that we persist, published or not, and loved or unloved: we persist.

And this is: "Something Like a Sonnet for Phillis Miracle Wheatley":

> Girl from the realm of birds florid and fleet
> flying full feather in far or near weather
> Who fell to a dollar lust coffled like meat
> Captured by avarice and hate spit together
> Trembling asthmatic alone on the slave block
> built by a savagery travelling by carriage
> viewed like a species of flaw in the livestock
> A child without safety of mother or marriage
>
> Chosen by whimsy but born to surprise
> They taught you to read but you learned how to write
> Begging the universe into your eyes:
> They dressed you in light but you dreamed
> with the night.
> From Africa singing of justice and grace,
> Your early verse sweetens the fame of our Race.

And because we Black people in North America persist in an irony profound, Black poetry persists in this way:

> Like the trees of winter and
> like the snow which has no power
> makes very little sound
> but comes and collects itself
> edible light on the black trees
> The tall black trees of winter
> lifting up a poetry of snow
> so that we may be astounded
> by the poems of Black
> trees inside a cold environment

Maureen E. Ruprecht Fadem

■

The Interval

for Reetika Vazirani, and her Son

Reetika Vazirani (1962–2003) was an award-winning poet. Born in Patiala, India, she and her family immigrated to the United States when she was six. Though she "never expected to be a writer, let alone a writer of poetry," Vazirani fell in love with literature at an early age, frequently copying poems she wished had been her own. A distinguished alumna of Wellesley College and the University of Virginia's MFA program, she would emerge as a widely acclaimed poetic voice in the 1990s. Over one hundred of her poems appear in numerous publications, including *Callaloo,* the *Kenyon Review, Ploughshares,* and the *Paris Review.* In 1995 she received the Barnard New Women Poets Prize for *White Elephants,* a book eight years in the making. She later described her first book as "a funeral for my father": though he died when Vazirani was twelve, it would be years before she knew that he had ended his own life. In a review for the *Nation,* Grace Schulman praised *White Elephants* for the "skill with which [Vazirani] creates poetry out of opposites: the sacred and the secular, exile and belonging, humour and wry sadness." Vazirani was the recipient of a "Discovery"/The Nation Award, a Pushcart Prize, the *Poets & Writers* Exchange Program Award, and several fellowships and writing residencies. Also a passionately engaged creative writing instructor, Vazirani was expected to join the Emory University faculty only a few months after her sudden death. In 2003, she won the Anisfeld-Wolf Book Award for her second volume of poems, *World Hotel.*

On July 18, 2003, the literary world was rocked by the violent deaths of Reetika Vazirani and Jehal Vazirani Komunyakka, her small son. Among those stunned into momentary silence—and a long, searching grief—was Maureen E. Ruprecht Fadem. A prize-winning scholar, Fadem was born in 1961 and raised in St. Louis. After working in finance for sixteen years, she moved to New York to study literature. Now a doctoral candidate at the Graduate Center of the City University of New York, Fadem focuses her research and teaching on postcolonial literature, particularly women's narratives of partition in Ireland and Asia. But here Fadem writes first as an undecorated reader, a woman who like us all must now read and love Vazirani's poetry amid the bloody footprints she left behind. In this remarkable prose/poem, two women/writers who never met come together, miraculously, through "the words of a dead poet and one mother's ability to hold onto them." At once a lyric eulogy and testament to the survivors of a world where "even the little children are swaddled in its fire," "The Interval" carries both the capacity of words to fail us and their miraculous power to connect us—one to the other—with their breath.

Drink / from my mouth.
Paul Celan

In music, "interval" refers to the pitch distance between two notes, the difference usually expressed in the number of steps between two distinct sounds. In language (a kind of music), "pitch accent" means the stress produced by a change especially a rise in pitch from spoken word to spoken word. In time (the space of music and language), "interval" is a bifurcated term, meaning: 1) the space between two objects or points; 2) the time between two events or states; 3) one of a series of distances covered at regular time increments with intermittent periods of rest.

"Interval": The pitch distance (being, in time and space) between two linguistic events with strikingly different tones in combination with the stress produced by the rise in pitch from the first set of words to the second and the changes called for in the field of such an occurrence.

I.

There is a time—the tense, present. It is a single, extended movement provoked by an incongruous interval: within seconds of receiving the death announcement the black book of prison writings arrives. It is a tiny, momentous clockturn beginning with death and ending in survival. One of those earth-shaking jolts when time, undermined, goes from humming along at a comfortable, invisible pace to trouncing (defiantly) out of control in a way that is not enlivening. It is a time of unnerved disarray that reverberates in the form of roiling aftershocks; that develops from a single step ("du-daaah") into a complex, protracted movement (a three-day rhapsody in presto, fortissimo); that gives birth (in time) to a dissident, searching urge: the impulse to reach outwards, eyes closed, blindly grasping after some unseen, misunderstood thing.

It begins on the 18th day of July in the year 2003 in the city of New York on the island of Manhattan, extreme northern territory. I am at home. I am seated in the chair belonging to the desk in a room belonging to me—my "study," a room with two tall, narrow windows facing the garden on the other side of the street, a garden with red flowers and lush foliage and children at play. I have just begun to write something when the news hits. The computer screen cooperates as I key in "words" ("Once . . .") ("upon . . .") once in a while pausing to watch the breeze through the trees through the windows, the green aural rush of ripe summer leaves bending en masse to the will of the wind; once in a while pausing to read.

This time, it is a series of crushing words that would (unsuspectingly) define the rest—the "news": "In Final Hours, Despair Defeated Poet; Indian-Born Writer Apparently Killed Herself [and] 2-Year-Old. . . ."[1] I can't understand. Reetika Vazirani (woman, poet, mother, lover) was dead at my age. She ended her life herself and took her son with her. I can't understand. But it sinks in, piecemeal: *A mother is dead. A child. A poet. She, who was to have become a doctor, became a poet instead, a writer of perfect sonnets.* I cannot understand this.

And I am shocked by how hard these words hit me, confused by the way everything stopped right along with them—the breeze, the play, the music, stopped. Whatever I'd been writing (something) stopped. *A mother. A child. Dead.* And then the buzzer sounds and I fly from the chair as if the building had gone up in flames, as if one of my children had arrived from somewhere far away after a long absence. Did I think she would be there? I press the enter button and listen to its high-pitched hum. Or did I expect another note, different words, tolerable news to flutter through the air through the doorway, land in my hands and cancel out the unbearable syllables of the moment? Perhaps that is precisely what transpires because the doorbell rings and I, hesitating, open my door upon a letter carrier with a book. (It is for me. It isn't her. It isn't my son. It isn't my daughter.) It is the thing I've been waiting for, the bleeding book about continued existence amid undreamed-of ferocity and carnage aptly titled, *This Prison Where I Live.* The book of survival against impossible odds; the book of choice. *A desperate mother. The woman poet who would have been a healer has brought her son's life to a brutal, premature end.*

An unfamiliar postman thrusts the ragged package toward me. I stare at it, momentarily, I don't accept it, right away, I try, unsuccessfully, to recall what I'd been writing. In the moment of ex-change—from his hands to mine—I think about the colors of the four corresponding hands, the corrugated yellow gold of his tiger's eye ring, how this ex-change is occurring in slow-motion-time, how I have never before seen this man. I raise my eyes to his wondering where Susie is today when, abruptly, the wrapper rips, snagged by the doorbell plaque, an earlier tear gaping now, and much to my surprise hundreds of prisoners' words start spilling out—"unheard-of violence" "shapeless nightmares" "trapped and suffocated" hurdle over the edges, "This is my sister here" tumbling onto my chest. A frenzy of English erupts the moment I break the seal (forcibly, this time) and remove the book, ordered sentences soaring into pandemonium—"frozen with terror" "a sea of nausea" "phantasms and terrible symbols." I catch and hold what I can. Still fix-ated on the news of the minute, I scarcely manage registering my aston-ishment over the fact that the thing is coming undone, furiously discharging stories of torture, hunger, cold, and madness by people who've been badly hurt but lived to tell the tale—"a circle without beginning or end," "a voice full of anger," "a language not understood."[2]

It's desperate for a reader, I think, *and self-destructing.* With aid of the postman, I lay my bundle on the bulky corner chair—dripping words, paper pages, spine, and decimated glue, back and front covers (frayed), recycled brown exterior wrap, cellophane interior wrap, packing tape. An oversized shooting fragment skids along the chair's edge, lands on the floor. We pause concurrently, almost imperceptibly, and read: "like a stone the foreign word falls to the bottom of every soul. 'Get up.'" The postman smiles brightly exposing the glint in his eye and his wide white teeth. *Perhaps you might have paid better attention,* he suggests all-knowingly, *perhaps you could have come to retrieve the book sooner?* With a pang of guilt and a pinch of annoyance, I promise to do better in any future like episode. He nods shrewdly, a supreme gesticulation. I thank and salute him. He makes for the next destination. Disappearing through the corridor, his cape catches on a current of wind through the tall hall window and billows a figure eight.[3]

I close the door leaning my back against it; I close my eyes folding my arms about myself; I swallow a mouthful of breath—it is an inverted sigh. *The woman poet, who, like me, loved Ghalib—a mother, babe in arms—followed her father to the edge of the world and jumped, eyes open, resolute.*

II.

I think about things—my doorway situation, my flawed posture, my over weight, that I'd forgotten the quarters (again), that I'd anticipated the book's arrival for weeks unaware it had been sitting on a post office shelf waiting for me. ("The woman who apparently slashed the left wrist of her 2-year-old son and her own Wednesday and then died with him in a pool of blood . . .") "July 7," the orange note read, "Will be returned to sender, July 22." ("[They] were found lying next to each other in the dining room . . .") As luck had had it (this time) the package and its contents were saved by an angelic postman, just in time. (" . . . Police called the deaths an apparent murder-suicide.") I think about my shabby bundle, do a little math and deduce, *I'm 11 days older since that book hit the shelf, started collecting dust, waiting.* Whereas two days from now I will have a birthday for the 42nd time. Which may mean I have finished changing, which may mean I can leave behind the struggle for augmentation, clarification, acumen.[4] Unsure whether that's good or bad news, I recall with some relief that my birthday will be spent with my Son. He is 22 years of age. He is a musicmaker. He is a breadmaker. He is a minor god. And—there is something inconceivable, perhaps even miraculous, about him.[5]

I am marking time. Because the news had come and couldn't be turned back. And I am getting a crick in my neck, perhaps also a headache, maybe even the jitters. And in the instant of time featuring terrible news and an exploding book, I'd been hurled madly about. And now, I am smarting. In this interval I travel from survival to its opposite and back again. (I was surviving before the "news" hit me like tumbling brickwork and caused a murmur in the regularity of my endurance. I had to face the fact of "deaths" and then became too swiftly obligated to accept the long overdue book of survival.) The second of these knowledges hits me, hard—like a wide-angled, close-range, unexpected slap, like the time I cooled off beneath the ventilation device in the doorway to my bedroom. And then fainted. And then woke up and wondered what had happened during this break in the time of my life. Only after which would the story be permitted to continue.

Until we get to today. A day on which I feel faint once again. A day on which unanswerable questions run (reckless) through my mind as I think through the preparations for the 20th. A day on which I find myself duty-bound to composing my meditations on the first real question. While the laundry is still in dire need. The dishes, on balance, far dirtier than clean. The books are piled high; they are dust-covered, anxious, awaiting their just desserts—a careful reading. Still, in the face of survival and its opposite, all these: trifling diversions from the question of the moment.

What is the color of survival—its temperament, temporality? Why is the opposite of survival the well-considered choice of some, and why do I crumble beneath someone else's tragedy, someone I have never known, someone I will never know? What is the language of survival, its words, syllables, phrasing, meter, rhyme scheme, line length? And how do prisoners and poets know? What happens when the surviving falls apart finally? When it's the end, and you know it? Does it melt (Virginia Woolf)? Fade (Primo Levi)? Scatter, spreading out and away like a net (Paul Celan)? The color of survival—is it White (for wicked indignance), Green (for the good fight), Orange (for ordinary chutzpah), Red (for Reetika Vazirani, for the revolution, the sunset, the rainbow—that miraculous fusion of sunlight and water droplets)? Red is the color of Love, the color of sex, the color of birth, the color of Ghalib's passion. Blood red roses say *I love you* and that means—I will survive. Red sequins on a glinty dress say *I want you* and that means, you and me—we survive together, our fused bodies standing as proof of the unassailable fact. A bloody delivery says *"Welcome, O life!"* and that means, I am prepared to take the first step towards death. Blood red beads make a trail of clinging droplets, they rest upon the outermost edge of each and every eyelash of the beloved poet, they say—*I lived on your promise.*[6]

I lived on your promise. Perhaps this is what I had (only moments ago) been writing. It wasn't an elegy or a eulogy or my life story translated from time into words on paper—becoming a body, in black and white. Perhaps it was a story, the beginning of a story: *Once upon a time I lived on your promise.* And now, several discordant cymbals are ringing orgy-like through my mind; they are saying *Wake up.* Now, I hold on to pieces of the (unreadable) book of survival and blood with my hands while my head holds on to the ineffable news of this (unlivable) interval, while my heart writhes, undetectably. I begin to realize that I can no longer continue like this—standing here, back against the door, eyes closed, arms hugging, slugging swells of air—can't hold on to all of this all at once, the words the book the pieces the poet's last poem my own lost words her lost Son. Now, my sixty little seconds—the mindless time between incidentals, between writing and whatever was to come next—the interval shudders trembles bends creaks collapses finally beneath its own weight: the incompatible juncture of survival and its opposite, the heavy time when (urgent) questions drop, crowding me drowning me and there is not a single answer in sight.

III.

Now, I am almost-9 again. The change is sudden and startling, like an unforeseen drop off in a fast-moving motorcar, like a book self-destructing before your eyes. It is an unforgettable July day in the year 1970, a suffocatingly hot humid midwestern day just before my 9th birthday, the day I could have died. I have come inside after playing in the gardens, picking flowers, singing "Edelweiss." I am tired from a long morning of play, and overheated. I stand in my bedroom doorway beneath a ceiling vent lately installed by my father and a pack of unfamiliar men. I am motionless and marveling at all the cold air billowing forth, drumming my face and neck. My chest. *It's a miracle,* I think, *it feels like heaven.* The brothers are playing ball in the yard, their yells and guffaws float up, fly about. The piano is in use on the first floor; it is a staccato piece—first mother, then her student, followed by mother again and then her student and so on. Most of all, there is an abundance of freezing air falling forcefully downwards as I stand staring upwards, its relentless purr suppressing all the other sounds, creating a dual reality effect—the present and its offbeat echo; the melody and its 1/3 up, 1/3 down relations. Meanwhile, the old oak tree sags hulkishly, waves and winks at me through three side-by-side windows.

What happens next, I can't readily recall. I believe I tumbled through space, lost myself and landed in an altogether different universe. Because all of a sudden it was a new day and I was outside again in the yard again in the gardens again and I was talking to an unfamiliar girl. A girl who looked like, me. (The first image: a girl, like me, amidst hundreds of fully blooming flowers.) We were the same height, the same weight, we both had long brownblack hair and searching, singing brown eyes. We wore white Keds and white bobby socks and two versions of the same outfit—a soft stretchy polyester bold-striped top with solid, permanently creased cropped pants (very "in" for the pre-pubescent in those days)—our clothes were red, except, the alternating color—the other stripe—it was white. I believe we were touring the gardens, and that we'd started with the vegetables then moved to the flowers because I could feel the sandy residue of tomato stalks on my palms, and I believe the tour was over because she was seated, cross-legged, right in the middle of one of mother's flowerbeds (the special red tulips). To me, this was nothing short of astonishing, and I stood outside on the grassy exterior. (People don't belong in flowerbeds; only flowers. And dirt. And water. And sunshine. Maybe a little breeze, too.)

At that time, mother was a master gardener; she'd planted flowers of assorted colors species and sizes in numerous geometrically shaped beds all around the yard. Whereas father planted the vegetables. With the help of grandfather, he graduated up to tomatoes eventually, which are peculiar, tricky, and in need of special help. (They require these sticks to hold them up, so they grow right. *Without those sticks,* father said, *they'd die on the vine.)* Father showed me how to know when the tomatoes were ready—they should be soft (but not too) and when you put a little pressure on them (gently, with your thumb and your forefinger) they ought to flow (slowly) back into smooth, perfect place. And—they had to be just right tomato red.

I looked around to see if mother was coming, but then the girl looked at me and she spoke to me (it was the thing I'd been waiting for) and I paid attention and forgot all about my mother.

"Weathered," she said, "I am dusk."[7]

What did she say? I asked myself. Perhaps I hadn't heard her properly. These words—though not understood—were too much of a downer for me. I tried to make out what she said and decided it had been: *"My head hurts, and it's almost dusk."* Which threw me for a serious loop since it was only midday and the sun wouldn't set for a long time. (Except "set" isn't really the right word in this instance. People say "sunset" when really they mean "sundrop"—like clockwork, the sun drops then rises every day, everywhere.) When I looked back at the girl and the flowers I was surprised because I couldn't see her. I thought she'd gone home (perhaps disappointed in me for a reason I wouldn't have understood) but then I took a second look and realized she was there, it was just harder to see her now because she was wedged between the tulips, lying on top of and in-between them on her side. Her left arm pillowed her head, her right arm and knees were folded into her chest, and she was holding something. (I couldn't see what it was—honest.)

Meanwhile, hundreds of red late-blooming lily-flowered tulips (also known as "Queen of Sheba" or *Tulipa,* part of the Liliaceae family) were in full bloom beneath and all around her—each one, a six-pointed star. Mother planted them two falls before when they were little bulbs. They bloomed last July for the first time and were in bloom again, fairly gloriously. (You see, tulips come back perennially, as promised.) She planted the tulips close together in a rectangular bed flanked on two sides by wild sweet alyssum (white, also known as *Lobularia maritima*) and on the other two sides by the bricks used to build my home (reddish brown, also rectangular, alternatingly smooth then rough surfaced). The cinnamon logs were stacked in neat undulating rows packed tightly with slate colored cement that had at one time (sometime in the year 1921) oozed slightly between each one and had then hardened and was now very hard and dry and greyish black. Bordering the flowerbed was a row of funny-looking marble-colored rocks (they were silky and crystally with bumps like frozen bubbles) followed by the cheerful shamrock-laden greengreen grass (where I was standing) which led to the other gardens and to the porches and to my home. Dark green, white-speckled ivy (aka *Hedera helix,* part of the Araliaceae family) spiraled upwards, snakelike along the brick exterior wall, the vine's source a mystery never solved.

My home. I could read it talk about it re-member it—its structure contours history—but I couldn't understand my visitor. And it seemed to me that between us, things weren't going very well. She wanted to sleep, I wanted to play and I couldn't understand the sleeping. See, when I was almost-9, I didn't have a care in the world, and I didn't want one—didn't want to know or care about things like life (the meaning of) or death (the event of) or the Vietnam War or the fact that I could have died or the kinds of things detailed in father's beloved "news": "A Year After Moon Landing: Space Dream and Jobs Fade" "Laird Keeps Close Eye on South Vietnam's Economy" "New Bedford Gets Curfew To Ease Racial Tensions" "Cambodia's Young Women Are Taught the Art of War" "Blacks in South Africa Developing a New Awareness" "U.S. Assumes the Israelis Have A-Bomb." I knew and cared about and believed in things like my uniform breathing, my birthday, my brothers, my sisters, and my guardian angel. I believed in these things, and in getting up off the ground out of the flowerbed and back into the yard. And I couldn't understand rival views.

So, I decided to rouse her. I reached outward, toward her as far as my almost 9-year-old arm would go. (It was the arm with the hand with the flower.) I smiled as big as I could and in a loudish voice—the kind you use when it's time to get up and everybody's still sleeping—I said,

"Here, take my flower! Look, it's a red star!"

She looked at me, appeared baffled, seemed not to appreciate my words or my enthusiasm or perhaps me. We locked four brown eyes, two on two, for a few thudding, endless-seeming seconds. *This situation is either gonna grow up or die on the vine,* I thought. But I remained quiet. And she tried again,

"With myself and music I lie down."[8]

What does she mean? I took a look around, as if I might *see* the sound of music if only I *looked* for it, hard. But I couldn't see it. I couldn't understand. And I just squinted vaguely in reply hoping she'd read my confusion (this time) and clarify things for me. But she didn't answer my look with one of her own or offer anything further by way of explanation. Still, I waited for her for a long time. (I don't re-member how long. Long enough for a mood swing to blossom.) I was feeling angry or eager or agitated (just a little, maybe of all three, maybe just one). Perhaps it was desperation—after all, play friends aren't supposed to fall asleep on you in the middle of the flowers. After awhile I yelled out— somewhat heatedly, intent on projecting confidence into my optimistic (though anxious) cry—and I shook my flower, saying,

"There are flowers everywhere, but you must get up to see them. If we look, we will see their rainbow-like beauty together, and we will smile, together. *I promise!*"

Nothing. Not a sound, no movement. Feeling dejected, I slumped down on the shamrocks, cross-legged, and gazed up at a clear blue sky. I took a deep breath (sort of like sighing) and I closed my eyes and sat, head uptilted, basking in the sun's rays, the floating breeze, the rustling leaves and to myself and to no one at all I said, *She isn't gonna get up, is she?* See, this is how it was supposed to happen. I was to come to after my fall with exactly two remnants: the smell of the flower's stem and the moisture it leaves on the palm—the clinging dabs and droplets of memory, the material remains of a previous time. Which tell us: *Something occurred in the interval just before the present moment—a revolution perhaps, a story certainly—and now, it is over.* But, by the time I was finished basking and thinking and looked back, she was gone.

Sprawled like a hearthrug longwise across the doorway, I am half in and half out of my room. I awaken with a lurch, sit up and touch myself—face chest arms. Waking up takes time (this time) because I am stunned by the eerie mixture of dull sleepiness and loud ear-pounding surprise. I stand up hurriedly; it is almost a leap and I totter a little. I feel absurd, confused, unhinged. Slowly, I realize what happened: *The floor must have hit me, hard,* I think, *I could have died.* In the interval between hot and cold, I lost a piece of my life. But my flower is there, next to where I'd lain and when I bend down to pick it up I realize just how much my head hurts. And that I am cold. And that I'd passed out. And that I am inexplicably sad. Like me, my flower looks spent and sad and as I reach for it I try recalling where I was and then re-member (or decide) that I was having an extraordinary conversation with a girl. A girl who looked like, me. A girl who thought flowerbeds were sleepingbeds. A girl who vanished. Except that at the time I didn't know she didn't speak my language. Only after coming to did I realize I'd spoken to her in a language not understood. And that she'd said words I only thought I could hear. Despite matching eyes, our words were strange, one to the next. (Which means she doesn't know I've been waiting all these years to finish the story, to give her my flower, to make good on my promises—smiles, beauty, and a future.)

IV.

When I come back to the time and the news and the tremor of the present, I am slumped down on the floor, back against the door, knees folded upwards surrounded by arms, face down. I am wondering about the value of failed communication, I am disappointed that accidents happen I am angry about the absence of an angel at a crucial life-or-death moment. I pitch back and forth, from prickly hot rage to deep, raw understanding recognition.

And I am still reciting the line, *I lived on your promise* (no, not my words) and I am puzzled because I feel betrayed, as though a promise I can't re-member has been broken. I am wondering what one does with the time after a broken promise, when, despite being somewhere between the bizarre and the ridiculous, betrayal is the unfair rejoinder that refuses to correct or annihilate itself. *I lived on your promise* and now that you have taken your words and gone, all I have are unutterable turns of phrase and a shattered book.

And, still, I feel betrayed, still, I feel that I have died a little with you, still, I gasp for air, grasp after lost words, still, I do not know the color of your prison, its materials or location, its source or shape, windows walls contours, or who had the key, I don't know what you saw when you picked flowers on July mornings or who you saw when you looked at your Son, don't know where your lost moments have taken you or what terror drove you there, or why, where I saw red six-pointed stars you saw petals of blood,[9] why my flower says *"Love on!"* and your flower says *"I die a little more, every day."*

And now, I am alone with a burning sadness and the second real question: Is there a method for understanding our relative survivals our comparative deaths, a medium capable of providing safe passage over all that lies between them—so that, in the name of survival, the time the space the distance might be negotiable?

V.

It is morningtime on the 19th day of July in the year 2000 and 3 in the city of New York on the island of Manhattan, the northernmost region. (Long ago, this area was called "Shorakapok"—a Lenape word which means "edge of the river.") I am at home. I occupy the chair by the desk by the window overlooking the park and the garden—greenery, flowers, children, trees, breeze (light, today). My preferred morning mug is filled with hot coffee (light, sweet). It drafts steamy whorls that disappear into thin air, one after the other, while the *New York Times* crackles (blackening my hands), smells (ever so slightly), speaks (as usual, unfathomably) saying: "Coup on Tiny African Islands Felt in Texas Oil Offices" "A Hip-Hop Fashion Bridge Across the Atlantic" "Palestinians in Nablus Fed Up

With Crime Posing as Jihad" "Homosexuality Issue Threatens To Break Anglicanism in Two" "AFTER THE WAR: POST-COMBAT FATIGUE; Extension of Stay in Iraq Takes Toll on Morale of G.I.'s" "AFTER THE WAR: INTELLIGENCE; British Arms Expert at Center of Dispute on Iraq Data Is Found Dead." I hear things: the trash is dragged to the stoop by Mendez, fast-paced high heels snap a determined beat along the sidewalk, fade, strollers ping pong carefree greetings back and forth across the street. I see things: the gardener—he's there in the park, quietly tending the plant life with a tranquil meditative hush about him as if composing carefully considered poems in his mind in perfect form while the trees watch over him, filtering sunrays, singing naturally.

Meanwhile, I am still trying to resuscitate yesterday's disremembered writing. I place my hands (still, hopeful) upon the keyboard. (I am angry, still.) I am still not composing my meditations on survival and its opposite. (I can't bridge the gap.) I am able to think, however: I think, *There is something to be said for living on promises.* And then (inexplicably) I re-member the full *sher*. It appends faithfulness and survival and promises with something else. It is the great Urdu bard, Mirza Ghalib—our mutually beloved poet. It helps me to think—it helps me to recite it aloud:

> *"I lived on your promise, because I knew it to be a lie*
> *For, wouldn't I have died with happiness, had I believed?"*[10]

A tragedy inhabits this little poem. It means we survive because we refuse faith, and we thrive for having been infidels. It means "life" is the superlative paradox because living on promises means dying by them too; and dying means having lived; and living is the long wait for something else. I think, *There is something to be said for a mother's Love*—its ferocity, its boundless, merciless, guiltless obedience. I think, *There is something to be said for the terror we live with*—and die with, and refuse to admit—to ourselves, to our lovers, to our mothers—for the rage I feel and refuse (even now) to confess. My rage is rooted in the pain-producing juxtaposition of certain (vitally though mysteriously) linked unknowns:

I do not know how the tortured prisoners survived all those vicious, pitiless trials, don't know how (even now) they speak of torture, hunger, cold and madness with lacerated tongues through parched cracked blood-stained lips; I do not know why mother and child are lost (together) to the impenetrable void despite their different standings relative to the question of the completion of individual change, don't know why they took their last (syncopated) breaths (together) in a pool of mixed blood, essential fluids mingled once more in that most final of moments; I do not know why there was no angel for them. (And I will cry for that immeasurable, incomprehensible, holy error in endless fits of memory.)

Faith. Despite the failures of angels, faith is what she turned to just before the end—faith. It is Ghalib's subject matter, too. The Argument: There is an antidote—someone out there who knows we exist, who will save us, just in time. A messianic angel. Our deliverer. She'll pick us up, dust us off, and give us our just desserts—a careful reading. If she does exist, we don't consider that she may not know us. We can't. It's too hard to know that and go on waiting. So, we await the savior's arrival, loyal in a rabid kind of way. Meanwhile, she's busy providing rigorous protection in an altogether different universe, insentient to all our "I's." Othertimes one accepts the cold hard fact of a godless universe unaware the goddess is right there hammering her fists on the dining table in furious feral abandon. But we can't hear her, or don't know how to. And (even now) we put those tiny ripples in the coffee, those mystifying clinks of knives and companion utensils down to natural or human error. (An imperceptible collision with a table leg; a too heavily placed bootprint in an adjacent dwelling; a window open shockingly wide just before a storm, the wind whistling.) We return to the newspaper, read on: ". . . The day before the bodies were found . . . she sought a meeting with a neighborhood priest and borrowed a Bible from a neighbor . . ."[11]

VI.

There is a time—the tense, present. It is eveningtime on a suffocatingly hot humid northeastern July day just before my 42nd birthday. I am at home. I am seated on the long couch facing the oversized corner chair containing the remnants of yesterday's explosion. I prefer averting my eyes staring instead through the two side-by-side windows facing the park and the sunset. I prefer listening to the far-off yells and guffaws of children at play, to the low whirr of the small fan on the windowsill. I prefer trees and their music. (Still, I do not know what to make of my shooting scriptures.) Like our beloved poet, I drink red wine and pay homage to lost souls. Like him, I am an infidel. But, when news comes, it changes me ("salvation"). And when books self-destruct I am alerted to distinct wisdoms of the ages for the first time (only now do I know that the whole world can come unhinged in sixty seconds flat). I think, *Perhaps this means I'm not finished, changing.* Perhaps this means the opposite of survival is the end of change, that the color of survival is the color of change, that the character of survival is to change, and, that you were finished, changing.

Angels come (my caped messenger), they fail (his absence in the District of Columbia on the 16th day of July in the year 2003 sometime after 8:00 A.M.), but every moment has an "I"—time is lived by someone, if there is no one there is no time. Perhaps this is what we live on: a moment, a movement, an episode—the space of an interval (a train, in motion) and the potential it promises to hold (a question, unanswered). Though invisible, it may be our only home despite the fact that we don't declare it, die for it, wait for it—breath held: the interval, and how in its persistence it is *lived.*

Once upon a time, a longsuffering old man called this *the interval of wakefulness.*[12] Intervals: in-betweens and gaps interludes and intermissions spaces of consequence event choice hesitation exhalation devastation symphony rhapsody ecstasy impulse denial hate insouiance Love—they constitute our "I's," our stories, our selves, our lives—they add up to a life lived in a distinct, extraordinary way. In these times— these present tenses—the color of survival is revealed. It is the moment of change (being, in 4/4 time), it is a kaleidoscope ("a constantly changing set of colors," "a series of changing phases or events") whose temperament and temporality are made anew each time, each time I say:

I listen I listen to you I listen for your story,
Can you hear me, listening?
I think I think of you I think of your life your death your promise your poem,
Do you hear me, thinking of you?

Perhaps this is the story I have since forgotten. The poet falls apart waiting for the recuperative response, a careful reader; I fall apart waiting for the animating stimulus, a carefully assembled poem. A careful reading, a careful reader: these are our needs, this, our condition. We wait to be read, holding this tragic posture to the end. We hold on knowing that what we hold on to (someone, something) might fall apart in our hands, unexpectedly explode, and drop us. We wait knowing that what we wait for (the something, the someone) may never arrive. But isn't it in this ex-change, in "writing" and "reading," in the forgotten incidental the accidental masterpiece that whatever is crucial,("survival") occurs? We misspeak, misunderstand, miss; we disremember, decode, decide and are often wrong; and yet we desire to recognize, connect, see, to be declared, acknowledged, Loved—to coexist in the mirror of someone else's eyes:

Ex-change: A rhapsodic movement in which words are uttered, gifted, hazarded by a speaker.
Ex-change: A rhapsodic response in which words are received, consumed, undertaken by a reader.

These ex-changes are imperfect and partial; ultimately they are failures, all; and yet, they are miraculous, beautiful, indispensable. Poetry, music, bread, words—that's where it happens, in the concurrent occurrence of language traveling back and forth in time (together with hits misses and misfires), gifted from writers to readers and back again. Despite its status as the essential ingredient, ex-change always occurs, like tragedy, in the certainty of its own failure:

Give me your language, a language I will not understand, then I may find my own,
Give me your words, words that will confound me, then I will discover my home.
Play the song that will shatter my heart, then I will know the color of Love,
Make me a promise you will break, then I will recognize the color of survival.

We survive and we die together. We change with words in time with others, by reading and being read, by undressing, all the way down to nothing, laying ourselves bare, and waiting. Being touched, in time. Touching back, in reply. It is a dance, this surviving. A fluid faltering movement, a wrong move touched off by a stray stimulus. Just one botched, stumbling pirouette is all it takes. An index finger taps my shoulder (twice, quicklike, "du-daaah") and I turn. I turn, and there is no one. I turn, and everything is new, again. These are words we say: "You," "I," "Love," but in the utterance we touch off a revolution, set the globe in motion, it spins—blurring the "You are Here" pointer, running the distinctions of place into geographical mélange.

We survive and we die together. When we say, "She was suicidal" "disturbed" "deranged," we cover her over with diagnoses verdicts rationalizations categorizations, we separate from us, ourselves her heinous act, its terror and ugliness, preserve and fortify the illusory divide between one "I" and the next, between tragedy and its opposite. In the light of my inadvertent meditations these seem like lies and happy fallacies. She was a woman who died by her own hand and took her Son with her. *Here is tragedy.* He would have made something—he could have made music and bread, he would have made Love and other sweet sounds—but he is lost, whatever he might have made, lost. *Here is tragedy.* And yet, here was a mother like all mothers, a woman like all women, a human being (hurt, desperate, damaged, broken) like all human beings. (A girl, like me.) Her crimes of passion—not so far from the rest of us, from humanity, certainly not far from "civilization" whose outstanding contributions to life on earth have been the relentless creation of dominions of terror; the proliferation of bigotry; the strategic planning of cruelty; the professionalization and romanticization of blood letting and other shocking sport. Slavery, genocide, the atomic bomb, the death "penalty"—all "modern." All part of the bizarre ex-change in the prison where we live. Allegedly, the quagmire of World War II "necessitated" the A-bomb; the quagmire of Vietnam, Agent Orange; the quagmire of Iraq, Smart Bombs. All these "quagmires" are, in all honesty, rather uncomplicated:

A "well-educated," "high-bred" European without a criminal record or a diagnosis had an idea; it caught on. Later, an Aboriginal child in Australia is savagely snatched from her mother so that she might be schooled in the ways and means of British barbarism; later, a West African child, soon to be renamed: "Phillis Wheatley," is placed on a ship (called "Phillis") so that she might learn the meaning of survival ("poetry") in a savage land (called "America"); still later, the corpses of children are piled high, a patriotic banner for the death makers and the marching soldiers singing, *"Seid umschlungen, Millionen! / Dieser Kuss der ganzen Welt!"*—*"Embrace each other now, you millions! / This kiss is for the whole wide world!*"[13] Child snatching, slavery, mass murder, as inexplicable and heartrending as the loss of sons at the hands of their mothers. We are brutes, all. And, we survive and we die, *together.*

I think, *It is all right.* It is all right to live. It is all right to stop, to discontinue the ex-change, to give up the long wait, to sleep, to die. It is all right to cry—for lost Sons, for the end of your individual change. I cry today knowing there will be other intervals. I cry today knowing that tomorrow, blood will flow—down stairwells streets sewers walls, myriad white sheets, across the playgrounds and the battlefields of Jerusalem Gujarat Belfast New York Hiroshima and Nagasaki ("civilization") it will rage on and on undying, in the night and in the day, steadfast and shameless it will roll on and on in hideous triumph ("civilization") until even the gardens and even the shamrocks and even the little children are swaddled in its fire—and, red lily-flowered tulips will bloom, somewhere.

VII.

Time is passing and I want to tell you about it before it's over. It is dusk on the 20th day of July in the year 2003 in the city of New York, Manhattan island, the northernmost neighborhood and former home of the Wiechquaesgeek Indians, a branch of the Lenape family. They used to grow corn and beans along Seaman Avenue, there by the park; and they danced, rousing the ancient dust into heroic drifts. That was before the island was overrun by Europeans and the previous residents (hundreds of Wiechquaesgeek families who'd been there long enough to give the place a name: "Shorakapok") got sick and died or were murdered, including the children. (I think, *On the ground beneath my feet and my first floor apartment—who lived there, once upon a time?*) I am at home. The sun is dropping. I am looking through the two side-by-side windows facing the park with its old oak trees and whistling wind, its playing children, its green and red flora. In my lap I hold a bundle of nerves requiring my attention. I study it assiduously as if a riddle that when worked out will reveal the mystery of the interval in which it is implicated. I contemplate what type of action is called for, now, in the interest of time.

Perhaps by now you have forgotten that today is my 42nd birthday. That my Son visits me today, that he is 22. Now, he is baking bread and clashing cymbals about with the sticks I gave him. My Son (the royal capitalization of "Son" being required in this instance, the boy is descended of an antediluvian line of wise and wandering stargazers and poets from the time before *all* our known prophets), he creates something altogether new in the adjoining room. He arranges dices chops heats cools countless bits and pieces of sustenance in such a way that they correspond compatibly, each one to the next. From the corner chair in the dimly lit living room, I watch him, lovingly and without strain, while he works. (I think, *He makes the world, again.*) Later, we will dine together, side by side. We will hold hands and pay attention, make good on the disbelieved promises, display a hitherto inconceivable discipline in our approaches to Love. We will endeavor—perhaps unsuccessfully to understand each other's languages, in every way, at every moment. But, it is not yet time.

Now, tears drip drop drip dampening the dry, raggedy glue of a broken bookspine. In another time, the book had flown into a rage and exploded in my arms, like a howling toddler beside herself with temper and tantrum, in need of Love; like a tree felling its leaves, burying the earth below in outrageous fury, in need of some sunlight and a little water–dying for a rainbow.

Now, the little book of woe and wounding is recast. It endures a complete reorganization until restored. Its pieces are located (first) and ordered (second). A slow meticulous process, a great perplexing puzzle: 1) perceptible sentences are re-built from scattered words (carefully), 2) disheveled pages are re-associated (sequentially, right side up), 3) front and back covers are bandaged (neatly, as possible) stemming the outward flow of matter best kept hidden, 4) remnants are recycled and rejected until there is nothing but the book. (I think, *Now, it resembles a somewhat more complete fragment of Sappho.*)

Now, I will read my resurrected *biblio*. (I am anxious, worried still about my lost words. Hopeful, still, in a dreamy childish way—like awaiting the tooth fairy or conferring with my guardian angel—that my words might still be found.) I read the patchwork story of someone else's dream, the dream of a prisoner:

> *My sister looks at me, gets up and goes away without a word.*
> *A desolating grief is now born in me, like certain barely remembered pains of one's early infancy. It is pain in its pure state*

a pain like that which makes children cry   *My*
dream stands in front of me, still warm, and although awake I am
still full of its anguish: and then I remember. . . .[14]

And then (inexplicably) I re-member the words of my dead poet: *It is*
what you do. The line is from "Dedicated to You," a poem that appends
faithfulness and survival and promises with something else. It wrests
my attention. It's the one about the dead poets: *Mirabai, Dickinson,*
Ghalib, Hayden. They're all there. It's about the moment of reading, the
gift of writing. I realize I misremembered the line just now: *It is the*
thing you do. Yes, that's it: *It is the thing you do*   *open a book.*

Now, I close the renovated prisoners' book placing it on the oversized arm of the bulky chair, gingerly (afraid of further flare-ups). And
in what seems (to me) like one small step—which is actually a leap and
several long running steps across two and a half rooms, from the living
room through the kitchen (past my Son) and on into the long hall
where hundreds of neatly arranged, categorical, alphabetical, dusty
books lie in wait, it is the interval (the space, the time, the distance)
between two books in which I say the words aloud, with an urgency
suggesting these are the most meaningful words I have uttered in forty-
two years. I arrive at the bookcases, follow them all the way down to
the last one—section S ("Sappho") through Y ("Yeats")–my hand skids
along innumerable spines until I find it in the V's ("Vazirani"). The
book is dust-covered, anxious, in need of a careful reader. I blow the
dust from the cover into thin air, watch it scurry through the light and
then it opens (reluctantly, a sulk it seems to me) and I locate the pages
and find the words I've been looking for. I recite them aloud,

> *It is the thing you do*   *open a book . . .*
> *you leaf through to see*
> *which words are dedicated to you.*[15]

Indeed, I think, *the words are a mirror.* You leaf through, find your
words, find your self, re-member again. Survive, again. Poets reach
toward us with hands with flowers with words, sustain us with bits of
language harmoniously combined, risked, presented. The words of poets
intersect our times, outline pathways, suggest plausible answers, ring the
bells of our lost effects. Your words make a place for me, a destination I

can see my way into, offer me the much-repeated all-important step I might decide to take, give me dreams and apparitions I can explicate, stories I might re-member or compose anew. Your words return like a gift I grasp after, receive and embrace. And the whole universe (it seems to me, now) depends in that moment on the words of a dead poet and one mother's ability to hold on to them.

Despite our failures and our humanness, our terror, our rage—you (the writer) die taking me some of the way with you, I (the reader) live bringing you part way into my world, into my words of Love, injury and fury, into a story about a broken promise, a burning sadness—a desolating grief triggered by the disappearance of my sister:

> In the story, you died at home, you were with me, and you were surrounded by the most stunning flower in the world—the lily-flowered tulip, part lily, part tulip. You see, you had finished changing. And, so you decided to stop. Just stop. When you left, you rescinded your promise to the world taking the beautiful something you had made for us away with you—the gift you couldn't leave behind, couldn't give away, after all. (You were left behind, once. To you, it would have been an unthinkable wrongdoing to leave and leave your gift behind.) And I knew that despite your tragic misgiving, and notwithstanding my mottled rage, I loved you. Once upon a time, you lived and died in our mother's garden, surrounded by the beautiful something she had made for us. This is what I remember, now. It is not true. It is not false. It is my story.

Your words, my words, the words of our beloved poet and many wounded prisoners—they are indivisible, all. Linked by messengers and other interlocutors, these words establish a set of filial relations, form a chain of exchange that enables my survival in the face of myself, in the face of you, in the face of our Sons and our Daughters, of humanity, even in the face of "civilization." Your words authorize my survival: my utterance, my dedication to you—the words I say now and again and again: "You" "I" "Love"

NOTES

1. Quotation is the title of the *Washington Post* article: "In Final Hours, Despair Defeated Poet; Indian-born Writer Apparently Killed Herself, 2-Year Old in D.C. Home," by David A. Fahrenthold and Simone Weischselbaum, *Washington Post* Staff Writers. (Friday, July 18, 2003, page A1).

2. Quotations in this paragraph from Primo Levi's "Dreams in Auschwitz," in *This Prison Where I Live,* ed. Siobhan Dowd. (Cassell, 1996): 121.

3. From "Dreams in Auschwitz," 122 (see note 2).

4. Alludes to a line from Vazirani's poem "Memory I": " (he was forty-two and had finished changing)." This poem is about her father, who committed suicide when Vazirani was twelve years of age. Poem published in *The Literary Review:* http://theliteraryreview.org/Featured_P&W/Reetika_Vazirani/vaz2.htm

5. All parenthetical quotations in this paragraph from the *Washington Post* article previously cited (see note 1).

6. Quotation in this paragraph is from James Joyce's *A Portrait of the Artist as a Young Man* (1916).

7. From Vazirani's poem "Saris of Kasturiya," published in *Monsoon Magazine:* http://monsoonmag.com/poetry/i3rvazirani1.html

8. From "Saris of Kasturiya" (see note 7).

9. The title of a novel by exiled Kenyan writer Ngugi wa Thiong'o, *Petals of Blood* (1991).

10. Couplet from a well-known *ghazal* by legendary Urdu poet Mirza Asadullah Khan Ghalib (1797–1869). The original Urdu *sher* reads: "tere waade par jiye ham, to yeh jaan jhoot jaanaa, / ke khushi se mar na jaate agar atbaar hotaa."

11. Quotation from the *Washington Post* article previously cited (see note 1).

12. From "Dreams in Auschwitz," 120 (see note 2).

13. From Friedrich von Schiller's "Ode to Joy" and the 4th movement of Ludwig von Beethoven's 9th symphony.

14. The final quote (slightly manipulated in appearance) is from "Dreams in Auschwitz," 120 (see note 2).

15. From Vazirani's poem "Dedicated to You," which was published in her last collection of poems, *World Hotel* (Copper Canyon Press, 2002).

Edwidge Danticat

■

Women Like Us

Among the most celebrated young writers in contemporary American literature, Edwidge Danticat is an award-winning author of novels and short fiction. Born in 1969 in Port-au-Prince, she started her "writing hobby" when
she was nine years old. With her brilliant debut, *Breath, Eyes, Memory* (1994),
Danticat exploded onto the international literary scene as a writer to watch,
according to the *New York Times.* Her unforgettable renderings of life and politics in Haiti, and the resilience of Haitian women throughout the diaspora,
have captured imaginations around the world. Author Paule Marshall
impresses upon us the literary and historical significance of Danticat's work:
"A silenced Haiti has once again found its literary voice." But Danticat maintains that her voice is only one among millions, and recently gathered a small
selection from this chorus in *The Butterfly's Way: Voices from the Haitian
Dyaspora* (2001). Like Sophie Caco, the young protagonist of *Breath, Eyes,
Memory,* Danticat moved to the United States when she was twelve, joining
her resettled parents in New York. After studying French literature at Barnard
College, she entered Brown University's MFA program. There she finished
work on *Breath, Eyes, Memory,* which began as "an article for a New York City
teen newspaper" that she wrote during high school. In 1995 she published
Krik? Krak!, a collection of short stories, and made history as the youngest
writer to be nominated for the National Book Award. Set in 1937 during the
dictator Rafael Trujillo's brutal massacre of Haitians living on the Dominican
border, *The Farming of Bones* (1998) was voted one of the best books of the
year by *People, Entertainment Weekly,* the *Chicago Tribune,* and *Time Out New
York.* Danticat has won numerous honors for her work, including a Pushcart
Prize and fiction awards from *Essence* and *Seventeen.* The editor of *The Beacon
Best of 2000: Great Writing by Women and Men of All Colors and Cultures,* she
also teaches creative writing in New York and Miami.

With this graceful essay, Danticat remembers the daily resistance and
artistry of Haitian women. Here she offers tribute to the "kitchen poets" of
her childhood, women who "make narrative dumplings and stuff their daughter's mouths so they say nothing more." Though she is urged into silence by

the women who loved her most, it is ultimately through her mother, and her mother before her, that Danticat locates the source of her undaunted voice— and the inspiration to raise it. Tracing their stories, she bears tender witness to the lives of "women like us," vowing that those "who lived and died and lived again" will remain unforgotten.

You remember thinking while braiding your hair that you look a lot like your mother. Your mother who looked like your grandmother and her grandmother before her. Your mother had two rules for living. *Always use your ten fingers,* which in her parlance meant that you should be the best little cook and housekeeper who ever lived.

Your mother's second rule went along with the first. Never have sex before marriage, and even after you marry, you shouldn't say you enjoy it, or your husband won't respect you.

And writing? Writing was as forbidden as dark rouge on the cheeks or a first date before eighteen. It was an act of indolence, something to be done in a corner when you could have been learning to cook.

Are there women who both cook and write? Kitchen poets, they call them. They slip phrases into their stew and wrap meaning around their pork before frying it. They make narrative dumplings and stuff their daughter's mouths so they say nothing more.

"What will she do? What will be her passion?" your aunts would ask when they came over to cook on great holidays, which called for cannon salutes back home but meant nothing at all here.

"Her passion is being quiet," your mother would say. "But then she's not being quiet. You hear this scraping from her. Krik? Krak! Pencil, paper. It sounds like someone crying."

Someone was crying. You and the writing demons in your head. You have nobody, nothing but this piece of paper, they told you. Only a notebook made out of discarded fish wrappers, panty-hose cardboard. They were the best confidantes for a lonely little girl.

When you write, it's like braiding your hair. Taking a handful of coarse unruly strands and attempting to bring them unity. Your fingers have still not perfected the task. Some of the braids are long, others are short. Some are thick, others are thin. Some are heavy. Others are light. Like the diverse women in your family. Those whose fables and metaphors, whose similes, and soliloquies, whose diction and *je ne sais quoi* daily slip into your survival soup, by way of their fingers.

You have always had your ten fingers. They curse you each time you force them around the contours of a pen. No, women like you don't write. They carve onion sculptures and potato statues. They sit in dark corners and braid their hair in new shapes and twists in order to control the stiffness, the unruliness, the rebelliousness.

You remember thinking while braiding your hair that you look a lot like your mother. You remember her silence when you laid your first notebook in front of her. Her disappointment when you told her that words would be your life's work, like the kitchen had always been hers. She was angry at you for not understanding. *And with what do you repay me? With scribbles on paper that are not worth the scratch of a pig's snout?* The sacrifices had been too great.

Writers don't leave any mark in the world. Not the world where we are from. In our world, writers are tortured and killed if they are men. Called lying whores, then raped and killed, if they are women. In our world, if you write, you are a politician, and we know what happens to politicians. They end up in a prison dungeon where their bodies are covered in scalding tar before they're forced to eat their own waste.

The family needs a nurse, not a prisoner. We need to forge ahead with our heads raised, not buried in scraps of throw-away paper. We do not want to bend over a dusty grave, wearing black hats, grieving for you. There are nine hundred and ninety-nine women who went before you and worked their fingers to coconut rind so you can stand here before me holding that torn old notebook that you cradle against your breast like your prettiest Sunday braids. I would rather you had spit in my face.

You remember thinking while braiding your hair that you look a lot like your mother and her mother before her. It was their whispers that pushed you, their murmurs over pots sizzling in your head. A thousand women urging you to speak through the blunt tip of your pencil. Kitchen poets, you call them. Ghosts like burnished branches on a flame tree. These women, they asked for your voice so that they could tell your mother in your place that yes, women like you do speak, even if they speak in a tongue that is hard to understand. Even if it's patois, dialect, Creole.

■

The women in your family have never lost touch with one another. Death is a path we take to meet on the other side. What goddesses have joined, let no one cast asunder. With every step you take, there is an army of women watching over you. We are never any farther than the sweat on your brows or the dust on your toes. Though you walk through the valley of the shadow of death, fear no evil for we are always with you.

When you were a little girl, you used to dream that you were lying among the dead and all the spirits were begging you to scream. And even now, you are still afraid to dream because you know that you will never be able to do what they say, as they say it, the old spirits that live in your blood.

Most of the women in your life had their heads down. They would wake up one morning to find their panties gone. It is not shame, however, that kept their heads down. They were singing, searching for meaning in the dust. And sometimes, they were talking to faces across the ages, faces like yours and mine.

You thought that if you didn't tell the stories, the sky would fall on your head. You often thought that without the trees, the sky would fall on your head. You learned in school that you have pencils and paper only because the trees gave themselves in unconditional sacrifice. There have been days when the sky was as close as your hair to falling on your head.

This fragile sky has terrified you your whole life. Silence terrifies you more than the pounding of a million pieces of steel chopping away at your flesh. Sometimes, you dream of hearing only the beating of your own heart, but this has never been the case. You have never been able to escape the pounding of a thousand other hearts that have outlived yours by thousands of years. And over the years when you have needed us, you have always cried "Krik?" and we have answered "Krak!" and it has shown us that you have not forgotten us.

You remember thinking while braiding your hair that you look a lot like your mother. Your mother, who looked like your grandmother and her grandmother before her. Your mother, she introduced you to the first echoes of the tongue that you now speak when at the end of the day she would braid your hair while you sat between her legs, scrubbing the kitchen pots. While your fingers worked away at the last shadows of her day's work, she would make your braids Sunday-pretty, even during the week.

When she was done she would ask you to name each braid after those nine hundred and ninety-nine women who were boiling in your blood, and since you had written them down and memorized them, the names would come rolling off your tongue. And this was your testament to the way that these women lived and died and lived again.

Eavan Boland

■

Letter to a Young Woman Poet

Extolled "one of Ireland's most important poets" by the *San Francisco Chronicle,* Eavan Boland is a leading voice in contemporary poetry. She writes frequently about the "common" experiences of womanhood and motherhood—defiantly reimagining a tradition "which simplified us as women and excluded us as poets." As *Publishers Weekly* notes, she "has long won admiration for verse that combines Irish postcolonial experience and Irish politics with an outspoken feminism." Not so easy, says Boland, who maintains that she is a poet and a longtime feminist, "not a feminist poet." All other things being equal, her coming of age in the wake of Ireland's violent partitioning—and into a long, predominantly male poetry tradition—figure prominently in her work as a mature poet. Born in Dublin to a painter and a diplomat, she and her family moved to London when she was six. At age eighteen she returned to Dublin to study English and Latin at Trinity College. That same year, she self-published her first poetry collection, the chapbook *23 Poems* (1962). She is now the author of nine major books of poetry, including *In a Time of Violence* (1994) and *Outside History: Selected Poems 1980–1990.* Her most recent collection, *Against Love Poetry,* was a *New York Times* Notable Book and a *Newsday* Favorite Book of 2001. Boland has won numerous honors for her poetry, including the Lannan Literary Award and the Irish Literature Prize. Her work is widely anthologized and has appeared in the *New Yorker, Atlantic Monthly,* and elsewhere. A professor of English, Boland directs the creative writing program at Stanford University. She has lived between the United States and Ireland since 1979.

Now proclaimed by the *Irish Times* as one who "has influenced the course of poetry during her own lifetime," Boland still remembers well her lonely initiation into a tradition "defined by and in our absence." More than a portrait of the poet as a young woman, Boland's evocative "Letter to a Young Woman Poet" is a loving, hopeful invitation to poetry's next generation— those unawakened, those uncertain, those unborn. Inscribing the history of women upon the poetic past, Boland opens the gates a little wider for the women who will change its future. Here she sits quietly writing, dreaming "as one writer who listens for the emergence of another."

I wish I knew you. I wish I could stand for a moment in that corridor of craft and doubt where you will spend so much of your time. But I don't and I can't. And given the fact, in poetic terms, that you are the future and I am the past, I never will. Then why write this? It is not, after all, a real letter. It doesn't have an address. I can't put a name at the top of it. So what reason can I have for writing in a form without a basis to a person without a name?

I could answer that the hopes and silences of my first years as a poet are still fresh to me. But that in itself is not an explanation. I could tell you that I am a woman in my early fifties, writing this on a close summer night in Ireland. But what would that mean to you? If I tell you, however, that my first habitat as a poet is part of your history as a poet: is that nineteenth century full of the dangerous indecision about who the poet really is. If I say I saw that century survive into the small, quarrelsome city where I began as a poet. That I studied its version of the poet and took its oppressions to heart. If I say my present is your past, that my past is already fixed as part of your tradition. And that until we resolve our relation to both past and tradition, we are still hostages to that danger, that indecision. And, finally, that there is something I want to say to you about the present and past of poetry—something that feels as if it needs to be said urgently—then maybe I can justify this letter.

And if some awkwardness remains, rather than trying to disguise it, I want to propose an odd and opposite fiction. If most real letters are conversation by another means, think of this as a different version. Imagine a room at dusk, with daylight almost gone. I can do this because I associate that light, that hour, with ease and conversation. I was born at dusk. Right in the centre of Dublin, in fact, in a nursing home beside Stephen's Green. Big, crackling heaps of sycamore and birch leaves are burned there in autumn and I like to think of the way bitter smoke must have come the few hundred yards or so towards the room where I was born.

And so I have no difficulty imagining us sitting there and talking in that diminishing light. Maybe the sights of late summer were visible through the window only moments ago. Fuchsia and green leaves, perhaps. But now everything is retreating into skeletal branches and charcoal leaves. My face is in shadow. You cannot see it, although your presence shapes what I am saying. And so in the last light, at the end of the day, what matters is language. Is the unspoken at the edge of the spoken. And so I have made a fiction to sustain what is already a fiction: this talking across time and absence.

But about what? What name will I give it? In the widest sense, I want to talk about the past. The past, that is, of poetry: the place where so much of the truth and power of poetry is stored. "Poetry is the past which breaks out in our hearts," said Rilke—whose name should be raised whenever one poet writes to another. But the past I want to talk about is more charged and less lyrical than that for women poets. It is, after all, the place where authorship of the poem eluded us. Where poetry itself was defined by and in our absence. There has been a debate since I was a young poet, about whether women poets should engage with that past at all. "For writers, and at this moment for women writers in particular," Adrienne Rich wrote eloquently in "When We Dead Awaken," "there is a challenge and promise of a whole new psychic geography to be explored. But there is also a difficult and dangerous walking on ice, as we try to find language and images for a consciousness we are just coming into and with little in the past to support us."

Then why go there? Why visit the site of our exclusion? We need to go to that past: not to learn from it, but to change it. If we do not change that past, it will change us. And I, for one, do not want to become a grateful daughter in a darkened house.

But in order to change the past of poetry, we have to know what happened there. We have to be able to speak about it as poets, and even that can be difficult. Ever since I began as a poet I have heard people say that fixed positions—on gender, on politics of any kind—distort and cloud the question of poetry. In those terms, this letter can seem to be a clouding, a distortion. But poetry is not a pure stream. It will never be sullied by partisan argument. The only danger to poetry is the reticence and silence of poets. This piece is about the past and our right as women poets to avail of it. It is about the art and against the silence. Even so, I still need to find a language with which to approach that past. The only way of doing that, within the terms of this fiction, is to go back to the space you now occupy: in other words, to the beginning.

■

When I was young I had only a present. I began in a small, literary city. Such a voluble, self-confident place, in fact, that at times it was even possible to believe the city itself would confer a sort of magical, unearned poetic identity. At night the streets were made of wet lights and awkward angles. Occasionally fog came in from the coast, a dense space filled with street-grit and salt and the sound of foghorns. By day things were plainer: a city appeared, trapped by hills and defined by rivers. Its centre was a squashed clutter of streets and corners. There were pubs and green buses. Statues of orators. Above all, the cool, solid air of the Irish sea at every turn.

The National Library was a cold, domed, and friendly building. The staircase was made of marble and formed an imposing ascent to a much less elaborate interior. Old books, shelves, and newspapers crowded a huge room. The tables were scarred oak and small lamps were attached to the edge of them and could be lit by individual readers. As twilight pressed on the glass roof where pigeons slipped and fluttered, the pools of light fell on pages and haloed the faces above them.

I read poetry there. I also read in my flat late at night. But the library was in the centre of town. Often it was easier just to stay in and go there and take a bus home later. There was something about the earnest, homeless feel of a big library that comforted me.

I read all kinds of poetry here. I also read about poets. I was eighteen. Then nineteen. Then twenty and twenty-one. I read about Eliot in Paris. And Yeats in Coole. I read Pound and Housman and Auden. It was the reading of my time and my place: too many men. Not enough women. Too much acceptance. Too few questions.

I memorized the poems. I learned the poetics—although I had no use for that word. But I had a real, practical hunger nevertheless for instruction and access in the form. And so I learned something about cadence and rhythm there. And something about the weather and circumstance of tradition as well. If I had known what to look for I would have had plenty of evidence of the tensions of a tradition as I read about the big, moonlit coldness of Ullswater and the intimacy of Wordsworth's hand-to-hand struggle with the eighteenth century. About the vowel changes in the fifteenth century. About the letters between John Clare and Lord Radstock. *Tell Clare if he still has a recollection of what I have done, and am still doing for him, he must give me unquestionable proofs of being that man I would have him be—he must expunge!*

When I came out of the library, I got on the bus and watched for ten or so minutes as the rainy city went by. During the journey I thought about what I had read. I was not just reading poems at this time, I was beginning to write them. I was looking for that solid land-bridge between writing poems and being a poet. I was taking in information, therefore, at two levels. One was simple enough. I was seeing at first hand the outcome of a hundred years of intense excitement and change in an art form: how the line had altered, how the lyric had opened out. I was also absorbing something that was less easy to define: the idea of the poet. The very thing which should have helped me transit from writing to being. But just as the line and the lyric had opened out and become volatile, the idea of the poet had drawn in, and distanced itself from the very energies the poems were proposing.

This made no sense at all. When I read poems in the library I felt as though a human face was turned towards me, alive with feeling, speaking urgently to me about love and time. But when I came across the idea of the poet I felt as if someone had displaced that speaker with a small, cold sculpture: a face from which the tears and intensity were gone, on which only the pride and self-consciousness of the Poet remained. I had no words for this. And yet I began to wonder if the makers of the poem and the makers of the idea of the poet could be one and the same. It was an amateurish, shot-in-the-dark thought. And yet all I could do was ask questions. What other way had I of dealing with a poetic past whose history I didn't know, and a tradition composed of the seeming assurance that only those it confirmed and recognized would ever be part of it? Besides, I felt my questions would bring me, if not to the front, at least to the back entrance of this formidable past. But if these were the gates, who were the gate-keepers?

Stay with the fiction. Imagine the light is less. That we can no longer see the water drops and wasps under the fuchsia. That the talk continues, but in a more mysterious space. I know when I was young I could barely imagine challenging the poetic past. It seemed infinitely remote and untouchable: fixed in place by giant hands.

And yet what a strange argument I am about to make to you. *That the past needs us.* That very past in poetry which simplified us as women and excluded us as poets now needs us to change it. To bring to it our warm and fractious present: our recent decades of intense debate and excited composition. And we need to do it. After all, stored in that past is a template of poetic identity which still affects us as women. When we are young poets it has the power to make us feel subtly less official, less welcome in the tradition than our male contemporaries. *If we are not careful it is that template we aspire to, alter ourselves for, warp our self-esteem as poets to fit.*

Therefore we need to change the past. Not by intellectualizing it. But by eroticizing it. The concept that a template of poetic authority can actually be changed, altered, radicalized by those very aspects of humanity which are excluded from it is at the heart of what I am saying. And yet these ideas are so difficult, so abstract that I sense them dissolving almost at the point of articulation. If you were not in a make-believe twilight in an unreal room in a fictive letter you might ask a question here. How can you eroticize a past? My hope is that this story—this strange story—will make it clearer.

When I was seventeen years of age I found myself, as many teenagers do, with time to spare between graduating from school and getting ready for college. Three months in fact of a wet, cool Irish summer. I lived in Dublin. In those times it wasn't hard to get summer jobs. So I got a job in a hotel just over the river on the north side of the city. I worked at housekeeping in the hotel. I carried keys and straightened out the rooms. The job was not difficult and the hours were not long.

The hotel was placed above the river Liffey and it was right at the end of one of the showpiece streets of Ireland. O'Connell Street. Its bridge, the widest in Europe, had once been a claim to fame when Dublin was a garrison city. On this street a group of Irish patriots in 1916 had taken their stand against British rule in Ireland. They had established themselves at the Post Office just above the river. The British troops had shelled the building. The position had fallen after a week of struggle and bloodshed. The patriots in the Post Office had been arrested and several of the leaders had been shot.

It was not hard when I was young to get off the bus on a summer morning beside a sluggish river that ran into the Irish sea, and walk straight into Irish history. There was the Post Office. Inside it was the bronze statue of Cuchulain with a raven on his shoulder. Here was the stone building and the remembered action. And all up the street, placed only fifty yards or so apart, was statue after statue of Irish patriots and orators. Burke. Grattan. O'Connell. Parnell. Made of stone and bronze and marble and granite. With plaques and wreaths and speeches at their feet. I got off the bus between the river and the hotel. And I walked past them, a seventeen-year-old girl—past their hands, their gestures, their quoted eloquence, all the way to work.

There was a manager in the hotel. He was a quietly spoken middle-aged man. He looked after all the inventory in the hotel and he sat in an old-fashioned office with a ledger and a telephone. One day one of the other girls there, a bit older than I was, told me something strange about him. She told me he had a wound which had never properly healed. Every day, she said, he went up to his room and dressed it and bandaged it. And I was fascinated in a horrified sort of way by the contrast between this almost demure man, with his dark suit and pin-striped trousers, wearing the formal clothes of small daily ceremonies, hiding his damaged secret.

But what I remember now is not exactly what I'm describing here. And that wounded man is only one part of the story. And the whole of the story is maybe not something I will be able to tell, not because I knew that man. Because I didn't. I spoke to him once or twice. Not more. Once I waited with the voyeuristic curiosity of youth, of which I still feel ashamed, at the top of the stairs to see him climb up to his room to dress that wound. But I never knew him. And never really spoke to him.

The story is something different. It has something to do with realizing that I could change the past. With going in every day to work in that hotel. With having my imagination seized, in a fragmented and distracted way, by a man whose body had not healed. And then, when the drizzling summer day was coming to an end, it had something to do with going out into the long, spacious street and walking down it to the river. Which also meant walking past the statues which had not moved or changed in the day. Which still stood on their columns, above their grandiose claims. It meant leaving the hotel with one idea of a manhood which had been made frail in a mysterious way and walking down a long, well-lit street where no such concession could ever be made. Where manhood was made of bronze and granite and marble. Where no one's thigh or side had ever been wounded or ever could be. But where—so intense was my sense of contrast—I could almost imagine that the iron moved and the granite flinched. And where by accident and chance I had walked not only into history, but into the erotics of history.

The erotics of history. In a certain sense I discovered my country by eroticizing it: by plotting those correlatives between maleness and strength, between imagination and power which allowed me not only to enter the story, but to change it. And yet at seventeen my own sexuality was so rudimentary, so unformed that neither I nor anyone else would have thought it could have been an accurate guide to the history I inherited. In fact, it served. I walked down that street of statues, a girl who had come back late to her own country. Who lacked its language. Who was ignorant of its battles. Who knew only a little about its heroes. And yet my skin, my flesh, my sex—without learning any of this—stood as a subversive historian, ready to edit the text.

If you and I were really there in that room with the air darkening around us, this would be a good place to stop. To be quiet for a moment. And then to start again. This time with another question. Is it possible to eroticize a poetic tradition in the way in which I eroticized my own history? Maybe the real answer to this is the most obvious one. The only way of entering the poetic tradition, of confronting its formidable past, is through a living present. And yet it hardly seems possible that the painful, complex, single present of any one poet could offer a contrast to a tradition. Despite that, what I am about to tell you is how I discovered it. Just how tentatively I put together my sense of being a poet with my sense of a past that did not offer me an easy definition for it. And how, in a house on a summer night, with sleeping children, when I wondered how to do it, I would think back to those summer mornings, that long street with its iron orators. Of looking up, made subversive by alternative senses of power and weakness. Of how I asked myself: Would I ever be able to eroticize this tradition, this formidable past, stretching back and reaching above, so that I could look up confidently? Could I make the iron breathe and the granite move?

■

When did I discover the past? Perhaps the answer should be, which past? My sense of it as a problematic poetic terrain came late. All through my first years as a poet it was just the place where poems I loved had been written, where patterns had been made which invited an automatic reverence I could not give. And so I continued to turn to that past to read those poems, but never to be part of the tradition they belonged to.

But when I married and had small children, when at last I lived at a distance from any poetic centre, things changed. I started to have an intense engagement with every aspect of writing a poem. So much so, that the boundaries between the edges of the poem and the limits of the world began at times to dissolve. I was fascinated by the page in the notebook on the table, with a child's cry at its perimeter and the bitterness of peat smoke at its further edge. I loved the illusion, the conviction, the desire—whatever you want to call it—that the words were agents rather than extensions of reality. That they made my life happen, rather than just recorded it happening.

But what life? My life day to day was lived through ordinary actions and powerful emotions. But the more ordinary, actual, the more intense the day I lived. The more I lifted a child, conscious of nothing but the sweetness of a child's skin, or the light behind an apple tree, or rain on slates, the more language and poetry came to my assistance. The words that had felt stilted, dutiful, and decorative when I was a young and anxious poet, now sang and flew. Finally, I had joined together my life as a woman and a poet. On the best days I lived as a poet, the language at the end of the day—when the children were asleep and the curtains drawn—was the language all through my day: it had waited for me.

What this meant was crucial to me. For the first time as a poet, I could believe in my life as the source of the language I used, and not the other way around. At last I had the means to challenge what I believed had distorted the idea of the poet: the belief that poetry had the power to dignify and select a life, instead of the reverse. That a life, in other words, became important only because it was the subject matter for a poem.

I knew from everything that I had read that the poets who changed the tradition first had to feel they owned the tradition. Instead, I had come slowly and painfully to a number of hard-won positions which did not feel at all like the privileges of ownership. First and foremost,

I had wanted to feel that those things I had lived as a woman I could write as a poet. Once I did that, I felt there was a fusion, a not-to-be-denied indebtedness between those identities: the woman providing the experience, the poet the expression. This fusion in turn created a third entity: the poet, who not only engaged in these actions, but began to develop a critique about them.

This critique may have had its origin in the life of a woman, may have begun in the slanted light of a nursery or a kitchen, but its outcome was about something entirely different. The interior of the poem itself: about tone, distance from the subject, management of the stanza. It was about the compromised and complex act of language. It was about the historic freedom of the poet, granted right down through the tradition—the precious and dignified franchise—to return to the past with the discoveries of the present. *To return triumphant to the present with a changed past.*

I did not have that sense of entitlement. The interior sense that I could change poetry, rather than my own poems, was never exactly there. But if the tradition would not admit me, could I change its rules of admission? Either I would have to establish an equal relation with it, or I would have to adopt a submissive posture: admiring its achievements and accepting its exclusions. Yet what tools had I to change the resistances I felt around me and within me? Certainly neither intellectual nor theoretical ones. Gradually I began to believe that the only way to change a tradition was to go to the sources which had made it in the first place. But what were they? Intuitively I felt that the way to touch them was by reaching back into my own imagination, attempting to become not just the author of the poem but the author of myself. The author, that is, of myself as a poet. This in turn meant uncovering and challenging the elusive source of authoring within the tradition which had made not only the poem, but also the identity of the poet.

Who makes a poetic tradition? Who makes the idea of the maker? "We are accustomed to think of the poet," wrote Randall Jarrell ironically, "when we think of him at all as someone Apart." But customs have to be made. They have to be stored deep in the culture and layered into habits of thought in order to change from custom into customary. Wherever the custom had started, I was certain it was a damaging, limiting one.

Of course it's arguable that I felt this because I was not an author in

that past: neither named nor present. But I don't think so. The truth was that in my reading—scattered and inexpert as it was—I had picked up a fault line: something strange and contradictory which I began to follow with fascination and unease. Obviously the language I use now is not the outcome of the perceptions I had then. I was young, badly read, just beginning. Nevertheless I know now that the fault line stretched from the end of the Romantic movement to the end of modernism. That it marked and weakened a strange, confused terrain of technical widening and ethical narrowing: just as the line and, the lyric began to grow plastic, open, volatile, the idea of the poet contracted, became defensive, shrugged off links with the community.
Here for instance is T. S. Eliot.

> We can only say that it appears likely that poets in our civilization, as it exists at present, must be difficult. Our civilization comprehends great variety and complexity, and this variety and complexity, playing upon a refined sensibility, must produce various and complex results. The poet must become more and more comprehensive, more allusive, more indirect, in order to force, to dislocate if necessary, language into meaning.

Our civilization. The poet must. This exclusivity was too pure for the warm, untidy enterprise of imagination as I understood it. What exactly was our civilization? Why should a poet try to reflect it in a dislocated language, instead of trying to find a plain and luminous one for standing outside that civilization?
    Further back again. Here is Matthew Arnold, seeming to claim for an art the devotions of a sect.

> We should conceive of poetry worthily, and more highly than it has been the custom to conceive of it. We should conceive of it as capable of higher uses, and called to higher destinies, than those which in general men have assigned to it hitherto. More and more mankind will discover that we have to turn to poetry to interpret life for us, to console us, to sustain us. Without poetry our science will appear incomplete, and most of what now passes for religion and philosophy will be replaced by poetry.

What higher destiny? What civilization? I repeat these questions only because it seems to me they have something to do with the fault line I spoke about. Reading through nineteenth-century poetry, even haphazardly, was to become an eyewitness to the gradual dissolving of the beautiful, maverick radicalism of the Romantic movement—where individualism was an adventure which freed the poet to experiment with the self—into a cautious and rigid hubris. Perhaps a sociologist or a historian could explain how the concept of the poet became mixed with ideas of power which had little to do with art and too much to do with a concept of culture shadowed by empire-building and conservative ideology. And how in the process men like Arnold and Eliot accepted the task of making the poet an outcome of a civilization rather than a subversive within it.

Whatever the causes, the effect was clear. Poetry in the last century had hit into a massive inconsistency which was not resolved in my century. One of the most vociferous movements in twentieth-century poetry—modernism—had been openly anti-authoritarian. "It was not a revolt against form," said Eliot, "but against dead form." But this apparent anti-authoritarianism had been built on the increasingly authoritarian idea of the poet as part of *our civilization* as called to *higher destinies*. The fault line lay here: the poets of the first part of the century had dismantled a style; they had not dismantled a self. Without the second, the first was incomplete.

Darkness. No trees. Not even outlines. Just the shadow of a profile and the sense of someone speaking. Let me remind you who I am: a woman on a summer night writing a fictive letter from a real place. Suppose I were now to turn a harsh and scornful light on my own propositions, and say why should a great tradition—a historic tradition of poetry with all its composure and assurance—be held accountable to the criticisms of a woman in a suburb?

The truth is simple: however wrong-headed my criticisms, I—no less than any poet who lifts a pen and looks at a page—was an inheritor of that tradition. The difference was that as a young woman I undertook that act in circumstances which were relatively new for a poet. Not in the London of coffee houses. Or in Greenwich Village. Or even in the city that was only four miles from me. But in a house with tiny children, with a washing machine in the background, with a child's antibiotic on a shelf and a spoon beside it.

And the fact was and is, that the words, decisions, insistences of poets and canon-makers—but more canon-makers than poets—had determined the status of my machines, my medicine bottles, my child's hand reaching up into mine. They had determined the relation between the ordinary object and the achieved poem. They had winnowed and picked, and sifted and refined. They had made the authority of the poet conditional upon a view of reality, which then became a certainty about subject matter and a prescription about language. They had debated and divided, subtracted and reduced the relation of the ordinary life to the achieved poem, so that it was harder than seemed right or proper to include the angle of light falling across copper, or returning to the kitchen from the gap between the poplar trees, into the poems I planned. It was harder than I thought proper to record the life I lived in the poems I wrote.

Gradually, it became apparent to me that the identity of the poet— on which was predicated the mysterious idea of the authority of the poet—had something to do with the permission granted or withheld, not simply to subject matter, but to the claim that could be made for it. Gradually I came to believe that in that nineteenth century, where Matthew Arnold proposed his higher destinies, the barriers between religion and poetry had shimmered and dissolved. Out of that had come a view I needed to challenge, which argued that the poem made the experience important; that the experience was not important until the poem had laid hands upon it.

Somewhere in that century, it seemed to me, if I could find it, would be a recognizable turning point, where the poet failed to distinguish between the hubris and the history, between the expression and the experience. And to which I as a poet—and I believed other poets like me from new and challenging constituencies—needed to return: to revise and argue and engage.

No light at all. Stars somewhere. And if this was a summer darkness in Ireland the morning would already be stored in the midnight: visible in an odd brightness to the east. I have finished talking. I have to finish also with the fiction of your company, and I am surprised at how real my regret is. Nevertheless this letter is still full of irony and hope. The hope is that you will read in my absence what was so thoroughly shaped by the irony of your non-presence. And despite the fact that this room, with its darkening window and its summer shadows, has only been made of words, I will miss it.

Occasionally I see myself, or the ghost of myself, in the places where I first became a poet. On the pavement just around Stephen's Green for instance, with its wet trees and sharp railings. What I see is not an actual figure, but a sort of remembered loneliness. The poets I knew were not women: the women I knew were not poets. The conversations I had or wanted to have, were never complete.

Sometimes I think of how time might become magical: How I might get out of the car even now and cross the road and stop that young woman and surprise her with the complete conversation she hardly knew she missed. How I might stand there with her in the dusk, the way neighbors stand on their front steps before they go in to their respective houses for the night: half-talking and half-leaving. She and I would argue about the past. Would surely disagree about the present.

Time is not magical. The conversation will not happen. Even writing this letter to you has been flawed by similar absences and inventions. And yet there is something poignant and helpful to me in having done it. If women go to the poetic past as I believe they should, if they engage responsibly with it and struggle to change it—seeking no exemption in the process—then they will have the right to influence what is handed on in poetry, as well as the way it is handed on. Then the conversation we have had, the letter I am just finished with, will no longer have to be fictions.

What is more, the strengths that exist in the communal life of women will then be able to refresh and renew the practice and concept of the poetic tradition. Thanks to the women poets in the generation before mine—poets such as Adrienne Rich and Denise Levertov—many of those strengths were already there when I started out. But I believe words such as *canon* and *tradition* and *inheritance* will change even more. And with all that, women poets, from generation to generation, will be able to befriend one another. And that, in the end, is the best reason for writing this letter.

Acknowledgments

There is an old Spiritual that I love: *My soul looked back and wondered how it got over.* Looking back, I know that this road is paved with the love, support, and inspiration of those I am privileged to call family and friends. You know who you are, and I know what it is to be blessed.

I am also grateful to the collective members at South End Press for showing me such generosity and faith as I wrapped up *Word.* In every way, it has made all the difference.

At the Feminist Press, I thank everyone I've had the privilege of working with there: amazing staff, past and present, and of course some of my favorite authors on the planet. I especially thank Jean Casella for offering me this remarkable opportunity, Dayna Navaro for yet another stunning design, Gloria Weiner for more reasons than I could name here, and Danielle Bonnici, a gifted poet, fierce negotiator, and true reader. And I must send mad props to the "title crew"—Lissa Fox, Sunny Maguire, and Jessica Roncker. *That* was a close call. . . . I also gratefully acknowledge Jamie Stock, whose creative work and superb research during this project's early stages is evident in all that is good in the finished volume.

Thank you, Suheir Hammad, not only for writing a graceful and incisive foreword (while touring!) but for reading the manuscript again and again, offering so generously of your fine critical eye and beautiful spirit. I've cherished your presence and your gifts. And many thanks to Nancy Yap for handling the business end, and with such grace. Special thanks must also go out to Victoria Sammartino, founder of Voices UnBroken, for her tireless work in (re)connecting writers on the inside with their craft and their audiences. I also thank Judith Clark and Maureen Fadem for the privilege of working with you on your manuscripts and under very tight schedules. I'm thrilled and inspired by all that your voices bring.

Finally, my gratitude to all the writers, not only for granting permission to print their essays here (often for free), but for doing what they do in the world, no matter what.

Most of the essays in *Word. On Being a [Woman] Writer* first appeared, sometimes in a slightly different form, in other publications. We gratefully acknowledge the following sources:

Alexander, Meena. "Lyric in a Time of Violence." Copyright © 2003 by Meena Alexander. From *Fault Lines: A Memoir.* (second ed.), New York: The Feminist Press at CUNY, 2003. Reprinted by permission of the Feminist Press.

The Feminist Press at the City University of New York is a nonprofit literary and educational institution dedicated to publishing work by and about women. Our existence is grounded in the knowledge that women's writing has often been absent or underrepresented on bookstore and library shelves and in educational curricula— and that such absences contribute, in turn, to the exclusion of women from the literary canon, from the historical record, and from the public discourse.

The Feminist Press was founded in 1970. In its early decades, the Press launched the contemporary rediscovery of "lost" American women writers, and went on to diversify its list by publishing significant works by American women writers of color. More recently, the Press's publishing program has focused on international women writers, who remain far less likely to be translated than male writers, and on nonfiction works that explore issues affecting the lives of women around the world.

Founded in an activist spirit, the Feminist Press is currently undertaking initiatives that will bring its books and educational resources to under-served populations, including community colleges, public high schools and middle schools, literacy and ESL programs, and prison education programs. As we move forward into the twenty-first century, we continue to expand our work to respond to women's silences wherever they are found.

Many of our readers support the Press with their memberships, which are tax-deductible. Members receive numerous benefits, including complimentary publications, discounts on all purchases from our catalog or web site, pre-publication notification of new books and notice of special sales, invitations to special events, and a subscription to our email newsletter, *Women's Words: News from the Feminist Press*. For more information about membership and events, and for a complete catalog of the Press's 250 books, please refer to our web site: www.feministpress.org.